ETHNOGRAPHY

as a Pastoral Practice

AN INTRODUCTION

Mary Clark Moschella

THE
PILGRIM
PRESS
Cleveland

*I dedicate this book to my students at Wesley Theological Seminary,
whose courageous work enlivens these pages.*

The Pilgrim Press
700 Prospect Avenue
Cleveland, Ohio 44115-1100
thepilgrimpress.com

❀ Printed in the United States of America on acid-free paper
that contains post-consumer fiber.

12   11 10

Library of Congress Cataloging-in-Publication Data
Moschella, Mary Clark.
    Ethnography as a pastoral practice : an introduction / Mary Clark
Moschella.
        p. cm.
    Includes bibliographical references and index.
    ISBN-13: 978-0-8298-1774-4 (alk. paper)
    1. Christianity and culture. 2. Ethnology – Religious aspects –
Christianity. 3. Pastoral counseling. 4. Pastoral psychology. I. Title.
BR115.C8M675 2008
253'.7 – dc22
                                                    2008008150

Contents

Foreword

Mary Moschella dedicates this wonderful book to her students at Wesley Theological Seminary "whose courageous work enlivens these pages." Before readers even see the table of contents, they see the heart of the book — listening to and learning from others. Moschella calls the book a roadmap, and indeed it is. It offers practical guidance for enacting ethnography as a pastoral practice, and it does so with captivating prose and simple clarity. Moschella herself calls ethnography a messy and muddy process, but she has superb mapping expertise. She knows the ethnographic and pastoral theology literature well and is able to translate it into maps and travelers' guides that people can follow with ease. This is an art, and Mary Moschella is an artist.

Moschella is also a stunning practical theologian. She is able to inspire students, pastoral leaders, and congregations to study the *texts* of their communities, to discern the rich and colorful *textures* of those communities, and to weave vivid *textiles* from their study. The textiles are the written narratives of the communities or even the sermons that pastoral ethnographers preach in their congregations, offering people pictures of their common life, complete with differences, conflicts, interpretations, and hanging threads. In this book, Moschella teaches readers her method of practical theology, a method that can be practiced in congregations as well as the halls of academia. She describes the elements of her method as listening, conversing, co-authoring, re-authoring, interpreting, and writing. In so doing, she reveals how deep wisdom can be uncovered in the process of engaging a community's puzzles, stories, counterstories, secrets, images, and metaphors.

This book does something that is even more radical, however; it raises a nagging question and opens the door to a powerful answer. The question is the relation between the pastoral role of listening, observing, being with, and interpreting a community and the prophetic role of transformation. These two roles are often defined as sharply different, even antagonistic. Scholars writing on the history, forms, and functions of ministry have traditionally described a tension between priestly and prophetic ministries. Mary Moschella writes as if they were not antagonistic, but intertwined; herein lies her contribution. Curiously, she lays the groundwork early in the book: "Hardly anyone who echoes Isaiah's response to the divine call, 'Here am I, send me!' (Isa. 6:8), envisions a life dedicated to maintaining the status quo." Later she describes listening as "a liberating practice, a practice that validates and honors another person's experience, insight, and soul." Still later, she quotes a student as saying, "This study helped me to love the congregation more fully and with a greater understanding of who they really are." Moschella suggests that the threads of a minister's prophetic call, together with listening and understanding, can lead to profound transformation.

More boldly, I want to say that she has unraveled the bifurcation between prophetic and priestly ministry, between working for social transformation and tending the communal life of a congregation. To make this case, I will join Mary and share a story. Recently, I was co-leading a discernment process in a large church conference, as conference delegates prepared to make decisions on resolutions and future actions regarding gay marriage. The conference was divided on the issues, and I had been asked to design a process for communal reflection. I was happy to do this, but my prophetic impulses made me wish that I could, instead, take a stand and proclaim it loudly. Whereas that would have been appropriate at another time, it was not what I was asked to do at that moment. Further, the body itself was not asked to share their prophetic proclamations either, but to share their life stories, ethical dilemmas, perspectives, and questions.

Together with a colleague, I designed and led a process that took place over two and a half days. Toward the end of the process, one woman came to me and said, "You are leading me to a place I do not want to go." I was surprised at her comment, as I thought that I was working hard not to lead in a particular direction, though this person knew me and my particular perspectives well. When I asked her to tell me more, she said that she had been engaged with several pastors and laity through the two days of discernment, and they were talking more honestly and respectfully than they had ever talked about this subject before. She realized that, as she listened, she was changing her own views. As I listened to her, I realized that a more profound transformation was taking place in her than a battle of ideologies could have produced. She was being transformed from the inside out, and it was leading her to advocate social transformation that she herself could not have imagined a short time before.

This story, together with Mary Moschella's panoply of stories from her students and her own work, suggest to me that Mary's (partly implicit) thesis is correct: that people change more profoundly, that their passion for prophetic ministry and social transformation is enacted more fully, when they engage in listening, observing, and learning from one another. Who would have thought such a thing? Mary Moschella did! She has pointed the way for ethnography as a pastoral practice, and she has done something even more subtle and powerful. She has pointed the way to prophetic ministry through the very processes that she describes. Listening and learning leads to envisioning and empowering, which then leads to transforming the world. May it be so!

Mary Elizabeth Mullino Moore
Candler School of Theology,
Emory University, Atlanta

Preface

This book offers a way for religious leaders to harness the power of social research to transform a group's common life and its purposeful work in the world. Through ethnographic listening practices, pastors and rabbis can begin to hear their communities' stories, told in many voices and versions. By weaving these stories together, leaders can "read" the theologies that are expressed and enacted in the everyday life of the group. Then, by sharing their research results back with their congregation or agency, leaders can stimulate more honest theological reflection and trusting relationships within the group. This process sows the seeds for spiritual and social transformation within the faith community and beyond.

Several years ago, in a course I took on "Interpreting Religious Practice," a student colleague, who was also a pastor, undertook a study involving members of his own congregation. This student's research yielded a dramatic transformation in his relationships with his church members. It was as if a curtain of pretense had been lifted, and instead of "playing church," both pastor and parish had started to become real with each other. This striking result inaugurated my thinking about teaching ethnography as a form of pastoral ministry, in and of itself.

For the last seven years I have been privileged to teach classes in "Ethnography for Transformation in Congregations and Communities" at Wesley Theological Seminary. In these classes, students engaged in research projects of their own design report eye-opening encounters within the congregations or agencies in which they serve. These students ask the members of their faith communities straightforward questions about their religious practices, such as, "Why do you come to church?" and, "What do you do there?"

Such ethnographic research is tilted toward the concrete, material, cultural, and social dimensions of faith. In observing and listening, and in studying related historical documents, students gather broader views of the congregations, schools, or agencies that they serve. Student researchers look at issues of social and financial power, intercultural relationships, race, religious difference, gender, and sexual orientation, to name just a few. Through their questions, students probe for values that lie beneath the level of cheerful or grudging compliance with official religious teachings, and probe dissent as well, eliciting new information and honest responses that often surprise and move them.

To my joy, some of this honest and deep sharing spills over into our classroom discussions. I am privileged to hear about life-changing experiences and insights gleaned through students' ethnographic endeavors. This sometimes sparks a kind of parallel process in the classroom, where students' personal stories and vocational hopes and dreams, fears and frustrations are spoken out loud. The classroom can become a community of trust, where rigorous analysis and searching questions are shared and met with mutual encouragement and engaging discussion. My hope is that classes, pastors, and other groups of researchers using this book will also experience a kind of parallel process, in which the practice of honest dialogue and open sharing enlivens the experiences of teaching, learning, and collegial peer review.[1]

It is my students' fine and daring work that has convinced me of the necessity of writing this book. Students asked for a "roadmap," a guide that brings together practical tools with pastoral theological reflection on the processes of conducting, writing, and sharing pastoral ethnography.[2] This book is my response. Because my students' ethnographic projects have been so

1. For a fascinating study of ethnography in the classroom, see Ernest T. Stringer et al., *Community-Based Ethnography: Breaking Traditional Boundaries of Research, Teaching, and Learning* (Mahwah, N.J.: Lawrence Erlbaum Associates, 1997).

2. This request for a roadmap is no doubt related to students' experience with a popular guide to New Testament interpretation, co-authored by my colleague Sharon Ringe. See Frederick C. Tiffany and Sharon H. Ringe, *Biblical Interpretation: A Roadmap* (Nashville: Abingdon Press, 1996).

remarkable, I refer to many of them here, with permission.[3] These projects appear as case studies, exemplifying the topics covered in each chapter, demonstrating a range of contexts for such study, and illustrating notable results.

The practice of ethnography can be fun because there are so many surprises involved in the research process. Where we thought there was unanimity, we find oppositional views. Where we thought people were boring, we hear outrageous stories. Where we thought we understood a certain tradition or dynamic, we turn up new questions.

Ethnography can also be muddy and confusing for the pastoral researcher. In the face of this confusion, it may be tempting to rush in and impose a unified theological vision or a structured business-model program upon the congregation, school, or agency. Research methods teach us rather to slow down and "hang out" for a while in the mud, paying attention and suspending judgment, until we begin to get our bearings. The research findings that are presented here show that it is worth the time it takes to listen to and to watch people as they perform their faith, trying to see what they are doing or saying through their actions and interactions within a particular local context.

This is not to suggest that social research will yield a unitary, fixed, or final picture of group life, a completed puzzle where all the pieces fit. People are more complicated than that. Yet through ethnographic research, we can glimpse a kind of "snapshot" of

---

3. I have received written permission from my former students for my references to their work. These students had previously secured written permission for their research and related publications from their research partners. In most cases, we have agreed that the names of all parties and organizations involved be changed in order to protect the privacy of the persons and groups represented in these studies. In order to add another layer of protection, I have changed some of the identifying details in the cases presented. In a few cases, such as when the research has already been published, or when the authors requested it and their consent forms allowed it, I used the authors' actual names. This book has received an ethical review as a part of the process of testing standards for establishing Human Subjects Policies and Procedures at Wesley Theological Seminary, under the oversight of the Academic Dean's office. Those policies are now under final review by Wesley's legal counsel and will soon be available for public examination.

group life.[4] It will represent a biased and partial view of the group, to be sure. There are limits to what anyone can see from a given place in a given time.[5]

Nevertheless, this snapshot is sufficient material to work with in order to begin to move into more honest engagement with the people we serve. "This is how it looks to me," we say in our summary of the study. "Have I got that right?" And, "What am I missing?" Entering into the pastoral practice of seeing and being seen, hearing and being heard on this deeper level is unsettling at times. We might experience cognitive or emotional dissonance when a deep disagreement opens up, for example. Or we may feel vulnerable when one of the faithful points out our misunderstandings or flawed habits. Yet it is this very unsettling feature of the process that may constitute what James Loder called the "transforming moment," the occasion for new insight to dawn and for new, more responsive pastoral practices to be imagined.[6]

The first time I taught a doctor of ministry class on ethnographic listening and pastoral transformation, my students looked at me with seemingly incredulous eyes. These individuals were already accomplished spiritual leaders; many of them did not want to take on the dry work of observation. They did not want to ask their people questions without offering them pastoral consolation; they did not want to make up forms and surveys and do anything quite so dull and mechanical as counting responses. They did not tell me these objections in so many words at first, in accordance with the usual codes of classroom etiquette. Yet one blessedly honest woman's response to my blithe admonition that "you can't expect a congregation to change if you're not willing to be transformed yourself," said it all: "But I don't want to change."

4. Nancy Tatom Ammerman, Arthur E. Farnsley et al., *Congregation and Community* (New Brunswick, N.J.: Rutgers University Press, 1997), 40.

5. For an essay on the interplay of "sight, cite, and site" in religious narratives, see Thomas A. Tweed, "Introduction: Narrating U.S. Religious History," in *Retelling U.S. Religious History,* ed. Thomas A. Tweed (Berkeley and Los Angeles: University of California Press, 1997), 1–23.

6. James Loder, *The Transforming Moment,* 2nd ed. (Colorado Springs, Colo.: Helmers & Howard, 1989).

Generally speaking, we don't want to change. We want others to change and fulfill our visions of what is good and just and hopeful. Nevertheless, transformative pastoral leadership requires open engagement and attentive listening to the lives of particular people and communities. Religious leaders have to be willing to be curious, to be surprised, to be moved. In a genuine relationship, the "I-Thou" sort of relationship of which Martin Buber spoke, we strive to respect the other as subject rather than object.[7] When we develop the ears to hear our people in their cultural complexity, we will likely come to appreciate them more, to feel compassion, admiration, or to understand a bit more about them. We may be challenged, or touched, or relieved and grateful to hear what our research participant has to say to us. Honest engagement requires this: that our view of a person, a community, and ourselves be enlarged in some way. As will become clear in the forthcoming case examples, it is this dynamic of mutually expanding awareness that harbors the potential for transforming a community's shared faith practices. Religious leaders are not removed spectators, but critical participants in the process.

My students at Wesley Seminary deserve most of the credit and thanks for this book, which would not have been possible without them. They have taken the tools of pastoral ethnography and employed them in many creative and courageous ways, launching themselves into deeper and more engaged ministries. I wish I could name each person here, though confidentiality agreements prevent this. I am grateful also to my students whose work is not cited here; they have also contributed in significant ways. I thank Dean Bruce Birch at Wesley Theological Seminary for encouraging my teaching in this area. Associate Dean Lewis Parks supported my engagement in the subject by continually requesting the course in Wesley's doctor of ministry program. I am grateful to President David McAllister-Wilson and the Board of Governors at Wesley for granting me a sabbatical leave during the fall of 2007 in order to work on the manuscript.

---

7. Martin Buber, *I and Thou*, trans. Walter Kaufman, 2nd ed. (Bel Air, Calif.: Hesperides, 2006).

I thank the Wabash Center for Teaching and Learning in Theology and Religion, which funded this writing in its early stages in the summer of 2006 with a Wabash Fellowship. I thank the faculty and colleagues of the 2005–6 Wabash Workshop for Pretenured Faculty, who nurtured and inspired me in thinking about teaching the course and writing the book. In particular, I acknowledge and thank Paul Myhre, Lucinda Huffaker, Nadine Pence Franz, and Richard Ascough. Special thanks go to Mary Elizabeth Moore and Willie Jennings, who read and commented on early drafts of the first two chapters. Mary Elizabeth Moore suggested the term "pastoral research." Workshop colleagues Jeffery Tribble, Boyung Lee, Jeanne Hoeft, Marion Grau, and Lisa Hess, among others, offered helpful conversation, good humor, and encouragement.

I am indebted to the work of many teachers and scholars. In particular, I want to acknowledge Ann Taves, whose class on interpreting religious practice led me to the idea for teaching ethnography as a pastoral practice. This book in many ways is an offshoot of that course. The work of authors in sociology of religion, ethnography, and qualitative study, together with the contributions of authors in pastoral and practical theology, constitute the warp and woof of this interdisciplinary weaving.

I especially want to acknowledge the work of researchers Nancy Ammerman and her co-authors; of Martyn Hammersley and Paul Atkinson; and of Jennifer Mason. I also want to acknowledge the work of pastoral and practical theologians Elaine Graham and her co-authors, as well as that of Herbert Anderson and Edward Foley; and of Edward Wimberly.

As always, I am grateful to the Society of Pastoral Theology for the camaraderie of friends and colleagues who stimulate and encourage my work. Kathleen Greider is a trusted mentor and friend. Bill Clements has offered me encouragement and insight. I thank Bonnie Miller-McLemore for her interest and support of this project. I also thank Leonard Hummel and Jane Maynard for reading a précis of the project and for their friendship and shared interest in the intersection of pastoral theology with the lived religion paradigm. The work of Carrie Doehring, Emmanuel Lartey, and Christie Neuger, among others,' underlies this project. I thank Susan Dunlap for her interest and enthusiasm for this work. Special thanks go to Pamela Cooper-White, Herbert Anderson, Janet Schaller, and Eileen Campbell-Reed, who read and commented on drafts of individual chapters. I especially thank my friend and colleague Charles J. Scalise, who read the entire manuscript and offered vital feedback.

I am also grateful to the Association for Practical Theology, which invited me to present portions of this work at its annual meeting in 2006 at the American Academy of Religion annual meeting in Washington, D.C. My colleague David Mellott is a key conversation partner in ethnography and theology. I thank Lawrence Golemon of the Alban Institute for inviting me to participate with other scholars in a series of think tanks on the topic of narrative leadership and formation.

Kathie Hepler of the Wesley Writing Center shared her literary expertise, helping me enormously with chapter 8. My thanks to Howertine Duncan of the Wesley Seminary Library, who filled my numerous interlibrary loan requests in her kind and speedy fashion. I thank the good people at The Pilgrim Press who have worked with me and improved this book in many ways: Timothy Staveteig, Ulrike Guthrie, John Eagleson, and Joan Blake, among others. I thank Carol Jackson at Weaving a Way for the use of the beautiful cover photograph of a collaborative weaving project.

I thank my many friends, colleagues, neighbors, counselors, as well as my church, my pastor, and my online writers' group for upholding me and for encouraging me to stay focused on the work of writing. This list includes, but is not limited to, Beverly Mitchell, Michael Koppel, Sondra Wheeler, Amy Oden, Denise Dombkowski Hopkins, Allison Smith, and Donna Firer. I acknowledge my parents, Sabino and Carmela Moschella, for their unflagging confidence and love. I am grateful to my husband, Doug Clark, who read the entire manuscript and offered helpful feedback. I thank Doug, Ethan, and Abbey, for their patience with the demands this writing placed on my time, energy, and attention. I also thank them for their complete willingness to celebrate

every minor triumph along the way. I am grateful to our minia-
ture Schnauzer, Maddie, who always knew just when I needed
to be walked. Finally, I am grateful to the mystery of life itself,
which continues to sustain and amaze me every day.

I hope that this book will be a resource for students, religious
leaders, and communities of faith who gather together in the bold
hope that they can help generate transformational, faithful, and
life-giving change in this world.

ETHNOGRAPHY
as a Pastoral Practice

Introduction

Great religious leaders are women and men who discern a prophetic call to change the world. Dreams of transformation —
both spiritual and temporal — motivate and inspire these leaders. In seminaries and theological schools, leaders such as these
are challenged to enlarge their views of God and humanity and
to imagine a more just and life-giving social order. Hardly anyone who echoes Isaiah's response to the divine call, "Here am I,
send me!" (Isa. 6:8), envisions a life dedicated to maintaining the
status quo.

Yet new pastors, rabbis, and other religious leaders are often
stymied when they attempt to practice prophetic pastoral leadership. Even highly gifted and talented individuals run into the
predictable barriers of institutional life: interpersonal conflict,
economic constraints, and dogged resistance to change. No matter how good your theology or how inspired your vision, these
walls rise up to meet you. To convey your convictions in a way
that makes an impact on the group is much harder than you ever
imagined. Coping with the quotidian power struggles enacted on
boards and committees or the persistence of prejudice and bias
or the sheer drain of time and energy required for institutional
maintenance — these can wear you down. After a few months or
years of trying, a painful truth dawns: the communal practice of
faith is gritty, messy, even morally flawed. As she wrestles with
constraints and compromises, a pastor's prophetic edge may be
blunted, her spirit dampened. The hope of creating change, of
making a difference, can elude even the most inspired pastoral
leader.

This book offers seminarians and religious leaders a way of
staying focused on the goal of spiritual and social transformation, even when up against these institutional walls. Ethnography,

3

the tool that I am proffering, may seem a surprising choice, especially coming from a pastoral theologian. Yet when conducted and shared as a form of pastoral practice, ethnography can enable religious leaders to hear the theological wisdom of the people, wisdom that is spoken right in the midst of the nitty-gritty mundane realities of group life. Ethnography practiced in this way can enhance the quality of relationships in the community, so that the local walls of institutional life will become less mysterious and less formidable. The pastoral practice of ethnography can engender conversations that transform the way things work within a faith community and beyond it.

What Is Ethnography?

Ethnography is a way of immersing yourself in the life of a people in order to learn something about and from them. Ethnography as a pastoral practice involves opening your eyes and ears to understand the ways in which people practice their faith. This method, described more fully in chapter 1, entails observing people's actions and interactions, and asking them to share their stories with you. Ethnography is also about writing. In a pastoral context, it involves recording your observations and reflections, analyzing them, and creating a narrative account of the people's local and particular religious and cultural life.

Ethnography can be practiced as a form of pastoral listening and care[1] in the work of prophetic leadership. Perhaps that still sounds implausible. After all, pastoral care, many think, is about visiting the sick or counseling people through a family crisis. This model of care has long employed the biblical metaphor of the good shepherd: the pastor leaves behind the ninety-nine sheep on the hill in order to go off and seek the one who is lost, bringing this sheep back into the fold.

This model of individual care, while still honored, is now supplemented with pastoral theological models of care for all the

---

1. John Patton describes the pastor as a "mini-ethnographer." See John Patton, *Pastoral Care in Context: An Introduction to Pastoral Care* (Louisville: Westminster John Knox Press, 1993), 43–45.

sheep. The concept of ethnography as a pastoral practice grows out of some of these new models, particularly the communal contextual model of care.[2] This model gives rise to questions such as: "How can a pastor or a rabbi care intelligently for the whole congregation and the wider community of which it is a part?" And, "How can the congregation itself begin to respond in more faithful and prophetic ways to the 'living human web(s)' of life both within and beyond the local community?" This pastoral practice is communal (it involves the whole "flock") and contextual (it addresses particular, local communities in their sociocultural complexity).[3]

Ethnography as a pastoral practice also draws from narrative models of theology and care. Narrative models recognize the importance of storytelling as a hallmark of human experience. We shape our lives and give meaning and coherence to them through telling personal stories, family stories, group stories, faith stories, and cultural histories. Likewise, we are shaped by the familial, cultural, and religious stories that we hear — from parents, schools, media, and houses of worship — all around us. Our lives are embedded in stories that influence us and describe the range of possibilities that we can imagine for our lives.[4]

---

2. John Patton coined the phrase, "communal contextual paradigm for pastoral care." Patton, *Pastoral Care in Context*, 4. Numerous pastoral theologians elaborate upon this concept. See, for example, Kathleen J. Greider, Gloria A. Johnson, and Kristen J. Leslie, "Three Decades of Women Writing for Our Lives," in *Feminist and Womanist Pastoral Theology*, ed. Bonnie J. Miller-McLemore and Brita Gill-Austern (Nashville: Abingdon Press, 1999), 21–50.

3. For an overview of these changes in the field of pastoral theology, see Nancy Ramsay, ed., *Pastoral Care and Counseling: Redefining the Paradigms* (Nashville: Abingdon Press, 2004). The term "living human web" is an expansion of Anton Boisen's concept of "living human documents." See Bonnie J. Miller-McLemore, "The Living Human Web: Pastoral Theology at the Turn of the Century," in *Through the Eyes of Women*, ed. Jeanne Stevenson-Moessner (Minneapolis: Fortress Press, 1996), 9–26.

4. For examples of narrative models of pastoral theology and practice, see Christie Cozad Neuger, *Counseling Women: A Narrative, Feminist Approach* (Minneapolis: Fortress Press, 2001); Edward P. Wimberly, *Recalling Our Own Stories: Spiritual Renewal for Religious Caregivers* (San Francisco: Jossey-Bass,

Practitioners of narrative therapies for individuals suggest that change comes about when we tell our stories, listening for themes and subplots, and identify the guiding myths or the underlying convictions by which we live. Articulating and evaluating these myths can then lead to a re-authoring process, wherein we begin to change our actions and attitudes and thereby begin to author — claim authority over — new, more intentional plotlines. By altering the stories we tell ourselves about ourselves and about the world, we can start to imagine new ways of conducting our lives. Conversely, by trying out new ways of acting in the world, we can create new stories, new themes and convictions.[5]

The pastoral practice of ethnography can bring a congregation into an analogous co-authoring process. This works by allowing the people to articulate their stories and reflect on the composite themes and subplots that come to light. The congregation can then begin to reevaluate and intentionally revise its corporate story, entertaining new ideas and engaging in new religious practices. Listening to complex local stories can help a congregation get unstuck from the tyranny of tradition and the ubiquitous reasoning of "We've never done it that way before!"

Ethnography also works by helping pastoral leaders get a feel for the undercurrents in the life of the community: the parking lot grumbling, the petty rivalries, the tight-lipped resistance that may be just under the surface of the parishioner's polite but terse, "Nice sermon, pastor." These undercurrents also tell a story — probably a different story than the one inscribed in official theologies or mission statements. Observing and listening to these stories can help pastors discover and name some of the issues that form the undercurrents of communal life. Once these issues are heard and explored in open conversation, the invisible hold of the undercurrents is usually diminished. It is not that the

1997); and Carrie Doehring, *The Practice of Pastoral Care: A Postmodern Approach* (Louisville: Westminster John Knox Press, 2006).

5. See Michael White and David Epston, *Narrative Means to Therapeutic Ends* (New York: W. W. Norton, 1990). White and Epston highlight the connection between knowledge and power, relying on the work of Michel Foucault.

undercurrents subside, necessarily, but they become less mysterious and unpredictable. Leaders can navigate better in currents whose patterns they recognize and understand.

These currents are often not noticeable at first. Several years ago, I went on a weeklong group kayak trip in the San Juan Islands off Puget Sound. In this beautiful part of the Great Northwest, the clear blue water is surprisingly forceful. Depending on the weather and time of day, strong currents can form and quickly become dangerous to recreation-seekers. I was a novice kayaker going on this trip; I knew nothing about currents. Fortunately, the trip leaders were highly skilled and well informed. They directed us: they told us when to depart and in which direction to paddle. Every time we landed on another island beach, the leaders studied their charts. One afternoon, the kayaks were packed and ready to go, but the leaders hesitated. They paced across the sand, trying to decide whether or not we should make the next crossing. Finally, one said, "Let's go, now!" and the entire group quickly boarded and paddled across the way as fast as we could. That night, we learned that a small boat had gone down just a little bit later in the day while trying to make that same crossing.

Doing ethnography is like studying navigational charts. Leaders who use ethnographic research can come to understand the currents of institutional life and how they can suddenly become treacherous. The forceful water doesn't go away as a result of studying it and being aware of it, but the study can help you learn how to navigate in it. When you learn a bit about the local community, its history and ecology, its beauty and its hidden currents, you will find out how to navigate in these particular waters, to get where you — and your group — want to go.

An Example: Racial Undercurrents

For an example of how ethnography can work as a pastoral practice, let's look at the story of "Ken," an African American student pastor in a cross-cultural appointment who enrolled in a pastoral ethnography class. When he started this class, Ken had been serving in a troubled congregation for almost four years.

The congregation was a small, all-white Protestant church in a rural southern state. As he set about to study his congregation, Ken discovered a record of remarkably brief pastorates in the history of the church. He concluded that one of the "plotlines" in this church's story had to do with the laity running the church and, more often than not, also running the minister out of town.

When Ken designed his interview questions for his ethnographic study, he wanted to understand why the people seemed so resistant to change. Ken asked his people a few simple questions about change, including this one: "How do you perceive change in the church?" To his surprise, several parishioners brought up the issue of Ken's race as an example of a big change in the church. Though the people had never before broached this subject with him, Ken soon discovered that his "racial background" had been a major topic of conversation among the membership. Members had been trying to discern his exact ethnicity and race, as some suspected he was Indian, and some Hispanic/African American. They described their experience of Ken's interracial appointment to their white church as "a shock." One member told Ken that a majority of the males in the congregation were once members of the KKK.

Ken was astounded to hear this, as were his teacher and colleagues in the ethnography class. Perhaps the most surprising remarks came next. "But you loved us and that is what changed my mind about you," a former Klansman told Ken. Other church members offered similar sentiments. Ken was moved by these comments. While it was disturbing to hear about the intensity of racism in the church, it was also a relief to have it named and out in the open. The sentiments had been there all along, functioning as emotional undercurrents in the church's life. But once the parishioners told him, honestly, how they had been experiencing him, Ken gained a clearer grasp of the strange emotional undertow that had made his work so difficult. It made sense to him now. Ken also knew that it took courage for these men to speak so boldly and to express their feelings of attachment to him so directly.

Ken understood the poignancy of these conversations; he felt validated in his pastoral role. The interviews confirmed Ken's understanding of his calling and Christian practice, which he describes in the following way: "To be in line [with Christ] means you love even when you do not trust; yet you are assured and you continue to walk together."[6] These conversations helped to bring to voice the growing trust between Ken and his parishioners; they also contributed to Ken's understanding of this shared theological vision.

Not every pastoral research project is as strikingly beneficial as this one. Sometimes people resist the research process, and sometimes people feel misunderstood rather than fully heard. Nevertheless, this example demonstrates two potential benefits of what I call "ethnographic listening." The first benefit is the way in which the power of unspoken prejudices or invisible undercurrents can be neutralized when brought out into the open. Ken's conversation with his congregants helped diminish the hold of the shameful racist secret. The conversation didn't overcome racism, but it made it possible to name and discuss this dynamic and its role in the congregation's history. This kind of open disclosure robs a shameful secret of some of its power.

The second benefit for congregational leaders, pastors, or rabbis engaged in ethnographic study is that they can get to know their people in a slightly different manner than usual. Ken's parishioners might never have had these conversations had he not asked them certain key questions, and asked them in a particular way. When Ken asked, "How do you perceive change in the church?" he was not asking as if there were one clear, theologically or morally correct answer. Rather, Ken was offering an honest and open question. Given that people often perceive pastors as morally authoritative, judgmental, or both, adopting the stance of a researcher can provide the pastor with a more neutral, less charged place to stand in the relationship. In the

---

6. "Ken," "Ethnography and Congregational Transformation at (a Protestant) Church," unpublished paper, December 9, 2004, Wesley Theological Seminary, 20.

role of a researcher, one asks questions in the spirit of curiosity, paying attention to and trying not to influence the answers. This dispassionate posture allows the parishioner to speak more freely.[7] Even though some respondents to questions will be more circumspect than others, and even though some will lie, an observant pastor-researcher will be rewarded with much helpful information.

Ethnography yields broad perceptions that come in to the researcher through all the senses. Paying attention to the sights, sounds, smells, and tastes related to group life will give the pastor a fuller and richer understanding of the complexity and variety of cultural stories within a congregation or a community. The pastor as learner can better "read" some of the shared knowledges and habits that constitute what people often call "the culture of the congregation."[8] In these ways, the practice of ethnographic research can become a form of holistic pastoral listening that attends to the range of meanings, experiences, desires, and theologies that congregations express not only through their words but also through their lives.

Relationship to Congregational Studies

The idea of using ethnography in congregations is not new. Authors in the field of congregational studies have already demonstrated many key techniques for this kind of study. Additionally, sociologists of religion have pointed to the ways in which social research carried out in congregations and neighborhoods can enlighten local ministries and missions. These authors have shown the value of gathering critical demographic and historical data about the congregation and its neighborhood, data

---

7. Of course, pastors and rabbis will retain their status as religious leaders in research relationships to some degree, even though they attempt to step away from an authoritative role when conducting research.

8. See, for example, Ammerman et al., *Congregation and Community*, 54–59; and Anthony B. Robinson, *Transforming Congregational Culture* (Grand Rapids: Wm. B. Eerdmans, 2003).

that can inform a congregation's sense of purpose and planning for the future.[9]

What is new is a focus on the ways in which the ethnographic encounter itself, through the processes of gathering and analyzing and sharing data, can profoundly affect the members of the group, the pastoral researcher, and their shared life together. Significantly, researcher Lynn Davidman notes, "the telling of lives always changes those lives."[10] Research changes lives. While anthropologists and historians may have lamented the social science equivalent of the Heisenberg Uncertainty Principle (that the research process always has an impact on the findings), for religious leaders, this principle is a boon. Pastors and rabbis searching for ways to inspire spiritual growth and social transformation can make use of the life-changing potential of ethnographic study.

Pastoral theology has always been concerned with the telling of lives and the changing of lives. Over the years, pastoral theologians have used differing metaphors to describe the role of religious leaders in promoting personal and social change. Words such as "healing" (Seward Hiltner), "growth" (Howard Clinebell), and more recently "emancipatory praxis" (Brita Gill-Austern), "liberation" (Carroll Watkins Ali), "resisting, empowering, [and] nurturing" (Bonnie Miller-McLemore), all point to the religious leader's role as an agent of justice-oriented transformation.[11]

9. See, for example, Nancy T. Ammerman, Jackson Carroll, Carl S. Dudley, and William McKinney, *Studying Congregations: A New Handbook* (Nashville: Abingdon Press, 1998); and Helen Cameron, Philip Richter, Douglas Davies, and Frances Ward, eds., *Studying Local Churches: A Handbook* (London: SCM Press, 2005).

10. Lynn Davidman, "Truth, Subjectivity, and Ethnographic Research," in *Personal Knowledge and Beyond: Reshaping the Ethnography of Religion*, ed. James Spickard, J. Shawn Landres, and Meredith B. McGuire (New York: New York University Press, 2002), 19.

11. Seward Hiltner, *Preface to Pastoral Theology* (New York: Abingdon Press, 1958); Howard Clinebell, *Basic Types of Pastoral Care and Counseling: Resources for the Ministry of Healing and Growth*, rev. ed. (Nashville: Abingdon Press, 1984); Brita Gill-Austern writes, "Emancipatory praxis will use whatever tools it has at its disposal to struggle against oppression and to further individual and social transformation," in "Pedagogy under the Influence of Feminism and Womanism," in Miller-McLemore and Gill-Austern, eds. *Feminist and Womanist Pastoral Theology*, 151; Carroll Watkins Ali, *Survival and*

Ethnography is a tool that can spark such transformation in persons, communities, and social systems.[12]

Authors in pastoral theology have also called attention to the importance of description as a key element in practical theology.[13] These authors have inspired numerous others to use the tools of qualitative research and congregational studies in order to better understand and thus care intelligently for persons in their social contexts.[14] Building on these efforts, I want to focus our attention on the research process itself as a potential means of spiritual growth and social transformation.

A key element in using ethnography as a pastoral practice is that it becomes a form of pastoral listening. Pastoral theologians have long stressed listening skills as a critical dimension of care and counseling. Teachers of pastoral theology and care spend a great deal of time talking about the practice of listening. "Listen to what is said and to what is omitted," they say. "Notice the furrow in his brow or the special light in her eyes. Pay attention to the body language as well as the spoken word. Pick up on the particularities; consider the quirky or artful phrases." It seems simple enough, but patient listening is actually difficult to sustain.

Liberation: Pastoral Theology in African American Context (St. Louis: Chalice Press, 1999); Bonnie Miller-McLemore, "Feminist Theory in Pastoral Theology," in Miller-McLemore and Gill-Austern, *Feminist and Womanist Pastoral Theology,* 80. Some of these references are cited in Charles J. Scalise, *Bridging the Gap: Connecting What You Learned in Seminary with What You Find in the Congregation* (Nashville: Abingdon Press, 2003), 78–79.

12. See also Larry Kent Graham, *Care of Persons, Care of Worlds: A Psychosystems Approach to Pastoral Care and Counseling* (Nashville: Abingdon Press, 1992).

13. Don S. Browning, *A Fundamental Practical Theology: Descriptive and Strategic Proposals* (Minneapolis: Augsburg Fortress, 1991); Larry VandeCreek, Hillary Bender, and Merle R. Jordan, *Research in Pastoral Care and Counseling: Quantitative and Qualitative Approaches* (Decatur, Ga.: Journal of Pastoral Care Publications, 1994); and John Swinton and Harriet Mowat, *Practical Theology and Qualitative Research* (London: SCM Press, 2006).

14. See, for example, Leonard M. Hummel, *Clothed in Nothingness: Consolation for Suffering* (Minneapolis: Augsburg Fortress, 2003); Karen D. Scheib, *Challenging Invisibility: Practices of Care with Older Women* (St. Louis: Chalice Press, 2004); and Janet Fishburn, ed., *People of a Compassionate God: Creating Welcoming Congregations* (Nashville: Abingdon Press, 2003).

Lapsing into a mode of giving advice, becoming an expert, or pretending to be one is so much easier.

I stress the practice of listening because I believe that deep down, listening is a liberating practice, a practice that validates and honors another person's experience, insight, and soul. Many people in the world do not have the privilege of being heard. Some people go to their pastor seeking someone who has "the ears to hear" them in their sorrow, joy, or perplexity. Too often, religious leaders, pressed for time and short on patience, dole out platitudes or advice, but miss out on the chance to "hear someone to speech," in Nelle Morton's eloquent phrase.[15] Patient pastoral listening can empower a person to find her own voice.[16]

Ethnography, as I construct it in this book, is a form of pastoral listening that can analogously help a congregation or a community to find its collective voice. Ethnography can be used as a means for listening to a group, helping to call forth both individual and collective stories. This form of ethnography also involves a kind of "reflective listening" practice, analogous to the reflective listening that is a key component of basic pastoral counseling conversations.[17] In an individual pastoral counseling conversation, a rabbi might repeat or reflect a congregant's words, offering them back to the individual for clarification or validation. In a parallel way, the rabbi who conducts a study can offer back an ethnographic narrative to the congregation. This "reflection" can help the congregation find its voice, its purpose, or, as Tom Frank would put it, its soul.[18] The dialogical process of speaking and listening, reflecting back and being corrected, in the context of caring relationships, can be deeply healing and

---

15. Nelle Morton, *The Journey Is Home* (Boston: Beacon Press, 1985).

16. This is not to suggest that pastoral listening alone is sufficient for healing all wounds, personal, spiritual, or political. Finding voice is one component of empowerment. See Michelle Tooley, *Voices of the Voiceless: Women, Justice, and Human Rights in Guatemala* (Scottdale, Pa.: Herald Press, 1989).

17. For an example of reflective listening, see Charles W. Taylor, *The Skilled Pastor: Counseling as the Practice of Theology* (Minneapolis: Augsburg Fortress, 1991), 31–38

18. Thomas Edward Frank, *The Soul of the Congregation* (Nashville: Abingdon Press, 2000).

liberative. This ethnographic engagement becomes a catalyst for healing and freeing a community up for change.

How This Works

When a pastor or religious leader steps back a bit into the role of a pastoral researcher, the asking of questions and the telling of lives that result can have a profoundly deepening effect on the leader's relationship to the people that he or she is entrusted to serve. New knowledge is uncovered or generated, together with the new experience of telling and hearing it. This happens, in part, because many people, when asked outright about themselves and their backgrounds, their practices, and their faith, tend to be forthcoming and honest; they are often grateful to be heard.

As different sides of various issues and practices get spelled out through the process of interviews or anonymous surveys that strive to be nonjudgmental, and diverse persons get a chance to speak their truth, the level of honesty and depth in the interrelationships will likely increase. This alone will enhance the spiritual quality of life in the group. Honest and clear communication tends to increase the personal well-being of the members of the group as well as the overall quality of group life. When things go well, both the pastor and the congregation, as "co-researchers," tend to become more comfortable and caring in their interactions through the research process. One student writes, "Conducting this study has shown the congregation that I am interested in their story. I tried very hard to appreciate and honor all the stories that I heard. This study helped me to love the congregation more fully and with a greater understanding of who they really are."[19]

When pastors engage as many persons as possible in the research and then analyze the accumulated data, a fuller picture of the congregation and its diverse constituents emerges. Suddenly, the pastor gets a clue about the reason two factions seem to be warring; the undercurrents start to make sense. While at times

19. Author Anonymous, Title Anonymous, unpublished paper, Wesley Theological Seminary, April 24, 2007, 29. Used by permission.

pastors may be shocked or disheartened at what they hear, they will be able to navigate congregational life better when they know and understand the deeper currents that have been holding things in place.

Further, when a pastoral researcher is able sensitively to report back the results of the study and analysis to the congregation as a whole, the benefits of reflective listening become clear. The members of the group may be genuinely surprised at the collective picture of themselves and their history that the pastor assembles and then holds up to them in a kind of mirror. They may be moved at the beauty that their religious leader sees in them, beauty they had not previously perceived or experienced in themselves. Likewise, they may be disturbed at the flaws the mirror reveals. They may also disagree with the pastor's interpretations of them. The pastor is, after all, offering back something more like a portrait than an actual reflection in a mirror. The results of the study (the pastor's portrait of the people) will inevitably be flawed and partial. The portrait will reveal only as much as the pastor can see, hear, and comprehend.

The pastor who is brave enough to offer his or her flawed portrait back to the people will likely hear a range of the members' responses. In this way, sharing research results leads to more dialogue, as the pastor listens again to the people's perceptions of themselves and their leader. The pastor then gets to see something of himself or herself in the mirror as well, as the people share their observations and insights, their "views from the pews." While this process usually will not be painless — most congregations can spot their leaders' flaws instantly and describe them in frightening and sometimes contradictory detail — such honest encounters will disclose impressions and information that the pastor can use, if willing, to help the group give birth to a new future.

One of the key assumptions in narrative therapy is that although change is difficult, it is possible.[20] Those who practice individual narrative therapy have discovered that when individuals realize the impact of their personal histories upon the various

---

20. Wimberly, *Recalling Our Own Stories*, 74.

story lines, themes, and myths with which they have been composing their lives, there dawns a recognition of a certain amount of freedom to change. Something analogous happens for groups of people such as congregations, agencies, or communities when they come to recognize themselves as embedded in a particular corporate story.

Traditional attitudes and activities, when examined and discussed from diverse angles through ethnographic research, tend to loosen their stultifying grip on group life. It is not that ethnography convinces people to "dump" old customs wholesale. It is rather that the group becomes intentional and aware of what it is doing and why. Once the social meanings preserved in traditional practices are explored — seen and heard and openly discussed — the group may consciously decide to critically retrieve or reappropriate tradition. The group, in the context of caring and honest relationship with its leader, can then take the authority needed to alter the themes of its future chapters. In this manner, a humble research process can spark personal, spiritual, and relational growth and create openings for communal and social change.

One example of a research project that prompted a dynamic of communal growth occurred in Manchester, New Hampshire, where an oral history project was undertaken with three hundred former textile mill workers. The researchers were not religious leaders, and they were not trying to instigate personal or communal change or transformation. Their intention was merely to record interviews in order to fill out the historical record on the Amoskeag Mills, once the world's largest textile company.[21] At first, the oral history researchers had a hard time getting former mill workers to agree to the interviews. Many of the workers felt that their work lives were unremarkable, that textile work was

---

21. Tamara Hareven, "The Search for Generational Memory," in *Oral History: An Interdisciplinary Anthology,* ed. David K. Dunaway and Willa K. Baum (Walnut Creek, Calif.: Altamira Press, 1978), 241–56. For a full-length description of this research, see Tamara K. Hareven, *Amoskeag: Life and Work in an American Factory-city* (New York: Pantheon Books, 1978).

generally looked down upon, and that the traumatic closing of the mill in 1936 was too painful to recall.[22]

Their attitudes changed after an exhibit opened in a Manchester museum, documenting the architectural design of the city, the urban plan, and the experiences of working in the mill that had been recorded in the interviews. No one expected the exhibit to be a popular success — it was meant for architects or preservationists. But a funny thing happened in the community as word spread about the exhibit. As the former mill workers who had been interviewed went to see the exhibit and rekindled their memories, word of the exhibit spread. Tamara Hareven, one of the researchers, writes, "Most striking were recurring scenes where old former workers searched for their relatives in huge historic group portraits of the workers, where grandparents led their grandchildren through the exhibit, often describing their work process of 30–40 years earlier."[23] In the five weeks that the exhibit ran, twelve thousand people came to see it. As former co-workers recognized each other, they began to see themselves and their stories as part of a larger story, a story that had historical significance. Hareven describes what happened among the people as a "collective identification" with the old work place.[24]

After the exhibit, the oral history interviewing continued, but it took on a completely new character. Former mill workers started volunteering to be interviewed, recalling their work experiences with a new pride. The research process, together with the exhibit, became a catalyst for a dramatically new sense of shared worth among the former mill workers. The research became "a common community event."[25]

This example demonstrates the kind of growth and healing that can emerge, even unintentionally, from a research process that is shared or "reflected back" to the community in some way, shape, or form. In this case, it was an architectural museum exhibit that was the medium for the "reflection" in which people came to see

---

22. Ibid., 248–50.
23. Ibid., 250.
24. Ibid.
25. Ibid.

themselves with new eyes. As we will see in chapter 9, many creative forms are available for offering a community's story back to it. The point is that qualitative research projects can be designed within congregations and communities in order to spark growth in personal and communal self-awareness. The energy that this process generates can be harnessed to help the congregation move forward — to author a new chapter of its shared life. Once the practice of honest dialogue is established, new possibilities for the community's life together can be negotiated with vigor.

Ethnography thus used as a pastoral practice can subvert institutional pressures to maintain the status quo by helping a faith community recall its stories, its strengths, its soul. While the research process itself is time-consuming and challenging, strategically, it is time well spent. It is time that will take the pastoral researcher into the lives of the people, into their histories, and into their confidence. Though the issues unearthed through this process may be daunting, the overall increase in honesty and mutual trust that emerges can lead to spiritual growth and more conscious, intentional religious practices. In the sharing of stories and in the pastor-parish dialogical encounter, faith is quickened. In this "potential space"[26] lies the opening through which a congregation may access new, creative, and transformational practices.

How to Use This Book

This book is a roadmap for students, pastors, and religious leaders who want to get started in ethnographic listening as a form of pastoral theology and practice. The best way to learn how to use this research tool is experientially — by undertaking a pastoral research project. I suggest that master's level students who are in ministry settings such as student pastorates or field education placements (after acquiring permission) conduct their research in their ministry settings. Likewise religious leaders in doctoral level

---

26. This term comes from the work of Donald Woods Winnicott, *Playing and Reality* (New York: Routledge, 1971).

programs will benefit from doing their research in their current contexts of ministry.

The book's ten chapters correspond roughly to the number of weeks in a semester of teaching, allowing time along the way for some class sessions where students share their work in progress. The course can also be taught in two semesters, which provides more time for the research and writing of ethnography and also for a carefully executed sharing event, when each researcher shares his or her results back with the group and enters into deeper dialogue and discussion. I have laid out the material in such a way that each chapter introduces readers to both concepts and practical steps involved in the research process. Students will be learning theory, theology, and practice together.

While I have tried to break down the steps into a somewhat logical sequence, bear in mind that ethnography is not a simple or linear practice, like walking from point A to point B. To use a metaphor offered by my colleague Boyung Lee, ethnography is more like embarking on a journey, and stopping along the way to see what strikes you, what you want to photograph, whom you might meet along the way, and where you would like to eat lunch.[27] By engaging in ethnography as a pastoral practice, new layers of complication, new side trips, are added. You might find that after a few days or weeks at this, you alter your travel plans, perhaps going back to where you started, with new questions and new angles to explore. This is a natural part of the journey. Throughout the excursion, the choices continue, not only through the activities of research design, getting permissions, and data-gathering, but also in modes of analysis, styles of writing and presentation, and in engagement in continuing dialogue with your participants as co-researchers. The progression through all of these steps and phases is more spiral than linear. While not a simple map, this book offers you a view of the terrain, a lay of the land that is pastoral ethnography.

---

27. Conversation at the Wabash Workshop for Pre-tenured Theological Faculty, Crawfordsville, Indiana, July 15, 2005.

Readers who are not using this book as a classroom text will have different challenges. I strongly suggest that you try out these ideas and practices in the company of colleagues rather than alone. For example, middle-level denominational leaders could convene groups of clergy to work through the book together. Ethnographic studies could also be used as case studies for peer groups in pastoral care and counseling as well as with CPE residents and supervisors in training. Pastors, therapists, and teachers doing research need to have peers or supervisors or both who can review each other's work. Because ethnographic research and writing is highly subjective, we need input from others who can help us think through the process and help prod our self-awareness along the way. Perhaps more important, because ethnography as a pastoral practice raises significant ethical issues, we need colleagues to hold us accountable. Religious leaders and researchers, like doctors, must adhere to the injunction to do no harm. I describe ethical issues as well as practices of accountability in detail in chapter 4; for now, it is critical that would-be pastoral researchers understand that this is not a journey to be taken alone.

A good way to understand ethnography is by reading clearly written ethnographic accounts. For this reason, I use numerous examples in the course of the book. I also offer a short list of recommendations for further study at the end of each chapter. These resources are chosen from a number of academic fields: religious studies, congregational studies, pastoral and practical theology. Reading ethnographic accounts that exemplify the principles and skills as they are being learned can be particularly helpful.

I refer to my former students' work in order to demonstrate a range of settings, theologies, and practices that pastoral ethnography can profitably address. The studies highlighted here address numerous topics, including the intricacies of church growth, community relationships among differently abled residents of a retirement home, and the child-rearing practices of single parents raising African American boys in southeast Washington, D.C. Other topics that students have chosen to study include the practice of alternative (praise) worship services in a large Protestant congregation and a Jewish congregation's practice of *Tikkun Olam* (see below p. 48). This is just a sample of the range of topics available for study. There are endless possibilities for research projects related to the practice of faith.

Chapter 1 offers a working definition of ethnography and explores the meaning of culture. Here I illustrate some of the ways in which ethnography can be used as a pastoral theological tool in the life of a community. I describe the role and posture of a pastoral ethnographer with the help of a hypothetical example. I also explain the meaning and significance of reflexivity. Finally, this chapter offers a process for starting to identify your own research question in the context of your religious leadership.

Chapter 2 takes you a step further on the journey by explaining the terrain of ethnographic study. Religious practice and *habitus* are the stuff of pastoral research, and they are fraught with theological significance. This chapter helps you clarify your research question and focus it around religious practice. Utilizing Jennifer Mason's taxonomy of intellectual puzzles — developmental, mechanical, comparative, or predictive — can help sharpen the focus of your research.[28] Each type is illustrated with actual case examples, drawn from students' work as well as from published studies.

Chapter 3 goes into the basics of research design, suggesting ways to match your research questions to some of the tried and true ethnographic methods, including qualitative interviews, participant observation, research teams, and survey instruments. I draw out the case examples used in chapter 1, demonstrating how these various research methods can be used to help answer particular kinds of research questions. A basic outline for research design is laid out in detail.

Chapter 4 discusses the importance of ethical care and respect for the relationships that ethnography involves. When people are gracious enough to participate in research with us, we owe them a

---

28. See Jennifer Mason, *Qualitative Researching,* 2nd ed. (Thousand Oaks, Calif.: SAGE Publications, 2002).

high degree of ethical accountability in the conduct of the research and in our use of the results. Here I describe issues of access, authority, and power in social research relationships and guide you through the important work of obtaining informed consent and anticipating the benefits and risks of the research. Practices of accountability to colleagues and Institutional Review Boards are explained. It is through the high quality of ethical discernment we exemplify in the practice of research that we can communicate and start to bring about the liberative relationships that our theologies proclaim.

Chapter 5 sends you out into the field, prepared to keep track of your learning. Here I explain the many practical issues related to data collection: keeping field notes, making recordings, taking pictures, and keeping an ethnographer's journal. Consistency in recording your observations, impressions, and responses to what you learn is critical to this process. Transcription and ethnographic software can be helpful in this task, and I describe their benefits and uses, along with many examples of these and the other procedures.

Chapter 6 articulates in greater depth the intricacies of ethnographic listening. Some ways to listen help elicit the deeper stories that people are often longing to share. Some cues can help you pick up on themes and metaphors embedded in personal stories. Importantly, there are ways to listen for silences — to note the pauses and "sighs too deep for words" (Rom. 8:26). Persons will express their own deep theologies when we take the time to ask and pay attention in a disciplined and compassionate way. In this chapter I explain the similarities and differences between pastoral counseling and ethnographic listening and provide guidelines to help you keep your research role clear and comprehensible to your participants.

As you continue on your ethnographic journey, you will begin to accumulate experiences and data. Chapter 7 explains how to organize your data by looking for patterns and associations in them and sorting out the puzzle pieces. This chapter also summarizes some basic methods for analysis and interpretation of interviews, public events, written documents, and material cultural evidence. The work of analysis lays the groundwork for writing a coherent and reliable ethnography.

Chapter 8 helps you compose your pastoral ethnographic narrative. Understanding your own story, voice, and theology in the narrative is critical. This chapter explains some of the basic principles of ethnographic writing and explores a variety of styles, structures, and conventions that ethnographers from diverse fields have tried. A process for theological reflection helps you weave together a narrative that proclaims your faith in relation to the practices and values of the group. The chapter includes a concise rubric for writing pastoral ethnography.

Chapter 9 describes how to begin the exciting work of sharing your findings. This important work involves the community in weaving a theological narrative that brings together stories human and divine. Sermons, large-scale presentations, and small group discussions are addressed as possible avenues for this sharing. As you create a communication event, anticipate receiving feedback that challenges and potentially enlarges your theology and pastoral identity. This chapter identifies strategies for responding to both positive and negative feedback. Nurturing the conversation, the back and forth of dialogue, helps the community discern its own theological commitment to change and transformation.

In chapter 10, I discuss ethnography for transformation and describe the process of co-authoring the future. The chapter emphasizes the importance of honoring creativity throughout the ethnographic journey and explores the benefits of artistic expression as a resource for change. Musical events, theatrical productions, and "participatory aesthetics" have helped communities tell their stories and proclaim their values. This chapter summarizes the challenges and benefits of ethnography as a pastoral practice and highlights the hope of prophetic transformation.

Ethnography as a pastoral practice can help us fulfill the prophetic injunction to "love kindness, do justice, and walk humbly with your God" (Mic. 6:8). It is my hope that this book will help religious leaders and congregations respond to this ancient and enduring call. Religious transformation will always remain a somewhat mysterious process. Nevertheless, we can take steps that help invite openness to God's presence in the midst of the mundane transactions of group life. As the power to speak and the shared wisdom of the group emerge through the practice of ethnographic listening, a space for the new opens up and fills us with hope.

For Further Study

Frank, Thomas Edward. *The Soul of the Congregation.* Nashville: Abingdon Press, 2000.

– O N E –

Getting Started

Understanding Ethnography

You can observe a lot by watching.

— YOGI BERRA

Ethnography is a form of social research used by sociologists, anthropologists, historians, and other scholars to study living human beings in their social and cultural contexts. Participant observation is the hallmark of this kind of social research. Ethnographers go to the places where people live, work, or pray in order to take in firsthand the experience of group life and social interactions. For example, an ethnographer studying a congregation will visit that congregation — perhaps many times over the course of a year or more — in order to observe as many aspects of congregational life as possible. Events such as worship services, staff meetings, and potluck suppers are of interest, as are office interactions and parking-lot debates. Ethnographers pay attention to mundane sights and smells and sounds and gestures. These are all elements of the cultural life of the people. Ethnographers notice the material dimensions of life, the financial workings of an organization, the power-relations between people, as well as their poetic or artistic artifacts and expressions. As Yogi Berra puts it, "You can observe a lot by watching."[1]

---

1. This quotation and the others used as epigraphs in each chapter can be found in Yogi Berra, *When You Come to a Fork in the Road, Take It!* (New York: Hyperion, 2001). Berra claims that he received his nickname "Yogi" from his early baseball teammates because he did observe a lot; his teammates thought his sitting and watching posture, with his arms and knees folded, resembled that of a Hindu Yogi (66).

Ethnographers also read a great deal. Historical records, worship bulletins, newsletters, and by-laws are raw materials to examine. Most important, though, ethnographers get to know the people in a particular place, interact with them, and form relationships. Ethnographers take lots of notes and may make photographs or audio or video recordings in order to preserve detailed impressions of their encounters. Ethnographers also make use of statistical and quantitative data, such as demographic information, attendance records, and membership rolls. However, the emphasis is on qualitative rather than quantitative study.

Ethnography was once considered an objective social science, something akin to naturalism. It was thought that by observing people in their local habitat one could perceive the habits, customs, and styles of a group of people in action and reach clear and irrefutable descriptions of them. Though ethnographers continue to strive for accuracy in their observations and validity in their analyses, it is now widely recognized that human social life cannot really be studied in its natural state, undisturbed by the researcher. Briefly, this is because researchers are a part of the world they are trying to study.[2] An objective, bird's-eye view of human society is not really possible.

An ethnographer's view of human society is always constructed from a particular site, which is both geographical and cultural.[3] Because a researcher can see only so much from where he or she is standing, both literally and imaginatively, ethnographic accounts are partial and biased rather than exact and objective. Borrowing from the words of the hymnist George Rawson, we can say that ethnographic writing will be limited "to our poor reach of mind, to notions of our day and time, crude, partial and confined."[4]

2. Mason, *Qualitative Researching*, 191; Martyn Hammersley and Paul Atkinson, *Ethnography: Principles in Practice*, 2nd ed. (New York: Routledge, 1995), 21.

3. For a fascinating essay on the significance of social and geographical sites in narratives of American religious history, see Tweed, "Introduction," *Retelling U.S. Religious History*, 1–23.

4. George Rawson (1807–89), "We Limit Not the Truth of God," in *The New Century Hymnal* (Cleveland: Pilgrim Press, 1995), 316. Rawson originally wrote the hymn in the 1850s. The refrain is attributed to the seventeenth-century

Ethnography involves the study of human culture. But what is culture? The meaning of this term has evolved over a long history of usage. It began as an agricultural metaphor for the "cultivated mind," implying spiritual, artistic, and intellectual refinement. Culture was once associated with "high culture," as opposed to popular ways of life, which were judged inferior and superstitious in comparison. Over time, the concept of culture was transformed into an anthropological term. Anthropologists began using the word in the plural, viewing the world as populated by "cultures," meaning distinct ethnic or geographic groups. Culture later came to be associated with the meaning dimension of social life and related to groups' values and norms for living.[5]

Against this modern anthropological view, postmodernists have pointed out that human culture is not one unified and coherent thing out there for us to study. Indeed, many have challenged the idea that ethnic or religious or regional groups are essentially similar — that we congregate in "bounded cultural wholes."[6] Cultural groups are not as unified or internally consistent as we might think. A diversity of opinions, ideas, and styles resides within as well as among social and ethnic groups. In our intercultural world, members of diverse social groups are continuously interacting and influencing each other. It has also been noted that power relations, as well as cultural systems of meaning, influence the way we live. No set group of cultural characteristics can be used to define or describe human clusters — whether they are ethnic, racial, religious, or geographic. People are far too complicated, changeable, and cantankerous to fit neatly into such categories.

For our purposes, we can think of culture holistically as the stories that guide our lives, the systems and symbols that we believe in and live out through our actions. Our cultural stories are

---

Puritan John Robinson. The earliest source for the refrain is Governor Edward Winslow in *Hypocrisie Unmasked,* 1646, which attributes the statement to Robinson's 1620 address to the Puritans on their departure for the New World.

5. Kathryn Tanner, *Theories of Culture: A New Agenda for Theology* (Minneapolis: Fortress Press, 1997). See part 1 for a clear exposition of the history of the term.

6. Ibid., 21.

intertwined with power relations. Ethnographers set out to study all of this — cultural stories, theologies, and artifacts, human actions and interactions, and the power arrangements that are intertwined with these. Researchers know that our lenses of analysis and our categories are cultural products, too. Like the people we study, we live in complex worlds of meaning and construct our stories and conceptual categories using the tools we find at hand.[7] We cannot stand outside of culture in order to study it.

Ethnographic accounts are also limited by time. For example, an annual ritual such as a Seder supper changes, slightly or significantly, each time it is performed. The subject of social research is something moving and fluid rather than fixed or stable. For this reason, social research has aptly been called "a snapshot, taken at one point in time."[8] It is a partial and biased glimpse of a changing social world.

This snapshot is influenced by the researcher's attitudes and inclinations and by his or her motivations for doing the research. What does an ethnographer choose to focus on, to photograph? What does the ethnographer overlook or leave out? What bothers the researcher about this picture? Ethnographic narratives depict the researcher's perceptions of the picture, and not merely the picture itself.

Even when researchers are scrupulous about gathering accurate data, things will be missed. Diverse angles of light can affect what one sees on a particular day. There is a good deal of interpretation that goes into the processes of seeing, recording, and analyzing observations. Even recording a description full of details and nuance — the venerable practice of "thick description" — is an interpretive activity.[9] Additional layers of interpretation are involved in the processes of analyzing data and attempting to

---

7. Here I refer to an important essay introducing the notion of "tool kits" by Ann Swidler, "Culture in Action: Symbols and Strategies," *American Sociological Review* 51 (April 1986): 273–86.

8. Ammerman et al., *Congregation and Community*, 40.

9. The phrase "thick description" comes from the classic work by Clifford Geertz, *The Interpretation of Cultures: Selected Essays* (New York: Basic Books, 1973).

find patterns in them. At the point when ethnographers "write up" their narratives, interpreting data, building arguments, and formulating conclusions, the author's voice in the narrative is especially pronounced. There is no getting away from the reality that ethnography is a theory-laden endeavor that reflects the categories and presuppositions of the researcher.

Because of all of this, ethnographic accounts and explanations are better understood as narratives than as scientific treatises. Ethnographers engage in the communal life of people, gather data and analyze them (one hopes) with honesty and rigor, and then construct accounts of their experiences, their findings, and their conclusions. However rigorous, these accounts are neither definitive nor fixed; they are interpretations.[10]

Perhaps an ethnographic narrative can be more accurately compared to an impressionist painting. An impressionist painting conveys the richness and expanse of the artist's insight and his or her ability to express it. Such a painting can be beautiful and inspire a vivid understanding of its subject matter, but the viewer always knows that the painting is a painting and not the subject matter itself. Similarly, an ethnographic narrative may be a beautiful and telling representation of the social life of a group, yet it always remains a construction, a story about the author's experience of the group, and not the group's shared social life itself.[11]

Hypothetical Example: A Church Supper

Imagine two ethnographers setting out for a downtown First Congregational Church supper, notepads in hand. One of them is Sue, a bright young woman who happens to be a vegetarian. As Sue enters the church basement, she is struck by the sight and smell of heaping mounds of red meat on the platters on the serving table. Feeling a bit queasy, she politely fills her plate with the

---

10. See Norman K. Denzin, *Interpretive Ethnography: Ethnographic Practices for the 21st Century* (Thousand Oaks, Calif.: SAGE Publications, 1997).

11. For a more thorough explanation, see Pierre Bourdieu, *The Logic of Practice* (Cambridge: Polity Press, 1992).

only available menu options: white rolls and Jell-O salad. Sue's vegetarianism is related to her faith; she sees it as an expression of her values of nonviolence and respect for life. Sue is mulling this in the back of her mind and feeling somewhat annoyed as she takes a seat at a half-empty table. She tries to enter into conversation with the couple seated next to her. They are naturally reserved folks. They don't say much. They do ask Sue why she isn't eating anything, and she mumbles that she isn't too hungry.

Sue makes excuses and leaves the supper as early as she can. Back in the car, writing up the evening's events, she doesn't have too much good to say about this encounter. While Sue knew enough to expect that meat would be served at the supper, she did not anticipate that it would be so prominent and bloody and that little else to eat would be offered. She is still hungry and annoyed as she settles down to write in her ethnographer's journal. In the margin of her notebook, where she writes her personal responses to events, Sue comments that the people at this supper, like the food, seem dull and unengaged with any theology or ministry.

Meanwhile, Sue's colleague Mike, a gregarious man in his forties, arrives at the dinner a little later. He is hungry when he gets there, and he finds the food delicious. He sits down at a busy table and has a fascinating conversation with the church elders. They tell their stories of growing up in this church and invite him to tell his own story. Mike enjoys himself. He stays for quite a while and notices that as the evening goes on, men who appear to be homeless are coming in from the streets and helping themselves to dinner. Later, Mike stays up late writing at length in his ethnographer's journal, describing the delicious food, the interesting people, and their friendly and generous practice of sharing their meal with street people.

This hypothetical example dramatizes the possible divergence in two ethnographers' experiences at the same event. Sue's vegetarian sensibilities and her physical sensations of queasiness influence her experience of the church. The shy people she sits near and her own discomfort combine to make this an unpleasant and short evening for her. Her field notes are brief, but her negative impressions are strong. They stay with her and "come out" in her writing.

Meanwhile, Mike's impressions of the same evening and group are, in many ways, quite the opposite of Sue's. A carnivore himself, Mike enjoys the hearty meal. He is having a good time, and coincidentally he finds the people to be both fascinating and faithful. He observes their camaraderie with the homeless folks, and feels that he has experienced a kind of communion, a holy feast.

Of course, Mike's narrative account will barely resemble Sue's. Though both may strive for accuracy, noting the items on the menu, and so on, the overall feel of the two human encounters will be dramatically opposed to one another. If they were to compare notes, both Sue and Mike might be shocked. Whose version would be right? Mike has a more generous and appealing view of the church, but Sue's observations and experiences, though less extensive, are also valid.

Reflexivity

The contrast in Sue's and Mike's "moods and motivations"[12] comes into play at least as much as those of the people whom they are trying to study. Because of this unavoidable reality, ethnographers now know that in order to study a group of people, they must also study themselves. Such self-study is termed "reflexivity." To continue the illustration, Sue, upon reflection, will wonder how her vegetarianism is coloring her view of the people at the supper. Similarly, Mike's self-reflection might lead him to realize that his hunger and gratitude for a good meal are influencing his positive experience of the dinner and appraisal of the church folks. Both Sue and Mike also need to think about how their presence at the dinner influences what takes place there. Are the church members at the dinner trying to behave well — being extra polite, for example, or trying to sound "spiritual" — because they know that researchers are recording their conversations? Are some of the "regulars" staying away because they don't

---

12. Geertz, *The Interpretation of Cultures.*

want to be studied? Reflexivity means that we take seriously our own role in the research and our influence on the results.

Reflecting again on Sue and Mike and their two views of the dinner, we wonder: could their two accounts be reconciled? Or, taken together, do they each offer a piece of the puzzle, suggesting a larger picture that is more complete by virtue of including two opposing views? Clearly, the two stories together would yield a more complex collage of perspectives on the church supper. Yet it is important to understand that even this larger collage would still be the outsiders' imaginative construction of what was happening at the supper. The insiders' experiences of the supper are going to be different. If the pastor (who is both an insider in some respects and an outsider in others) were to do this research, still another experience of the supper would be generated. Furthermore, even a thorough and complex narrative description of this supper that privileges the voices of insiders, perhaps quoting them liberally, would still be limited by the scope of the author's observations, analysis, and interpretative skill.

Ethnography and Ministry: Why Bother?

Ethnography is a complicated, messy, and humbling endeavor. Why would a pastoral leader want to spend so much time on a complex and inexact research process? One of the main reasons for doing this work is to add some new knowledge to one's understanding of a group or of a particular religious practice. Even though Sue and Mike can't write the definitive story on these suppers, nevertheless their narratives can help readers imagine or get a feel for some important aspects of the supper. Careful attention to faith practices doesn't yield complete or final understandings of them. This disciplined form of attentiveness, however, does add new information and insight.

From a pastoral perspective, what is done with the ethnography is also crucial. The church supper narrative could be used to help insiders in this church see "in the mirror, dimly," in the words of Paul (1 Cor. 13:12). The Greek here, *en ainigmati*, literally means "in a riddle," as in the word "enigma." The narrative could help church members grapple with the riddle. If the stories that Sue and Mike piece together are shared with the church council or published in the church newsletter, then the members will get a glimpse of how they look to outsiders. The narrative could be used to start a conversation within the congregation about the supper ministry. Perhaps a small group of vegetarians stands at the margins of this hypothetical church, simmering with resentment for years over the focus on red meat served at the suppers. Hearing Sue's account of the evening, this minority might coalesce to start offering a vegetarian entree as an alternative to beef.

Or perhaps there are homeless folks in the neighborhood who have no idea that they are welcome at the suppers. Seeing the vegetarian group's new signs attached to posts in the neighborhood, they may decide to stop in next week and enjoy a hearty meal. Alternatively, Ed, a man living in a homeless shelter, might pick up a copy of the church newsletter, read Mike's version of the story, and become annoyed. Ed may feel that he was treated like a charity case the last time he went to the church supper. He begs to differ with Mike's cheerful description of how this church cares for the poor; he might even tell the church's pastor or janitor just how he feels about this condescension. The written narrative can help to get a conversation going.

These church supper stories are contested stories. Things look one way to a vegetarian and another way to a carnivore. Things look still another way to a hungry or homeless person. Now imagine how differences in other social factors, such as the race, language, or sexual orientation of the ethnographers or the diners might affect the narratives written and people's responses to them. Things can get messy.

In a way, though, the messy and contested nature of these narratives — the riddle they suggest — is what makes them so potentially valuable to pastors and other religious leaders. These accounts, when shared with insiders and with outsiders, can lead the congregation to some interesting and important insights. Until this study was done, who knew that Ed felt patronized or that the roast beef offended? Once these experiences are noted and

shared with the community, the possibility for an honest discussion is opened up. Likewise, the possibility for change — for
new practices such as vegetarian suppers to emerge — is also
created.

This doesn't mean that it will be simple for the group to figure
out how to make the dinners more welcoming to the folks from
the homeless shelter or more pleasing to vegetarians. Indeed, the
congregation may not even agree to these goals. But once the
conversation gets started in this way, the group's level of interest
and energy tends to increase. This is what makes ethnography
such a useful and theologically invigorating pastoral tool.

Why should ministers bother? Ethnography can help shine a
light on what matters to people in a community. Margaret Kornfeld, in her book *Cultivating Wholeness: A Guide to Care and
Counseling in Faith Communities*, uses the metaphor of cultivating the ground of community to describe a minister's role
in tending to the wholeness or overall health of the group. She
writes about what she calls "real communities" and "pseudo-
communities." She describes a real community as a place where
people are free to be themselves and know that they will be accepted, a place where conflict can be expressed and resolved,
and a place where diversity of opinion is honored. A pseudo-
community, by contrast, may seem friendly at first, but it is
really not a safe place in which to express an opinion that di-
verges from the group's stated values. If you are different in a
pseudo-community, you feel it immediately; you feel pressured,
not safe. You sense that you don't fit in, that there is no room for
difference of opinion, and you may "go into hiding."[13] These
two types of communities described here are somewhat over-
simplified; in actuality, I suspect that people experience most
groups in a mixed way — sometimes real, sometimes as false or
pseudo-communities. Communities are living and breathing or-
ganic entities; none is ideal or as deeply welcoming to all as we

---

13. Margaret Zipse Kornfeld, *Cultivating Wholeness: A Guide to Care and
Counseling in Faith Communities* (New York: Continuum International, 2000),
19.

might hope. Still, the contrast is helpful for us, as we think about the value of ethnographic research in relation to the overall health of a community.

Ethnographers strive to probe the diversity of cultural, social, and religious practices and attitudes in a community in a non-judgmental way. Because of this, such research can help create safe spaces in which honest opinions can be shared. When a religious leader, as "gardener," initiates the research with this goal in mind, he or she can help move a congregation from being a pseudo-community toward being a more real community, where "members can communicate honestly and without fear."[14] This is the kind of community or "ground" where deep spirituality can be cultivated and can grow and flourish.[15]

Ethnography can be especially useful for religious leaders who feel that their community is somehow stuck in the past, immobilized by some unfinished business. These leaders may have a whiff of what the trouble was about but feel reticent to stir up the past. However, if there are old secrets or traumatic losses that were never fully aired or resolved in the community, these can put a damper on the life and health of the current congregation. In congregations as in families, "unfinished business" can shut people down emotionally and spiritually.[16]

For example, when a community does not sufficiently grieve the loss of a beloved leader, the general level of energy and enthusiasm for engagement with a new leader is diminished. Similarly, if there has been an ethics violation by clergy in the past, and particularly if the matter was not publicly disclosed or openly addressed, the community's level of trust in subsequent leaders will likely be compromised.[17] Allowing people to tell their stories of life in this community, including the good, the bad, and the

---

14. Ibid., 21–23.
15. Ibid., 18–35.
16. See Edwin H. Friedman, *Generation to Generation: Family Process in Church and Synagogue* (New York: Guilford Press, 1985), 44–45.
17. For a book-length treatment of the subject of congregational healing after clergy misconduct, see Beth Ann Gaede, ed., *When a Congregation Is Betrayed: Responding to Clergy Misconduct* (Herndon, Va.: Alban Institute, 2005).

ugly, is a critical pastoral task that can help people heal and free them to move on with strength and vigor.

This may sound counterintuitive. People are often ashamed of congregational secrets, worried about the group's public image, and thus try to move on quickly and forget about old wounds. But real community can't thrive if stories are not told. Walking into charged memories, with great care and sensitivity, is really the most direct route *through* the trouble and into the freedom of new life. Ethnography can be a vehicle for honest sharing about the group's past and thoughtful discernment of God's presence in the group's story, which helps to get the group "unstuck."

Ethnography can also help you build a community that can allow for and come to appreciate diversity within its ranks. When we think of building a sense of community in a congregation, many pastors or leaders intuitively want to help people bond. We try to find some commonality in people's experiences that will make them feel close. When people talk about themselves, they say things like, "I know what you mean," or "That happened to me once, too." Ethnography, interestingly enough, takes us in the opposite direction — toward becoming a stranger, even in a familiar setting. Ethnography keeps an eye out for what is different, what is particular about this person, this group, this place.

Theorists in the field of intercultural counseling describe something analogous when they talk about "interpathy."[18] Interpathy requires the listener to notice differences between one's own and the counselee's cultural experience, rather than trying to collapse them into a false bond based on the idea that "we are really all the same." Human beings do have some commonalities, but real relationships also attend to the differences, the particularities of each other's lives. Learning to recognize and honor differences, rather than either ignoring differences or trying to rule them out, is an important dimension of becoming a genuine community.

---

18. David W. Augsburger, *Pastoral Counseling across Cultures* (Philadelphia Westminster Press, 1986), 14; and Aart M. van Beek, *Cross-Cultural Counseling* (Minneapolis: Augsburg Fortress, 1996), 35.

When you are a part of a group, it is harder than you might think to attend to differences. Doing ethnography in a setting in which you really are a stranger — say, Samoa[19] — is much easier. There you would know that you don't understand why people are doing what they are doing. But closer to home, in our own congregations, we are so accustomed to the way things are done, that we don't even see the questions that would stick out for newcomers. We have to work to slow down and pay attention.

Ethnography gets us to ask ourselves the kinds of questions that might be obvious to a three-year-old, such as, "Why are people acting funny in this church?" (Or, as one of my children once asked when walking into a Catholic church for the first time, "Who is that man up there and why is he wearing a dress?") An ethnographic disposition pays attention to the things people do automatically in this particular place and tries to understand the rhyme and reason behind them.[20] Differences become interesting rather than threatening when we take this attitude. It is a mindful outlook: diversity and disagreement don't ruffle our feathers so much as pique our curiosity.

A religious leader is well positioned to do ethnographic research in a community. A pastor, rabbi, minister, or spiritual teacher lives in the tension between being a member of a community and one set apart from it in order to perform a leadership role. Tom Frank calls this a *liminal*[21] role, "standing on the threshold of insider and outsider status."[22] Effective religious leaders understand that they are not just members of the tribe. Pastors may live in the same community and share many aspects

---

19. This is, of course, a reference to Margaret Mead's pathbreaking anthropology in Samoa. See Margaret Mead, *Coming of Age in Samoa: A Psychological Study of Primitive Youth for Western Civilisation* (New York: William Morrow, 1928).

20. The phrase "ethnographic disposition" comes from Frank, *The Soul of the Congregation*, 65.

21. Victor Turner introduced this nineteenth-century psychological term into the study of anthropology. See, for example, Victor W. Turner, *The Ritual Process: Structure and Anti-Structure* (Chicago: University of Chicago Press, 1969).

22. Frank, *The Soul of the Congregation*, 82.

of life with the people, but in order to lead they must maintain some critical distance. Rather than merging with the community, good religious leaders work at staying spiritually focused and self-differentiated.[23] They are thus well situated to engage in participant observation and to pay attention to the community in disciplined ways.

Some readers may feel that the focus of ethnographic study seems to be misdirected. As a religious leader, isn't one's gaze supposed to be on God rather than on the people? And isn't the leader supposed to offer some authoritative theological knowledge and moral guidance rather than asking the people questions all the time? Don't congregants expect some wisdom from theologically trained leaders? Isn't this the reason that congregations pay ministers? To be sure, theology was (and in some places still is) thought of as special knowledge that teachers and leaders should interpret and explain and teach to the people. Pastors were supposed to be duly orthodox in their theology so that they could instruct the laity and apply the correct theological and ethical principles to the challenges, ministries, and mission of the local congregation. Congregants were supposed to be compliant, receptive to the wisdom of the ordained leader.

In recent years, however, many have come to understand that faith doesn't usually work this way, if it ever did.[24] Practical theologians have challenged not only the top-down authority system such a model implies but also this way of thinking about the relationship between theology and practice.[25] A close look at the

23. Friedman, *Generation to Generation*, 228–49.
24. Certainly there have been historical and philosophical shifts from hierarchical models to more democratic understandings of ministry. For a description of these, see Brooks E. Holifield, *A History of Pastoral Care in America: From Salvation to Self-Realization* (Nashville: Abingdon Press, 1983). However, the question about the interrelationship between theological interpretation and practice can be posed in the context of earlier eras as well as our own. See, for example, Ann Taves, *Fits, Trances, and Visions: Experiencing Religion and Explaining Experience from Wesley to James* (Princeton, N.J.: Princeton University Press, 1999). For a classic on English dissent, see Erik Routley, *English Religious Dissent* (Cambridge: Cambridge University Press, 1960).
25. Browning, *A Fundamental Practical Theology*, 42–54; Elaine L. Graham, *Transforming Practice: Pastoral Theology in an Age of Uncertainty*

ways people practice their faith complicates the seemingly simple, causal relationship between theological ideas and actions. Religious practices do not necessarily emerge out of beliefs. Instead, things are done for all kinds of reasons — some having to do with habit or tradition, others with style or aesthetic preference. Indeed, more than a few religious practices seem to have little, if anything, to do with the stated theology of the group.

Any pastor can attest to the truth of this in congregational life. For example, a congregation may preach the abundant love of God but manage its finances in a stingy and mean-spirited manner. A leader may preach about peace, while the congregation sings hymns that glorify war and triumph. A group's mission statement may proclaim God's hospitality, while the same people who wrote that statement turn away those visitors whose lives do not conform to conventional patterns. Is the problem that people are not faithful enough to their shared theology? This may be part of it. But when there is such an obvious disconnect between stated theology and regular religious practices, the reasons are probably deeper and more complex. Most likely, the pastor's preaching does not reflect the whole congregation's views. Typically, people within a congregation have their own diverse opinions on matters of war and peace, money, love, and exclusion. Some will disagree with the pastor, whether they speak up about it or not.

What can a leader do if this is discovered? Simply preaching harder at the people isn't going to change the way they do things. Congregations are complicated social organizations. James Hopewell, in his book *Congregation,* put it this way: "Despite our aspirations, congregations are not timeless havens of congenial views or values. By congregating, human beings are implicated in a plot, in a corporate historicity that links us to a specific past, that thickens and unfolds a particular present, and that holds out a future open to transformation."[26] Because of this

---

(Eugene, Ore.: Wipf and Stock, 1996); Elaine Graham, Heather Walton, and Frances Ward, *Theological Reflection: Methods* (London: SCM–Canterbury Press, 2005).

26. James F. Hopewell, *Congregation: Stories and Structures* (Minneapolis: Fortress Press, 1987), 160.

"corporate historicity," people get accustomed to doing things in particular ways. Often a certain kind of logic is presented to explain what people do in congregations. But as sociologist Pierre Bourdieu might say, the logic of these practices "is not the logic of the logician."[27] Here is the key point: practice does not always follow from theology. In fact, sometimes it is the other way around. Sometimes we can't even know what a congregation's theology really is until we look at what the people there do — how they practice their faith.

Another reason for doing ethnography is to discern the particular theologies that are embedded in that "corporate historicity" and thick unfolding present. Sometimes, by studying a congregation's practices — the things they do and reasons they give for doing them — we can get a vague sense of where God is in all of this. Some authors use the metaphor of "excavating" to describe the uncovering of theology or values that undergird religious practices.[28] By digging around and studying and talking about religious practices, we can sometimes come to understand the layers of meaning that are obscured from our view. When we start to think about religious practices as the bedrock of the community's theology and values, we get a sense of how exciting and spiritually enlivening this work can be. Ethnographic study can bring us into deep theological discussions. Rather than imposing abstract doctrines upon the people, the pastor as ethnographer becomes an interpreter of the theology that the people are already expressing through their lives.[29]

So instead of using theological reasoning to summon a reluctant congregation to affirm his own agenda for faithful action, a pastor doing ethnographic study is more likely to engage the congregation's current faith practices in theological reflection. By acknowledging the theological wisdom that is already there in

27. Bourdieu, *The Logic of Practice*, 86.
28. For example, see Graham, *Transforming Practice*, 140.
29. Elaine Graham asserts that "pastoral theology is not legislative or prescriptive, but interpretive. It enables the community of faith to give a critical ᵇblic account of its purposeful presence in the world, and the values that ᵃpe to its actions" (Graham, *Transforming Practice*, 208).

the congregation, in the way people live, and relating this to the scriptures or doctrines of the faith, a pastor can lead, not as one with power over the people — as an authority figure to be followed (or resisted) — but as a sensitive and perceptive leader, one who has eyes to see and ears to hear the faith of the gathered community. Ethnographic study helps the pastor articulate his or her perceptions of the living faith of the people, their history, and their current longings. When these perceptions are shared and discussed, lively, creative, and intentional new practices can emerge.

A True Story: The Mystery of Church Growth

Let me illustrate this dynamic by going back to the first case study I brought up in the introduction — the one involving Ken, the African American student pastor serving an all-white southern congregation. Ken's initial research questions had to do with change in the congregation. He felt that the congregation was afraid of change. He noted that during the first year of his appointment to this congregation, he had welcomed twenty new people into membership there. However, in his words, "seven were run off within the first three months of their joining." The "old members" were driving new people out and meanwhile encouraging Ken as pastor to focus on getting back some of the former members who had left the church years ago.[30]

Ken studied this problem by looking at church records of attendance and membership, but also by looking at the history of the area, which was a complicated one. To summarize briefly, Ken found that in the previous twenty-five years, many church members who were farmers had lost their land due to a painful takeover of the area by an electric company. Family farms had been put up on the auction block at the county courthouse. The church, which was once full of prominent farmers, had lost a great deal of its membership and its prestige. A few remaining families had taken over the governance of the church, and were

---

30. As noted in the preface, permission has been granted to cite this story.

accustomed to controlling their pastors, who, as we saw earlier, rarely lasted very long. The resistance to newcomers, who
were seen as wealthy "carpetbaggers," created a deep rift in the
congregation.

When he set out do some interviews for his ethnography assignment, Ken asked his members some key questions: How do
you perceive change in the church? Since you have been a member
of this church, how much change have you seen? How did it affect you? Do you like a big or a small church? Initially, Ken hoped
his people would come up with what he considered "faithful" answers to these questions. He hoped they would quote Jesus' Great
Commission in the Gospel of Matthew and describe a vision of a
large local church with a large mission to the world. The actual
answers Ken got to these questions surprised him a great deal. As
I noted in the introduction, one frequently identified example of
change had to do with accepting the pastor's skin color, a topic
no one had ever broached before. Ken describes the answers he
received to his question about preferred church size:

> The last question gave me a lot of insight into how my con-
> gregation thinks. Most of the people said they like a small
> church or medium church. Only three people said they liked
> a big church, while one did not care. However, the reasoning
> was what shocked me the most. Three members talked about
> knowing people and if [the church] gets too big, people will
> not know them. Four other people talked about how during
> communion I say everyone's name and if we get too big, I
> would not be able to remember them. Then the other two
> told about being lost and not having a place as what they
> feared the most.[31]

Ken came to understand the people better through this process.
Instead of judging them for turning newcomers away, now he
was able to view them with compassion, as people who had lost
a great deal in their recent history, people who valued the small

---

31. "Ken," "Ethnography and Congregational Transformation at (a Protestant) Church," 14–15.

size of the church because it gave them a place, a place where they were known and where the pastor could remember their names.

The research process changed the way that Ken thought about the people. In fact, it deepened his love for them. Looking back on this a few years later, Ken says that the ethnographic research helped him bring his people to "a place of healing and transformation," where the church has "doubled its membership and built on." In this case, the time that Ken took to probe his members to talk about change and church size was well spent. Through asking the people for their thoughts on these matters, Ken found a respectable theological inclination embedded right inside their resistance to church growth: the desire to know and be known. In the context of a church and local community that had undergone dramatic change in recent years, Ken found these comments all the more poignant. Ken's deeper understanding helped him appreciate his people and have patience with their need for control. Especially in light of the loss of status and economic power that the farmers had experienced, Ken could see the value in the expressed desire to insure that the church would remain a genuine community where the people would be recognized by name. Ken also changed through this process: rather than preaching the great commission at his people, he saw it as his calling to "get them to a place of healing and transformation." Paradoxically, this transformation eventually did include the numerical growth in membership for which Ken originally hoped. We can infer that the mutual trust that developed helped Ken and the church build a community that is more open and receptive to newcomers. Margaret Kornfeld might call this "a real community."

By now I hope that some of the benefits of ethnography as a pastoral practice are becoming evident. Social research can become a means for serving pastoral aims, such as improving the emotional/spiritual health of the community, the vitality of the people's spiritual and social engagement, and the community's openness to new people with diverse viewpoints and experiences to share. But in order to really learn about ethnography as a pastoral practice, you need actually to try it.

Finding Your Questions

So how does one get started in an ethnographic research process? The first task is to try to identify the questions that you have about the congregation, school, agency, or community that you want to study. In order to do this, start by simply going to the place or places where people congregate and taking a look around. Walk around the inside and the outside of the buildings and the neighborhood and see what you notice in the physical environment, what sights and sounds and smells accost you. Notice, also, what thoughts come to mind. Is there anything that you find puzzling about this place or the way the people here do things? Is there anything that bothers you about the community? At the start of a project, it is okay if your questions seem a little vague. You may have to get your feet wet in the research process before you can know what it is that you want to study.

Right from the start, realize that this project is going to involve you — your mind, body, soul, and spirit. Begin by attending to yourself, your role in relation to the group, your feelings about the people, your motivation for this study, and what you hope to gain from it. If you are studying a religious group, it is a good idea to articulate your own theology up front. What is your own worldview? How do you think people should live? Where is God in this institution you are studying? Do you have a vision of what hope and transformation would look like in this place? It is important to know yourself, where you stand, and, why you are considering this research. Writing about yourself in relation to your study will help you gain clarity; it will also make your role in the research more transparent to the eventual readers of your work.

When Ken started his research, he nosed around a bit in church records. That's how he found the striking list of rapid changes in pastoral appointments. He knew that his questions had something to do with change and church growth, but he didn't know much more than that. As Ken thought about it, he realized that he was unhappy about the way that the "old-timers" were treating the newcomers to the church. Ken clarified his own theology by explaining that he interpreted the Gospel of Matthew as requiring an expansive, growth-oriented model of ministry. He initially "read" his people as being unfaithful to this. Though Ken's understanding was to evolve, as was the people's, he had to start somewhere. Identifying his theological premise helped Ken find a focus for his research questions.

As you begin to think about your own theological assessment of the group you are studying, try not to worry about making your starting theology sound polished or perfect. Just keep it honest. Articulate your own stand, and if possible, offer a hunch or hypothesis about what you think is really going on with the people in the community at present. What change or growth do you think might be needed? Write this down. Sleep on it; write some more.

For Further Study

Becker, Penny Edgell, and Nancy L. Eiesland, eds. *Contemporary American Religion: An Ethnographic Reader*. Walnut Creek, Calif.: Altamira Press, 1997.

Hammersley, Martyn, and Paul Atkinson, *Ethnography: Principles in Practice*. 2nd ed. New York: Routledge, 1995, chapter 1.

Community / clique
Welcoming / unintentional
small / closed
Desire to grow / resistant
Generous / tight
Faithful / comfortable
Orthodox / rigid
Hopeful / cautious

- T W O -

Religious Practice

Clarifying the Questions

In theory there is no difference between theory and practice.
In practice there is. — YOGI BERRA

Religious practices, the stuff of focus in pastoral ethnography, carry or "body forth" theology in the world. As you continue to try to formulate your research questions, think about the religious practices in your setting. Consider practices of piety such as prayer and worship, as well as practices of care such as hospitality and practices of prophetic witness such as political advocacy.[1] Your research ought to probe the performed or lived[2] dimension of the congregation or group that you are studying. Religious practices constitute the shared religious life of a community. They function to hold traditions in place — and they play a key role in the course of innovation and change. Research that explores religious practices in fullness of detail will yield a nuanced portrait of the complex dynamics at play in the life of the group.

What Is a Religious Practice?

Growing up, you may have heard the aphorism "practice makes perfect." In this saying, practice means doing something over and again — such as riding a bicycle or playing the violin — in order

---

1. See, for example, Miroslav Volf and Dorothy C. Bass, eds., *Practicing Theology: Beliefs and Practices in Christian Life* (Grand Rapids: Wm. B. Eerdmans, 2002).

2. For an explanation of the term "lived religion," see David Hall, *Lived Religion in America* (Princeton, N.J.: Princeton University Press, 1997).

to improve at it. A religious practice is something people do over and again, with some regularity. Think of some common religious practices: worship services, singing hymns, the study of scriptures and commentaries. A religious practice usually involves action, although contemplation and any form of prayer certainly also qualify. To discover people's religious practices, start by looking at what people actually do in relation to their faith community, and how and why they do it. For example, congregations may practice love or justice through particular actions. (Of course, congregations may also be practicing some forms of exclusion or injustice, wittingly or unwittingly.) By studying over time the repeated actions and interactions of people in a particular group, one can catch a glimpse of theology as it is lived out in the life of the group.

Notice that these practices — or regular actions — come to life in the material, physical, and embodied aspects of faith more than in creeds or mission statements. Practices may seem a little less than theologically significant at first. Who cares where people sit in the sanctuary or who talks to whom at coffee hour? By homing in on religious practices in all of their social and material complexity, however, we are actually begging the question as to whether theology and practice can be separated at all. Studying religious practices, noting what people are actually doing, helps us hear what congregants are saying, not only with their words, but also with their lives. Some practical theologians call this approach "theology-in-action."[3]

This focus on theology-in-action is not new to biblical religions. The Hebrew prophets emphasized the need to do justice rather than make burnt offerings. Action for justice and liberation could be said to be one of the main themes in the biblical story. Elaine Graham and her colleagues trace a historical trajectory of emphasis on praxis or "value-committed action" from the Hebrew scriptures, to the New Testament, and all the way through to contemporary liberation theologians.[4] Since the 1970s, when

3. Graham et al., *Theological Reflection*, 170–99.
4. Ibid., 170–99.

Latin American liberation theologians proclaimed the value of *orthopraxis* ("right action"), over *orthodoxy* ("right doctrine"), numerous liberation theologies have developed.[5] These theologies focus on scriptural passages that identify Christ with the marginalized and find in such passages a divine "preferential option" for the poor and the oppressed. Implicit in these diverse liberation theologies — including black and womanist theologies, feminist theologies, third world liberation theologies, and, most recently, postcolonial theologies — is the call for doing social justice as a critical dimension of theology.[6] As Karl Rahner puts it, "Ideas alone are never the message of the gospel. Action is."[7] These theologians remind us that our practices proclaim what we believe in a profound way.

Similarly, some Jewish theological strands and traditions emphasize the critical importance of actions to care for the world as a theological and ethical obligation.[8] For example, the concept of *Tikkun Olam,* rooted in the book of Ecclesiastes (1:5; 7:13; 19:9), literally means, "setting straight" or "setting in order." In Reform and Reconstructionist Judaism, as well as in parts of Conservative Judaism, the phrase has taken on the meaning of "repairing the world through social action." Some see the obligation to repair the world as arising from the Jewish people's own experience as oppressed people, together with the biblical injunction in the book of Exodus, "You shall not oppress a stranger as you were slaves in the land of Egypt" (23:9). The mission statement of one Reconstructionist congregation puts it this way: *"Tikkun*

---

5. See Gustavo Gutiérrez, *A Theology of Liberation: History, Politics, and Salvation* (Maryknoll, N.Y.: Orbis Books, 1973).

6. See, for example, James H. Cone, *God of the Oppressed,* rev. ed (Maryknoll, N.Y.: Orbis Books, 1997); Delores Williams, *Sisters in the Wilderness: The Challenge of Womanist God-Talk* (Maryknoll, N.Y.: Orbis Books, 1993); Rosemary Radford Ruether, *Women and Redemption: A Theological History* (Minneapolis: Augsburg Fortress, 1998); Hyun-Kyung Chung, *Struggle to be the Sun Again: Introducing Asian Women's Theology* (Maryknoll, N.Y.: Orbis Books, 1990); and Kwok Pui-lan, *Postcolonial Imagination and Feminist Theology* (Louisville: Westminster John Knox Press, 2005).

7. Karl Rahner, cited in Graham et al., *Theological Reflection,* 196.

8. See Elliot N. Dorff, *The Way into Tikkun Olam (Repairing the World)* (Woodstock, Vt.: Jewish Lights Publishing, 2005).

Olam obliges us to help alleviate hunger, homelessness, disease, ignorance, abuse, and political oppression among all people. In addition, we have a responsibility to preserve the health of the global ecosystem upon which all life depends."[9] Here again we have the tacit understanding that religious practice is an inherent dimension of faith.

In pastoral ethnography, the focus on religious practice is important for two reasons. First, because theology and practice are intertwined phenomena, the study of religious practices will automatically involve us in theological reflection. While some practices are established as a result of theological reflection, this is not always the case. Theology can also arise out of practice.[10] For example, consider how a person who is singing a hymn in the context of a worship service can come to a new understanding of God. The study of practices can also reveal notable gaps between theology and practice.[11] We study practices in the hope of being able to "read" the theology they enact and evoke as well as the values that they suggest. Second, we focus on religious practice because practice is a key element in the process of change. As the double-entendre in the title of Elaine Graham's book *Transforming Practice* suggests, we, as historical agents, can change or transform our religious practices, on the one hand. Yet, on the other, religious practices shape us and have the potential to transform us, too. Research that attends to religious practices taps into this transformative capacity.

Many religious organizations, including seminaries and congregations, operate with a hierarchy of knowledge that places thought above action and emotion. In seminaries and theological schools, the so-called foundational disciplines such as Bible, history, ethics, and systematic theology are separated and often considered primary disciplines, while what is called the applied

---

9. Adat Shalom, *Tikkun Olam* Guidelines, 1995, 1–3. *adatshalom.net*.

10. Graham, *Transforming Practice*, 100.

11. See Amy Plantinga Pauw, "Attending to the Gaps between Beliefs and Practices" in *Practicing Theology: Beliefs and Practices in Christian Life*, ed. Miroslav Volf and Dorothy C. Bass (Grand Rapids: Wm. B. Eerdmans, 2002), 33–48.

disciplines, those related to the performance of ministry, are deemed secondary. Congregations often operate in ways that mimic this ordering of knowledge. If the sermon is theologically astute, it is assumed that the congregation will be persuaded to act faithfully. Congregations still tend to put orthodoxy logically ahead of orthopraxis, as if the latter is dependent upon the former. Groups will think their way into faithful action or social change, it is assumed. Yet the relationship between belief and practice — and therefore, change — is frequently more complex than that. As Amy Plantinga Pauw puts it:

> Beliefs about God are not pure truths grasped by a Cartesian ego and then "applied" to the messy, ambiguous, realm of practice. Religious beliefs are interwoven with a larger set of other beliefs and embedded in particular ways of life. They are couched in the language, conceptuality, and history of a particular people and reflect personal and communal experience and desires. Religious beliefs shape and are shaped by religious practices.[12]

Inspired preaching and thoughtful reflection on theological and historical traditions are important, even integral to authentic religious leadership. Yet the gaps between belief and practice suggest that real, transformative change — what pastoral theologians call empowerment or liberation — involves "personal and communal experience and desires." When you as a pastoral researcher become a student of what people already know and believe at this deeper cultural level, you tap into their potential for growth and change.

For all of these reasons, we need to pay disciplined attention to religious practices in all of their social, material, aesthetic, and theological complexity. Particular practices may get started for theological reasons — such as worshiping on a particular day of the week — but eventually they continue out of convention or the need for consistency and structure in social life. People choose some practices such as styles of worship because of aesthetic or

---

12. Pauw, "Attending to the Gaps," 36.

cultural preferences. Of course, theological motivations, stylistic preferences, and even material motives are usually braided together in practice. Many congregations pass the offering plate because income is needed to maintain the congregation's buildings and support the staff, while at the same time sermons are preached on the theology of stewardship. Financial incentives and theological convictions intermingle. When designing your research, pay special attention to this kind of confluence or conflict of interests. It is often at the points of intersection between what seems most earthly and what seems most transcendent that we can catch a glimpse of theology in action.

For our purposes, a wide range of activities can be considered religious practices.[13] Practices can be as active as preaching and as seemingly passive as meditation or glancing at a holy card. Serving dinner at the women's shelter can also be a religious practice. Just about any activity, if it is performed regularly and with a shared understanding of religious intent or meaning, can be considered a religious practice. Practice involving the more mundane and material aspects of community life, such as financial practices, the design and use of buildings, or food practices, may be rich with local theological meaning. Nothing can be deemed too secular to study, because the secular and the sacred, like the intellect and the spirit, and like theology and practice, dwell in us together. We are embodied human creatures, even as we reach toward the divine in our diverse expressions of faith. We dwell in complex cultural and material worlds that shape us even as we attempt to transform them and help to create more life-giving symbols and structures.

---

13. This point is debated in the literature. Some authors have a more restricted concept of religious practice and some focus more particularly on Christian practices. See Alasdair MacIntyre, *After Virtue: A Study in Moral Theory* (Notre Dame, Ind.: University of Notre Dame Press, 1981), 175; and Craig Dykstra and Dorothy C. Bass, "A Theological Understanding of Christian Practices," in *Practicing Theology: Beliefs and Practices in Christian Life* (Grand Rapids: Wm. B. Eerdmans, 2002), 13–32. I use a broader definition of religious practice, which is similar to that described by Kathryn Tanner in another essay in the same volume, "Theological Reflection and Christian Practices," 228–42.

Habitus and Social Memory

Religious practices, when they become habitual and are automatically or unconsciously performed, express the group's *habitus*. In particular groups, certain actions just seem "natural," at least to insiders. This is one of the reasons that moving to a new school, job, or congregation is difficult. The unspoken rules, habits, and styles have to be learned in order to get along well. Pierre Bourdieu defined *habitus* as "embodied history, internalized as a second nature and so forgotten as history."[14] A *habitus* incorporates the aspects of cultural life that we have learned so well that we have forgotten that we learned them at all.

When first trying to understand the concept of *habitus*, visit a religious group that is different from your own. If you are a Protestant, try visiting a synagogue service or a Catholic Mass. You will notice features of the sacred space and the ritual activities that are more or less unfamiliar to you. Patterned behavior will stand out to you when you are a visitor. For example, you won't know when to sit, stand, or kneel during the Mass. But you will see worshipers of all ages instinctively moving through these postures in a patterned way.

Recognizing such patterns in your own congregation or community is harder because they seem like "second nature." Even in so-called low church traditions in which the worship activities appear to be informal, people also behave in patterned ways. Insiders tend to believe that their way of doing things is just natural or normal. They don't have to think about what they are doing or what they expect to happen. Everybody knows what comes next. *Habitus* is this almost unconscious agreement that here we do things this way. Forgotten as history, it is experienced as just the way things were, are, and forever will be.

A *habitus* is expressed through the sense-worlds of the people in the group: the sight of art, architecture, or artifacts; the smell of

---

14. Pierre Bourdieu, *The Logic of Practice* (Cambridge: Polity Press, 1992), 56.

incense or special foods; the bodily feeling of kneeling in prayer or moving to music; the tones of the organ or the sound of the cantor singing; the taste of wine or grape juice or matzo. Styles, habits, customs, ethnic expressions, and people's ways of interrelating to each and to outsiders — these all express the *habitus*.

For example, denominational groups have particular habits and styles that can get captured in a characterization or caricature. The expression "holy rollers" is a designation of an emotional spirit or style of worship, often associated with Pentecostals. Or the phrase "the frozen chosen" is a designation attributed to Presbyterians who are judged to be completely unemotional. (Note that each caricature has a theological element). The *habitus* of a particular local group includes all of the aspects of communal life that have become habitual, or predictable, for that group.

Practices, places, history, and people contribute to a *habitus*. For example, consider the use of religious art, architecture, or artifacts. Congregational churches in New England with plain white walls and central pulpits were built to emphasize the centrality of preaching and hearing the word of God. The religious sensibilities of one who attends worship in this kind of space will be shaped in a particular way. The plain white walls will seem normal or natural to one who has always worshiped in this place. In the absence of décor, one learns to concentrate on God through thought, hearing, and word. By contrast, St. Peter's Cathedral in Rome, which was also built to proclaim the glory of God, was made in a different way. Its fine stone, wood, metals, sculptures, mosaics, paintings, and frescos draw the worshiper or visitor into a visual experience of grandeur, magnificence. One who worships regularly in this cathedral could find the New England Congregational white walls oddly empty, devoid of beauty, meaning, or inspiration. The regular visual experience of particular sacred spaces and objects will exert an influence on one's religious style, theology, and aesthetic sensibilities. Visual environments, including the look of landscapes and neighborhoods, help constitute and reinforce the *habitus*. People who habitually walk into a sanctuary are situated in worlds of preexisting meanings, values, and habits.[15] Visual practices and environments shape us, even as we enact and alter them, day by day.[16]

Particular places acquire meaning for individuals over time and through historical events and eras. When congregations struggle over rebuilding plans, part of what is at stake is the loss of accustomed visual environments that help to recall and reinforce the *habitus*. The sanctuary in which a couple was married, in which children were welcomed and loved ones were mourned, holds meanings and attachments for people. The building itself functions to recall its history. When the visual and physical environment is altered, a tangible marker of the past is disturbed. For this reason, changes to the environment are perceived as threatening to some members of the congregation. Sacred spaces trigger memories that make the past seem still present with the worshiper. Changes to the familiar sacred space could be experienced as a loss of coherence with the past, a loss of aids to memory.

One benefit for pastoral leaders who start to look at the religious practices and *habitus* of their congregations is an appreciation for the emotional costs of changing a sacred space, or a hymnal, or embodied expression of faith. Rather than deriding people for lacking the courage to risk change (and therefore, loss), pastoral leaders can use ethnographic interviews to allow people to articulate what is at stake for them, for example, when a congregation considers a particular kind of change. Simple questions such as, "What will be gained by this move?" and "What will be lost?" can help open up the grief and resistance that come with any significant change. When pastors and rabbis understand that certain losses provoke fear or uncertainty at the level of

---

15. For an analysis of situated knowledge, see Donna J. Haraway, *Simians, Cyborgs, and Women: The Reinvention of Nature* (New York: Routledge, Chapman, and Hall, 1991).

16. See David Morgan, *Visual Piety: A History and Theory of Popular Religious Images* (Berkeley and Los Angeles: University of California Press, 1998).

habitus, they may be able to respond more compassionately and even help to ritualize the grief that comes with these transitions. By recognizing the depth of emotion that such changes evoke, and honoring that by encouraging people to bring their experiences of loss to voice, pastors will help people to choose change consciously or to resist it thoughtfully.

When congregations or institutions consider moving, say, from a downtown location to a suburban one, an even greater challenge to the *habitus* of the group is at stake. The members may fear a loss of visual environments, a loss of group identity and purpose, a loss of relationships, or even a loss of a sense of history. The sense of safety and calm that comes from continuity in visual surroundings is often underestimated. If your institution is considering such a major move, then ethnographic study can help members enter into a process of mapping out what is at stake in terms of places, people, and history.[17] While people will still disagree about such large decisions, this sort of mapping of neighborhoods, the church's history, and the current process of deciding can help by bearing witness to the magnitude of the transition.

An artistic display or a public exhibit of your ethnographic findings can help the congregation cope during the actual period of change. Palpable reminders that link the current transition to the group's history and mission highlight the intentionality of the move. Artistic projects can help people express and process their grief over the loss of place, sacred space, or objects. When the experiences of loss and grief are openly discussed, the tendency toward unconscious sabotaging of the project is reduced. At the same time, imaginative creations and displays can help provide symbolic markers that help people feel grounded during the transition period. Charts or timelines can help make real the group's sense of hope while moving toward its goals.

---

17. One particularly helpful resource for this kind of study is Carl Dudley and Nancy Ammerman, *Congregations in Transition: A Guide for Analyzing, Assessing, and Adapting in Changing Communities* (San Francisco: Jossey-Bass, 2002).

Clarifying Your Question

As you try to clarify your research questions, think about how
your group's religious practices and *habitus* function in relation to
your question. What are the practices implicated in this question?
How can you begin to get at your question or questions? What
can you observe or query that would help address your curiosity?
Try to generate a list of religious practices that are related to
your question. Do you have some sense of an underlying ethos
or *habitus* that animates a given religious practice? Write down
your hunches. Then sift through them, perhaps in conversation
with another researcher, to try to gain a sharper focus on your
core question.

As you think about a particular religious practice, take a look
at what may already have been written about this. Others may
have conducted similar studies in other settings. Read to discover
the kinds of questions that others have asked and the different approaches they have taken. What is the new knowledge or
particular insight that you wish to gain? As you consider your different possible research questions, try to choose questions that are
possible to answer. A question such as, "What is the meaning of
the cross to the average Lutheran?" is overly broad, abstract, and
far-reaching. Aside from the fact that there is probably no such
thing as an average Lutheran (they're all above average, according
to Garrison Keillor), how could anyone really discover this kind
of knowledge?[18] By contrast, a more feasible question to pursue
might be, "How do students at this local Lutheran seminary employ the symbol of the cross in their practice of preaching?" This
question probes specific practices. Data related to this question
can be obtained in a number of ways: by listening to students
preach; by collecting their written sermons; by sitting in on seminary classes; by surveying or interviewing them to probe questions
that arise from these efforts.

---

18. See Mary M. Solberg, *Compelling Knowledge: A Feminist Proposal for
an Epistemology of the Cross* (Albany: State University of New York Press,
1997).

For another example, think back to the hypothetical church supper described in chapter 1. If a researcher wanted to explore the congregation's commitment to ministries of hospitality, where would he or she start? The question can't be answered merely by studying mission statements. The researcher needs one or more particular practices to study, such as the church supper program, in order to focus the question. There are many subquestions within the larger question about hospitality. The debate over vegetarian menus is one such subquestion. Try to clarify the practices and the larger and smaller questions that you may be homing in on. The focus on practice helps keep your work grounded in theology-in-action. Once you have a fair idea of the particular practice that you wish to study, think also about the kind of knowledge you hope to discover.

Research Puzzles

What exactly do you hope to learn about this? Jennifer Mason, in her foundational book on qualitative researching, outlines four types of intellectual puzzles that researchers might be trying to put together.

* Developmental puzzles — How did this come to be?

* Mechanical puzzles — How does this work (this way)?

* Comparative puzzles — How does this compare to that?

* Causal/predictive puzzles — How does this impact that?[19]

The kind of puzzle you choose at this early point in your process will affect the kind of argument that you are able to make later. Therefore, it is a good idea to think through these different approaches in advance.

---

19. Mason, *Qualitative Researching*, 18.

Developmental puzzles have to do with asking how something developed in a particular setting. You may be wondering, for example, how a congregation developed racist attitudes.[20] Or, how did this faith-based agency develop its current style of doing business? With this type of question, your eventual answer will involve an explanation of a meaningful process of development. You will write a narrative that elucidates the factors, events, theologies, or habits that, taken together, can help a reader see the logic behind the thing you are studying. Ken's study involved this kind of puzzle. At first it seemed odd to Ken that people in the church were driving off new members. But his research resulted in a narrative of the church's recent history that helped illuminate the logic of what was happening there. Mason points out that a developmental research question should lead you to create a textured and sensitive contextual narrative, rather than a simple explanation that caricatures people or their developmental processes.[21] This is a helpful caveat, in light of the common human tendency to develop simplified caricatures of people whose religious or political beliefs differ from our own.

Mechanical puzzles represent another kind of question. These questions query how something works and/or why it works in a particular way.[22] This type of question is especially useful for studying a religious practice that may seem strange to outsiders. When I studied Catholic devotional practices in a community of Italian immigrants in San Pedro, California, I wanted to understand the function of certain practices, such as praying before (or to?) statues that represented particular Catholic saints. This question took me inside the churches, the rituals, and the homes of the people. Answering this question involved observing the activities and artifacts related to praying, including posture, movement, and song, social gatherings, and expenses of time and money.

20. Ibid.
21. Ibid., 175.
22. Ibid., 18.

The question helped me explore the devotions and get a feel for what was transpiring in these practices.[23] Ethnography can help you delve into the workings of religious practices in diverse and complicated contexts.

The third kind of puzzle you might want to explore is the comparative puzzle. With this type of question, you are exploring how different social phenomena or groups compare to each other. You will eventually be explaining differences and similarities between the two. For example, if you want to understand the influence of affluence on charitable giving practices, you might study the giving patterns and expressed theological rationales for these among congregational members of diverse income levels. Or you could compare giving patterns and expressed theologies in diverse congregations. A third alternative would be to trace the development of traditions that shape the patterns and practices of giving among congregations in various denominations. This third alternative would involve both a developmental and a comparative question.

An excellent example of a larger-scale comparative study is described in the monograph *Being There: Culture and Formation in Two Theological Schools*.[24] The authors conducted parallel studies of two theological schools in North America, one that they considered an evangelical theological seminary, and one that they judged to be a mainline theological seminary. While the researchers asked a variety of kinds of questions and used different research instruments in the course of their ethnographic work at both schools, their overarching research question was a comparative one: what are the similarities and differences between the educational cultures at each of these institutions? Ethnography helped the researchers draw a comparison between the two

---

23. Mary Clark Moschella, *Living Devotions: Reflections on Immigration, Identity, and Religious Imagination* (Eugene, Ore.: Pickwick Publications, 2008).

24. Jackson Carroll, Barbara Wheeler, Daniel Aleshire, and Penny Long Marler, *Being There: Culture and Formation in Two Theological Schools* (New York: Oxford University Press, 1997).

groups that went beyond a simple statistical comparison to generate a nuanced narrative, full of contextual points of comparison and contrast.

The fourth kind of puzzle is a causal or predictive puzzle. Questions of this type try to get at the effect of one factor on another. If you undertake this type of puzzle, you might eventually try to predict the outcomes of a certain religious practice or teaching. Ethnographers don't usually arrive at simple or straightforward cause-and-effect statements, but rather at particular theories about causation in local settings and tentative predictions about how things might be similar or might vary in diverse contexts.[25] Research questions of this type sometimes include aspects of all the other types.

For example, a Wesley doctor of ministry graduate, David Bahr, conducted a study project for his thesis that addressed a causal or predictive puzzle. David was researching the effects of openly gay and lesbian United Church of Christ (UCC) pastors on the size and health of their "mostly straight" congregations.[26] David was aware that one of the objections some church members raise when they start to consider calling an openly gay pastor is the concern that hiring a gay pastor will either drive the straight (heterosexual) members away, or cause so many gay and lesbian new members to join that the church would become "mostly gay or lesbian." David found a way to test these predictions by identifying sixty-two UCC "mostly straight" congregations that called openly gay or lesbian pastors, and studying their attendance and membership levels before and after the arrival of the gay or lesbian pastor and over a period of years. It was a complicated project because many other factors besides the sexual orientation of a pastor could have a causal effect on the increase or decrease of membership and attendance rates. So David devised lengthy surveys that helped shed light on some of these other factors as well.

---

25. Mason, *Qualitative Researching*, 175.

26. David Paul Bahr, "Openly Gay and Lesbian Pastors Called by Predominantly Straight UCC Congregations" (D. Min. thesis, Wesley Theological Seminary, 2006).

Interestingly, David's study demonstrates a 10 percent or greater increase in membership levels for 51 percent of these churches.[27] This increase was made even more significant when David added a comparative component to the study, specifically, the aggregate membership and attendance levels of all UCC congregations in the United States over similar time periods. The churches led by openly gay and lesbian pastors looked to be thriving by comparison.[28] Similarly, this study challenges the fear that some people expressed that their churches would become predominantly gay or lesbian if they called an openly gay or lesbian pastor: this did not happen in these churches.[29]

These four different types of puzzles, and sometimes combinations of these types, can come into play in ethnographic research. Notice that they all revolve around rather basic questions: How did this (ritual, attitude, style, or practice) come to be (develop) the way it is? How does this (mechanical) phenomenon work, exactly? How does this compare to that? Does this theology or practice affect (cause or predict) that outcome? When you are able to focus your questions so that you know what kind or kinds of puzzles they involve, you are ready to begin designing your study.

I want to offer you a word of caution and a word of encouragement. First, the caution: ethnographic research tends to evolve and shift as you engage in it. You discover surprises and roadblocks along the way, so you have to stay flexible and creative and willing to let go of your first ideas if need be. Now, for the encouragement: remember why you are doing this. The benefits of the ethnographic journey will soon start to manifest themselves as you begin to see and hear the people with greater clarity. These first painstaking steps are setting your course for a transformative journey.

---

27. Ibid., 115.
28. Ibid., 111–16.
29. Ibid., 121.

For Further Study

Carroll, Jackson, Barbara Wheeler, Daniel Aleshire, and Penny Long
    Marler. *Being There: Culture and Formation in Two Theological
    Schools*. New York: Oxford University Press, 1997.
Graham, Elaine, Heather Walton, and Frances Ward. *Theological
    Reflection: Methods*. London: SCM Press, 2005, chapter 6.
Mason, Jennifer. *Qualitative Researching*, 2nd ed. Thousand Oaks,
    Calif.: SAGE Publications, 2002, chapter 1.
Volf, Miroslav, and Dorothy C. Bass, eds. *Practicing Theology: Beliefs
    and Practices in Christian Life*. Grand Rapids: Wm. B. Eerdmans,
    2002. See the essays by Craig Dykstra and Dorothy Bass, Amy
    Plantinga Pauw, and Kathryn Tanner.

- T H R E E -

Research Design
Sketching Out a Path

If you don't know where you are going, you will wind up somewhere else.   — YOGI BERRA

Creating a research design is crucial; it's like sketching out a path for your ethnographic journey. Although you can't entirely anticipate where this path will lead, the journey is best undertaken with intention, not as a haphazard ramble. Yogi Berra's words are apt: if you don't try to anticipate where you're going with your research, you'll end up somewhere else! The thought that you put into your research design at this early stage will significantly affect the direction and coherence of your overall project.

Bill Clements uses the analogy of a compass to talk about research design. Imagine standing at a high point with the ability to see out over a large terrain. Notice the compass point as you spy a route directly ahead. Then imagine shifting the needle's position just a few degrees to the right or left. Can you see the huge difference in the direction and endpoint of this new route? Research begins best when you both give thought to an overall strategy and try to anticipate where specific methods will take you. This effort will increase the precision and usefulness of your results.

As you consider your overall research design, think about how you can probe the practices and the *habitus* of your group. Move into what I call the ethnographic mind by thinking of your congregation, agency, or group as if it were a book. How would an outsider read it? What would be its theme, its underlying message? How would the chapters be arranged? Try to choose research methods that help you identify the theme or main story

63

that the book proclaims, through both word and deed. As you focus your questions more particularly on one or two religious practices, you can start to think of the particular practice you are studying as a chapter with its own thesis within a larger story. As you set about your planning, you will be trying to clarify your basic research question and selecting specific methods to help you puzzle out some answers.

Examples of sufficiently honed questions at this point include: How did this particularly strong ministry become what it is today? (developmental); How does the practice of spiritual journaling work in this setting? (mechanical); How do the various components of worship in one service compare to those in another? (comparative); Does this agency's practice of political activism increase the advocacy ministries of constituent congregations? (causal or predictive). A good research question is specific and concrete and leads you in the direction of observable data.

Matching Methods to Questions

Once you are clear about your main research question, the next step is to identify the particular methods that will help you glean the most pertinent data with which to answer your question. Recalling Mason's four types of research puzzles (developmental, mechanical, comparative, and causal or predictive),[1] we can go back to each research example used in chapter 2 to examine the particular research methods that were chosen for each kind of study.

Developmental Puzzles:
How Did This Come to Be?

Ken, the student pastor who wanted to address church growth, began with a question as to the reasons longstanding church members seemed to be driving away new members. Because

---

1. Mason, *Qualitative Researching*, 18.

this practice seemed to be inconsistent with the Christian theology Ken had been preaching and also counterproductive to the congregation's well-being, Ken was puzzled. He formulated a research question that is a developmental puzzle: How did this attitude develop? This question probes the *habitus* of the group, the history that is operative in the congregation's current practices. Ken looked for methods and resources that could help him get at this embodied history.

As Ken wondered what had happened that would cause church members to distrust newcomers, he eventually settled on four methods that could help him obtain data on this subject. They included: qualitative interviews with church members, reading the existing historical documents, listening to tape recordings found in the church office, and researching the history of farming and land buyouts in the church's geographical area. Developmental puzzles often involve a search for historical data in existing documents, including newspaper clippings, public town records, books, tapes, the organization's own records or archives, and websites. In addition to these sources, qualitative interviews can help elicit the historical memories and narratives people tell about an incident or an era.

Ken's research plan, like anyone's, was partly determined by the practical reality of what kinds of resources were available. In his case, a process of looking around in the church offices yielded considerable historical data in the form of written and taped records of church proceedings.[2] This data then helped Ken formulate his particular questions for his qualitative interviews. Similarly, the interviews yielded information about town history that Ken then researched through town records. You can see how various data sets and research methods can lead to the use of others. One of Ken's methods, qualitative interviewing, was particularly crucial to his growing understanding of his congregation.

---

2. For a good resource that discusses the practice of and ethics for oral history, see David K. Dunaway and Willa K. Baum, eds., *Oral History: An Interdisciplinary Anthology*, 2nd ed. (Walnut Creek, Calif.: Altamira Press, 1996).

Qualitative Interviews

Qualitative interviewing is one of the hallmark methods in ethnographic research. Many practical issues arise as you place interviews into your overall research strategy. These include: the length and number of the interviews, the place or places where you will conduct them, obtaining informed consent, the process for selecting particular persons to interview (and the rationale for these choices), plans for recording or transcribing interviews, and managing the time and expenses that interviews require. Interviews take time, and they necessitate many practical decisions. Some people do not wish to be interviewed, and you will have to respect this. If very few persons in the group are willing to be interviewed, you may then decide to select another method, such as anonymous surveys, which are usually considered less threatening.

Formulating interview questions is an important task in research design. Think about the kind of tone you want to set with your questions. Try your hand at writing down some key questions early on. A few simple, open-ended questions that probe current practices and personal stories are helpful for developmental puzzles. "What is your take on this?" you want to ask people. "Was it always this way?" If you want people to open up and share their stories, refrain from planning too many questions. If you go into the interview worried that all of your many questions must get answered, you may actually derail the natural flow of storytelling. With fewer questions, you can relax into listening to the stories people share. Allow enough time so that if a person starts to tell a story, you can let him or her keep going without interrupting too much.

Try to design questions that are nonthreatening. Refrain from asking questions that are too pointed. For example, if Ken had asked his members, "Why are you driving away newcomers?" they might have felt judged by their pastor and come back with harsh or evasive retorts. Instead, Ken asked, "Do you like a big church or a small church?" As Ken was puzzling over the possible reasons that church members were rejecting newcomers, he used logic to identify a basic question. Could it be that people preferred a small church? He put the question out in a casual way, inviting people to share their honest preferences. Asking journalism's famous five questions — who, what, where, when, and how — will usually help you get started. "Why" questions are more difficult to answer, so plan to use those more sparingly, and ask them later in the interview, after your conversation has moved to a deeper, more reflective level.

Once you have put some questions into writing, it is a good idea to test them out in some way. Questions that seem innocuous to you might strike someone else as pushy or prying. Ask your colleagues or research supervisors to help you at this point. If you are doing your research for a course, your class can be a good sounding board. You can also ask friends or a few trusted members of your congregation or another congregation to look over your questions. Ask them to identify any possible problems with the way the questions could be construed. Also ask your colleagues to review the logic of your choices. Do these questions fully probe the matter you want to understand? Take in the feedback that colleagues offer at this critical early phase.

At every stage of the project, remember to practice reflexivity. How would you answer these questions? What sorts of answers do you anticipate hearing from interviewees? Are you hoping for certain answers, and if so, why? The point is not that you are expected to be value-neutral, but that you understand your own biases, theology, and motivations enough to see how they are operating in your choice of methods and questions. One ethnographer puts it this way: "We are our own subjects. How our subjectivity becomes entangled in the lives of others is and always has been our topic."[3] The more you can be conscious and aware of yourself in this process, the more honest and transparent you can be in your questions and in the eventual process of ethnographic writing. Keep a running record or research journal

---

3. Denzin, *Interpretive Ethnography*, 27.

explaining your reflections upon your research decisions along the way.[4]

Mechanical Puzzles:
How Does This Work (This Way)?

The second kind of puzzle is the mechanical puzzle. Whether it is a large organizational structure, a small support group, or a personal conversion experience, your question is about how something works or functions. The example used in chapter 1 was of my own research in San Pedro, California, where I wanted to understand the function of Catholic devotional practices in the lives of Italian immigrants and their descendants. For that study, I used several methods in my overall research design, including the study of historical documents (there was a developmental component to this question as well), qualitative interviews, and participant observation. For studying the specific practice of praying before statues or pictures of the saints, participant observation was particularly useful.

Participant Observation

When puzzling over questions of how a religious practice works in a specific context, it is helpful to go to the places where people engage in this practice and spend time there, seeing what you can see. As Norman Denzin puts it, "The ethnographer who wishes to understand another has to build up an understanding based on an involvement in the subject's worlds of experience."[5] This understanding accumulates over the course of time spent with people and in their surroundings.

As you walk into a sanctuary where worship is practiced, for example, remind yourself to try to take in as much as you can, using all of your senses. It is wise to start out with broad "radar," being on the alert to notice the physical features of the space and

---

4. I will say more about research journals in chapter 4.
5. Denzin, *Interpretive Ethnography,* 35.

the experiential impact of whatever happens there, whether it seems religious or not. When I went into the sanctuary of Mary Star of the Sea Church in San Pedro, I tried to take it all in: the visual impact of the place, the number of people present at different times of day, the tone and feeling of various Masses, the imposing central altar with its towering marble statue of Mary (holding a fishing boat!), the electronic candles "burning" before the saints, the lists of prayer requests some of the devout left written down at various altars, the ethnic-looking features of the representations of the saints, the flowers left on particular saints' altars, the size and placement of the statues and stained-glass representations, the style of architecture, the occasional smell of incense, and the literature left on tables.[6]

Obviously, one could do a great deal of in-depth study on any one particular aspect of this experience. One could, for example, try to track down the details of the materials used to make each statue (some were made from imported Italian marble), the acquisition of each statue (who paid for each and decided on its placement?), the popularity and constituency of each statue (who knelt to pray before each statue and how often?), or the particular prayer petitions offered at each altar. Initially, I didn't know which aspects of the setting were going to be most helpful in my quest to understand how the devotions worked. So I tried to learn as much as I could about each these dimensions through observation, asking questions, and studying documentary evidence.

I also spent time in the sanctuary, "hanging out" in the sacred space to see what struck me and to monitor my own emotional experience of the place. One of the things that struck me when I would hang out in the sanctuary among so many life-sized or larger-than-life-sized statues was that I never felt quite alone in that space. This experience then became a piece of information for me to process and consider as I tried to understand the experiences of the devout, who often reported feeling a supernatural presence when in proximity to their statues or paintings of saints.

6. Moschella, *Living Devotions*, 3, 29–32.

I knew that my experience was not the same as those of the devout. Nevertheless, on some level, my own visceral experience helped me imagine what the devout were describing.

Participant observation, as noted in chapter 1, involves "being there" with people as they practice their religion. Religious leaders have a natural advantage in terms of gaining access to both the significant events in the life of a group and the mundane, ordinary times during which people practice their faith. Such access can be abused. In participant observation, as with any form of research, you will need to have the group's informed consent before you switch hats and take on the role of ethnographer, and especially before you begin to record your observations. (Chapter 4 will address informed consent and the ethics of ethnography in detail.) Before you ask for informed consent, however, you need to have some clarity about what it is you want to study and how you plan to proceed.

As you spend some initial time hanging out with the congregation, agency, or community, try to decide on which specific places or events you most want to focus. A great deal of material is available for study, and you will need to make tentative choices. As a religious leader-ethnographer, you probably won't be doing research full time, so it becomes especially critical to take practical limitations into account.

Hammersley and Atkinson say that this all comes down to a trade-off between the breadth and depth of investigation.[7] The broader your study, the less time you will have to pursue each experience in detail. However, broad-stroke portraits can reveal a great deal about a community. Pastors or rabbis who are just starting out in a new congregation might want to begin with a broad study that will provide clues to the *habitus* and the main themes in this particular congregation. Conversely, a leader who has been in a congregation longer may opt for a narrower field of observation, such as a particular committee whose meetings always seem to go awry.

---

7. Hammersley and Atkinson, *Ethnography*, 41.

While narrowing your choices can be difficult, keep in mind that this plan is tentative. If in the course of your research you find you are investing all of your energy in a particular issue or method that is leading nowhere, you will have to revise your plan. In order to discover this sooner rather than later, explore the existing resources for learning about your setting. Are there big annual events coming up? Are their archives to which you can reasonably hope to gain access? Who are the gatekeepers, the persons who control access to information and people? Talk over your question with a key leader or gatekeeper, and try to get a sense of whether there are resources available for you to explore, and whether your question seems pertinent and fitting to these individuals. As a time management strategy, starting with a study that is small in scope and adding something later is much easier than scaling back a huge project once it is launched.

Yet, stay flexible. If you know that a huge annual event or community-wide ritual is coming up on the group's calendar, it is wise to plan on going, even if you are not sure that you will learn anything that goes directly to your specific question. You don't want to skip the event, only later to realize its significance and have to wait another year to complete your research. Similarly, if an unplanned but significant issue or event comes along in the life of the group, pay attention. Check in with your gatekeeper or key informant on a regular basis, so that you will be "in the know." If you find out that something important is going on, be flexible enough to go where the action is.

Remember the two balancing acts involved in forecasting the best use of your use of time in participant observation: First is balancing between breadth and depth of inquiry. Second is the balancing between sticking to the plan and staying open to what comes up in the life of the group. Careful planning — as well as flexibility, intuition, curiosity, and peer-group consultation — can help you manage these decisions now and as your work unfolds.

Once you do focus in on a setting or settings for participant observation, pay attention to the experience in exquisite detail. For example, if you are wearing your ethnographer's hat at a governing council meeting and a visitor looking for financial help disturbs the meeting, pay attention to the entire interchange. Do not assume that the council's agenda is going to contain or limit the interactions you are observing. Early on, you will want to notice as much as you can — whatever happens or doesn't happen, the way that people speak to each other, the way decisions are made, who leads or influences the group and how. Is the visitor treated kindly? Does the group take time to listen or send the person away? Is the pastor expected to handle the interruption? Does anyone rely on religious resources such as scripture or prayer? Noticing the process of interaction as much as the content will help you see how the group operates as you try to solve your mechanical puzzle.

Comparative Puzzles: How Does This Compare to That?

The third category of research questions we looked at in chapter 2 is the comparative puzzle. You may be comparing two or more large entities — such as congregations or institutions, or two smaller subjects — such as two worship services within the same congregation. The example was from *Being There: Culture and Formation in Two Theological Schools.*[8] This example, as you might imagine, was a large-scale project emphasizing breadth of inquiry. In this study, there were four researcher-authors, none of whom were affiliated with either theological school. They split into two teams and worked intermittently on the project over a three-year period. They used a variety of research methods, including participant observation, interviews, the examination of material culture, and focusing on the printed word, including student newspapers, faculty publications, notices in mailboxes, postings on bulletin boards, and so on.[9] The authors' intent was to compare the effect of the two different institutional cultures — one evangelical and one mainline — on theological formation in each school.

---

8. Carroll et al., *Being There.*
9. Ibid., 7.

Research Teams

Large-scale comparative projects like this one will often benefit from a team approach to the research, rather than relying
on a single researcher. A group of researchers can allow you to
cover more ground. The research team can also provide a natural peer group for checking out the clarity and accuracy of each
researcher's observations and more subjective impressions of the
people and the setting. The broader range of viewpoints that a
team provides is a significant benefit to the research.

Some matters of concern for ethnography teams, however, also
need to be considered. The first is the need for some kind of consistency and clarity in the approach taken by each of the members
of the team. Two completely divergent approaches to research in
two settings will afford little basis for actual comparison. You
need to establish a broad consensus with your co-researchers
about the methods and questions you are pursuing in each setting. This will require ample time to meet and plan together at
the start of the project and at various points along the way.

Similarly, if you as a chief researcher decide to hire one or
more people to help you conduct the research or collect data,
you must allow enough time (and possibly, money) for training
your researchers as to how to proceed. It is not enough to hand
your employees a list of questions before they conduct interviews.
Interviewing is an art, and not everyone knows how to do it.[10]
Make sure that the interviewer understands the way you want the
interviews conducted — the tenor that you want set, the degree to
which you want the interviews to be open-ended and free-flowing,
or short and sweet and to the point, and so forth. You are aiming
for a kind of evenness in the research approach that will allow
you to make a fair comparison later on when you are analyzing
the data.

---

10. We will take up the art of interviewing in some detail in chapter 6. For
more help in thinking through the uses and conduct of interviews during your
planning stages, see Mason, *Qualitative Researching*, chapter 4, 62–83; and
Hammersley and Atkinson, *Ethnography*, chapter 5, 124–56.

Sometimes practicality dictates the need to have more than one researcher involved. For example, a former student in an ethnography class set out to study court mediation proceedings. In mediations, specially trained attorneys are hired to mediate legal disputes between two parties, with the hope of reaching a mutually acceptable solution without resorting to lawsuits. In this case, the student researcher, a mediator herself, was trying to ascertain the role of religious and ethical convictions in each party's thinking and participation in a mediation. She designed interviews to be conducted before and after several mediation proceedings. In order to conduct the interviews of the two parties at the same time, she needed to have at least one additional researcher working with her. She trained her researchers to conduct the interviews in a consistent way (with varying success), so that when she compared the parties' responses to interview questions, she would have a reasonably constant factor (the questioning) to use in her analysis.[11]

Thinking about the persons with whom you choose to work in any kind of a team project is important. In the *Being There* study, the four researchers were all theological educators. This background experience no doubt helped them design, conduct, analyze, and write up their study of theological schools. They were, in a sense, all insiders. But in another sense, they were all outsiders,[12] as none of them had any current or previous affiliation with either of the two schools they were studying. Interestingly, the group decided to divide up into teams in such a way as to make the maximum use of their felt cultural distance from the schools they studied. One of the schools they studied was considered more evangelical, and the other more theologically mainline. By background and experience, two of the researchers were more familiar with evangelical settings, and two with main-

---

11. Jane Juliano, "Lived Religion in Conflict: A Study of Spiritual Values in the Mediation Context," unpublished paper, Wesley Theological Seminary, December 16, 2004. Used by permission.

12. This recalls our discussion of liminal status in chapter 1; see notes 19 and 20.

line. The team decided to send the more evangelical researchers to the more mainline school and the researchers with mainline backgrounds to the more evangelical school. In this way, they hoped to maximize their capacity to observe and notice cultural phenomena that would stand out to the particular researchers in relief against their own backgrounds.[13]

If you are working on a broad comparative puzzle, you may still decide to work alone in order to have more consistency in the study. In this case, you can help limit your work by choosing one main focus for your study of each group. In a forthcoming book pastoral theologian Susan Dunlap offers an ethnographic and theological study of the respective practices of care for the sick in three distinct congregations. These include an African American Apostolic Holiness congregation, a Euro-American mainstream Protestant congregation, and a Latino Catholic congregation.[14] Though it has taken her several years to conduct the research herself, one advantage in her analysis and interpretation is that she herself as the researcher is a constant in all three settings. Though she no doubt is perceived differently and interacts differently in each setting, she is still a reasonably consistent presence in the research. By focusing on the same aspect of pastoral ministry in each church, she creates a stable axis for comparison.

In a situation where you are the pastoral leader, an interesting team approach to a large-scale study would be to involve church members in the conduct of the research itself. This is advocated in many self-study guides for congregations going through changes as well as in some of the congregational studies literature.[15] While this approach brings some challenges and risks, it also offers some potential benefits. First, if congregational members or lay leaders help lead the research, then they may have more access than you

---

13. Carroll et al., *Being There*, 7.

14. Susan Dunlap (Waco: Baylor University Press, forthcoming).

15. See, for example, Gil Rendle and Alice Mann, *Holy Conversations: Strategic Planning as a Spiritual Practice for Congregations* (Herndon, Va.: Alban Institute, 2003), especially, chapters 9 and 10, 113–37; and Ammerman et al., *Studying Congregations*, 9–10.

do to what has been called "the view from the pew."[16] Members may trust co-members more than they do a new pastor, for example, and they may be willing to share more openly. Second, the members who conduct the research will benefit from the experience enormously if they are well trained in listening and strive to remain nonjudgmental as they ask questions and learn more about members of their own group. Third, mutual relationships in the community could deepen, which could accrue to the well-being of the congregation.

If you decide to design your research to be co-led by members of the community, then some special concerns need to be addressed. A certain amount of training will be required, just as in the case of any other research team. The choice of particular leaders for this kind of study is also a critical one. The ethical constraints of research and the capacity of researchers to keep confidences must be fully thought through and addressed with the team, both in advance of the study and at various points along the way. Because qualitative research does lead to deepening relationships, it taps into a level of personal/spiritual vulnerability. Obviously, gossip would cause great harm to a person or a community that is just beginning to communicate at this level. Therefore, extra care must be taken to work with your member-researchers and be sure that they learn how to handle this new vulnerability with respect and care. Additionally, the pastor's relationships to the members of the research team will be challenged and possibly strained at times during the research process, as will relationships among team members. These relationships can grow and blossom as you work through the costs and joys of ethnography, but they will require your awareness, attention, and care.

The shared leadership route is both more challenging and potentially more liberative. If you think of your ethnographic research as a hike up a mountain, then this particular trail is a

---

16. See, for example, Lora-Ellen McKinney, *View from the Pew: What Preachers Can Learn from Church Members* (Valley Forge, Pa.: Judson Press, 2004).

steep one. The route has more hazards, especially if you are a novice. Yet it also has its advantages. It might get you there faster because you would have to start exemplifying more liberative relationships with your co-leaders sooner. For example, you would have to teach your co-leaders clear guidelines for interviewing and keeping confidences, all while demonstrating patient listening and thoughtful theological reflection on the process. From a pastoral theological perspective, the shared leadership form of ethnography represents a more communal approach, one that draws the laity into the pastoral practice. From an ethnographic standpoint, this approach takes seriously the term "co-researcher," which highlights respect for the subjectivity of the members of the group in the study. These are important pastoral theological matters to consider.

Causal/Predictive Puzzles:
How Does This Impact That?

The fourth kind of puzzle is the causal or predictive puzzle. If your research question has to do with the effect of one practice on another, such as the effect of wearing nametags on the return rate of first-time visitors to your congregation, then you are working on a predictive question. The example used in chapter 2 is David Bahr's study of openly gay and lesbian pastors called by predominantly straight United Church of Christ congregations. David used several research methods to get at the question of what kind of effect the presence of openly gay and lesbian pastors is having on the overall health of the UCC congregations that called them. Because David was doing a relatively large-scale study, participant observation was neither a feasible tool nor a necessary one, given the intent of his study. Research of documented statistics provided him with an important base of knowledge regarding membership, worship attendance, and church school attendance records. Additionally, David created a lengthy printed survey that served as the centerpiece of his research. This survey enabled him to collect both quantitative and qualitative data from each participating pastor.

Survey Instruments

A written survey is a useful instrument for gathering information and ideas from large numbers of people. Smaller research samples may allow you the privilege of establishing a deeper relationship with each person involved. Larger samples, in contrast, give you a broader view. They help you see the forest and not just the trees.

If you are working on a predictive puzzle, reaching greater numbers of people helps you establish more credible conclusions. For example, if David Bahr had chosen to survey only five pastors and their congregations, his findings would not have been so significant. A skeptical reader could say, "Okay, in these five churches, gay and lesbian pastors worked out. That could just be a fluke." Because he was able to locate and study sixty-two congregations, his conclusions are more substantive and harder to dismiss. The strong record of growth in attendance and membership in UCC churches that called openly gay and lesbian pastors is convincing because it is backed up by both quantitative and qualitative data. Surveys are also a good choice if you want to allow for a higher level of anonymity or confidentiality in the research process. Sometimes people are willing to express things in writing that they are not yet able to say out loud. While eventually you hope to be able to share findings and engage people openly, it is important to start the process at a comfortable level for the people involved. Surveys can be numbered without names, so that only you have a record of which name goes with which survey. Alternatively, surveys can be done anonymously, with no names recorded at all. A third option is that names can be optional. If you want to leave the door open for qualitative interviews to follow up on a survey, you can ask respondents to check a box and write down their name and contact information — or return a separate postcard or e-mail — if they are willing to be interviewed at a later date. Many excellent research projects include both a large survey sample and a smaller number of qualitative interviews that help elucidate the findings.

For example, a former doctor of ministry student whom we shall call "Pat" used a survey-with-interviews research design when she was trying to understand a failed ministry program in her church. Pat had been the pastoral staff member assigned to this particular program. At least some members of the ministry team were angry about the way the program ended, she knew, and some blamed her for its demise. Rather than sweep this under the rug, Pat bravely chose to explore this fiasco. She wanted to understand what had gone wrong from the people's perspective, and she wanted to use this understanding to help improve any future program's chances for success.

The anonymous survey option worked well for those who were angry but unable to address directly the deeper issues. A few people did put down their names and, when Pat followed up, agreed to allow her to interview them. This was a painful process because Pat did not agree with all of the perspectives being shared and because, as the researcher, she had to endure what she considered to be unfair criticism. Also, as a pastor, Pat was aware of some confidential information that she knew restricted her parishioners' ability to fully understand what had taken place in the context of the troubled ministry program. Of course, she could not break confidences, and therefore some misunderstandings could not be completely cleared up. Nevertheless, from her research surveys and interviews, Pat learned something valuable about how people had been perceiving her role in the ministry program. The combination of a survey and follow-up interviews proved to be an excellent strategy for achieving both understanding and, eventually, a sense of closure.[17]

Yet another way to do surveys is illustrated by the work of historian Thomas Tweed in his award-winning study of religious practices at a Cuban Catholic shrine in Miami.[18] For this study,

---

17. Likewise, the church members seemed to calm down and appreciate Pat more after these interviews and the eventual dialogue they spurred. Instead of "healing the wound ... lightly" (Jer. 6:14 RSV), Pat and the members of the former ministry project team were able to offer and receive real forgiveness for their mistakes before moving on. "Pat," "Learnings from Ministry to Instruct a New Lay Visitation Ministry," unpublished paper, Wesley Theological Seminary, February 23, 2005.

18. Thomas A. Tweed, *Our Lady of the Exile: Diasporic Religion at a Cuban Catholic Shrine in Miami* (New York: Oxford University Press, 1997). In his

Tweed combined historical research with ethnographic survey/ interviews. With permission, and wearing a researcher badge, Tweed stood on the steps at one of the entrances to the shrine with a clipboard, asking visitors as they left the shrine if they would be willing to spare a few moments for the twenty-question survey. He then asked the questions verbally (mostly in Spanish), and wrote down the answers as people spoke. By personally administering the surveys, he could get clarification when he did not understand an answer. He could also allow people to speak for as long as they were willing. Some conversations were brief, while a few went on for hours. In all, Tweed was able to record surveys from 304 visitors. He did not ask for names, so that anonymity would be assured.[19]

However you decide to conduct a survey, several issues need to be considered at the design stage. Whom do you wish to survey? Do you want a random sample, or a sample that is representative of various social groups? How can you get the best possible rate of return? What questions will you ask and how many? What deadline will you offer for the survey return? There is a particular need for careful thought about these questions if you are doing anonymous surveys, because you will only have one chance to get your answers. If you realize later that you forgot to ask an important question, you will not be able to add it.

When David Bahr set out to survey openly gay and lesbian pastors, his first step was to identify survey participants from the thirty-nine conferences of the United Church of Christ. This alone took a great deal of careful planning because the issue of sexual orientation is a sensitive one in the churches. He compiled his initial list mostly through contacting conference ministers with a thoughtful letter in advance of the study. When he started to receive names and churches, he created a contact database from there. In all, he compiled a list of 113 openly gay or lesbian pastors. Then he sent out numbered surveys with a one-

---

Appendix B, Tweed helpfully includes the English version of the survey he used, 146–47.

  19. Ibid., 6–8.

month deadline suggested. Because of time constraints, he could accept surveys only up to one week after the deadline. This well-constructed survey had the rather remarkable return rate of 75 percent.[20] (As a benchmark, researchers typically expect only a 10 percent survey return.)

Remember to include demographic questions, even if you are not sure how they will figure into your analysis. Questions that get at social location (such as gender, race, economic level, age, education level, sexual orientation, cultural and geographic background) may come up later as you look at your results and try to understand them.

When designing your questions, work as you would with qualitative interviews, namely, make a preliminary list of questions that can be shown to colleagues for feedback. Try to limit the number of questions you ask, so that recipients don't decide the survey will take too long to complete.[21]

David Bahr wanted his survey to answer a causal question, but he wanted a nuanced answer and not just a numerical one. In addition to asking for statistics and demographic information, he asked some "multiple choice" questions and some open-ended questions that left room for narrative responses. David tested his questions on a small sample of four pastors before sending out the survey. He did his best to vet the questions in advance, to make sure that the questions were clear and unambiguous and to take out or alter any questions that might be perceived as hurtful or leading. The responses he received to these narrative questions varied in length and depth, but many of them contained touching personal stories, which David was able to capture in his thesis narrative.

As in the case of other research methods, reflexivity is critical when writing a survey and testing a predictive question. In his paper, David was clear about his own theology and identity as an openly gay pastor serving in a mostly straight UCC congregation.

---

20. Bahr, "Openly Gay and Lesbian Pastors," 25–36.
21. For a helpful list of issues to consider in writing questionnaires, see Ammerman et al., *Studying Congregations*, 224.

He wanted to learn more about how similar pastors and churches were faring. He hoped his research would demonstrate that the churches that called openly gay and lesbian pastors were doing well, but he could not fully predict the outcome. By embarking on this study, he was taking the risk that he would turn up a large number of failed pastorates and unhappy congregations. David was pleased to discover that this was not the case in the majority of the churches he studied. There were, however, some very sad and painful stories of struggle for some of the congregations and the pastors involved. David includes these stories along with graphs that show the numerical growth or decline of the congregations. Though David undertook this research as an advocate, the quantitative data he collected make his results verifiable by outside researchers. His qualitative data add nuance, revealing that many of the pastors, even those whose congregations are thriving, experience their ministry as "both painful and liberating."[22] Because David is clear and reflective about his motivations and his role in the research, readers can follow the logic of his analysis and draw their own conclusions.[23]

The methods we have explored thus far do not represent a comprehensive list of the available research strategies and instruments. Many excellent handbooks, chiefly from the fields of congregational studies and ethnographic and qualitative research, can be consulted as you are deliberating about your research design. I suggest reading some of these in order to get an idea of the range of methods and the ways in which they have been tried and refined for different contexts.[24]

---

22. Bahr, "Openly Gay and Lesbian Pastors," 10.

23. The following are two good resources that describe "positionality" and "standpoint ethnography": Nancy A. Naples, *Feminism and Method: Ethnography, Discourse Analysis, and Activist Research* (New York: Routledge, 2003); and D. Soyini Madison: *Critical Ethnography: Method, Ethics and Performance* (Thousand Oaks, Calif.: SAGE Publications, 2005).

24. In addition to the books listed in "For Further Study" at the end of this chapter, see also Dudley and Ammerman, *Congregations in Transition*; Swinton and Mowat, *Practical Theology and Qualitative Research*; and Cameron et al., eds., *Studying Local Churches*.

Writing It Down

After you have pondered the various methods and options, your tentative plan needs to be put down in writing. Committing your research plan to paper will help you manage your time and delineate your next steps. Be as specific as you can be about the scope and limits of your work. Figure 1 offers guidelines for formulating your research plan in the form of key questions to answer. You should be able to complete the first five questions after reading this chapter. The final question, which has to do with the ethics of research, will be addressed next in chapter 4.

Writing all this down in the form of a narrative will help you gain clarity and perspective on your plan. Some of the writing you do now will become an important record of your ethnographic journey. Later, when you begin composing the larger narrative, you will want to recall how you started out and why. As you grow and change through the process of doing your research, you will want to be able to understand what happened — how you started out, and what, if anything, shifted for you in the course of the process.

Design a plan that you can bring to completion in a reasonable amount of time. Factor in extra time for scheduling interviews, dealing with occasional cancellations, waiting for surveys to be returned, or traveling to visit archives. Remember also that the processes of analyzing data, interpreting them, and sharing results with the group will require considerable time and energy. For a first effort, I recommend a modest project that you can see through to completion in three to twelve months, or within the limitations of your course schedule. If you would really like to do a gigantic study and this is your first time out, consider making this first effort a pilot study to test the waters. Alternatively, you could think of this as an opportunity to break down the larger study into manageable pieces and choose one smaller piece to work on first. Doctoral students may wish to take this approach: begin with a small study that can be done in a few months in a pastoral ethnography course, then build upon it or use the experience as practice for a larger study that fulfills a thesis or dissertation requirement.

Figure 1. Guidelines for Research Plan

Answer these questions in narrative form,
using 5–7 double-spaced pages.

1. Briefly describe the research upon which you are about to embark. What is the purpose of the study? How does your own theology inform or motivate your study? What change or transformation would you like to see in the community you are studying?

2. Try to narrow your focus to one or two research questions. What religious practice do you most want to explore and/or describe? What type of intellectual puzzle is it?

3. What ethnographic tools and methods will you use? Surveys? Interviews? Observation? Explain how the methods you select will help you "get at" your stated research question. Include a tentative list of the questions you will ask of your research participants. Be sure to include questions regarding demographic information such as race, gender, age, and so on.

4. What is the scope of your investigation? If using surveys or interviews, how many? If using participant observation, which events and how often will you observe them? Plan a reasonably modest study that you can accomplish, analyze, and describe in the time allotted. What are the limitations of your study?

5. Remember reflexivity: anticipate your role in the research relationship and its influence on the study. Explain your reasons for your research choices.

6. What is your plan for ethical accountability? Have you consulted with members of the group as you formulated your questions? Include a draft of your consent forms and IRB application.

So be bold — choose the method or methods that you think will help you answer your question. At the same time, be realistic. This is similar to planning a vacation in unfamiliar territory. If you plan to do too much in the time that you have, you may find yourself stuck on a tour bus or racing from one site to the next, but not able to relax and take in all of what you are seeing. (Students in ethnography classes may also find themselves requesting unlimited extensions in order to complete their assignments.) Plan like you would for a fascinating journey, and leave yourself some spare time so that you can comfortably add on a side trip once you get there.

For Further Study

Ammerman, Nancy T., Jackson Carroll, Carl S. Dudley, and William McKinney. *Studying Congregations: A New Handbook*. Nashville: Abingdon Press, 1998, chapter 7.

Hammersley, Martyn, and Paul Atkinson. *Ethnography: Principles in Practice*. 2nd ed. New York: Routledge, 1995, chapter 2.

Mason, Jennifer. *Qualitative Researching*. 2nd ed. London: SAGE, 2002, chapter 2.

Tweed, Thomas A. *Our Lady of the Exile: Diasporic Religion at a Cuban Catholic Shrine in Miami*. New York: Oxford University Press, 1997.

- FOUR -

Caring for Relationships

The Ethics of Pastoral Research

If you ask me a question I don't know, I'm not going to answer. — YOGI BERRA

Human relationships are at the heart of pastoral ethnography. Caring for these relationships requires scrupulous attention to the ethics of research. Regardless of the particular research question and methods chosen, certain ethical issues will arise in the course of this work. These include matters of informed consent, honesty and intellectual rigor, the sensitive handling of shared personal information, confidentiality, anonymity, and the exercise of authorial power. The way in which a pastoral researcher handles these obligations will have a significant impact upon the well-being of the community. In this chapter, we take up the ethics of research relationships as a constitutive feature of the goodness, hope, and justice to which the pastoral practice of ethnography aspires.

Contemporary ethnographic theory argues for the validity of the subjective understandings of researchers who learn about people through empathy and emotional intelligence, as well as through intellectual comprehension. Part of the wonder of the practice of ethnography is the way in which it opens up worlds of understanding among people. We have seen how healing, growth, and even new dimensions of truth can emerge from the interpersonal encounter. Additionally, ethnographic relationships, like all relationships, can be the cause of misunderstanding or even harm.

Because so much is at stake here, it is imperative that pastoral researchers gain ethical clarity and practice accountability in all stages of this work.

The ethics of pastoral research are tricky because the process of transformation that we are aiming for is not one-sided or limited to the so-called "research subjects." Ethnographic relationships always involve the person of the researcher as well as those who are sharing their stories. When pastoral leaders take on the ethnographer's role, they are engaging in research relationships with institutions and people about whom they care deeply. The researcher's emotional, spiritual, and professional interests will come into play. The ethical challenge of managing the complex role of pastoral ethnographer may be daunting or at times confusing; it must be handled with care.

Likewise, it may be confusing for people in the congregation, for example, when you begin to practice disciplined observation of your shared faith practices. Tom Frank describes the story of a parishioner leaning over the pew during a worship service and wryly asking the researcher, "Are you worshiping with us today or are you here as an observer?"[1] The new hat that you are wearing may confuse people; they may feel used, objectified, or uncertain. Because we are studying people's spiritual lives, extra care must be taken. We need to bring honesty and transparency about our motives to the ethnographic encounter. We need to bring reverence to research relationships. Reverence is profound respect and regard for the dignity of the persons and communities who allow us to see so much of themselves.

The ethical issues involved here are tricky, but not impossible to address. Nor are issues such as confidentiality or professional boundaries wholly new to pastoral leaders. One way to look at the ethical issues involved in the conduct and handling of pastoral ethnography is as an extension of some of the already familiar ethical dimensions of ministry.[2] The dynamics here are similar,

---

1. Frank, *The Soul of the Congregation,* 63.
2. For a good overview of ethical issues in the practice of ministry, see Joseph E. Bush, *Gentle Shepherding: Pastoral Ethics and Leadership* (St. Louis: Chalice Press, 2006). See also Carrie Doehring, *Taking Care: Monitoring*

but a bit more complex. In this chapter, we'll look at each ethical issue in turn, with attention to how these issues play out at each stage of the research — in the design phase, in the actual conduct of the research, and in the sharing of your research findings and interpretations. We will then review the basic practices that help to track and ensure ethical and legal accountability in research with human subjects. Throughout, the goal is to care for our research relationships by practicing justice or "right relationship"[3] with the people and institutions we serve.

Informed Consent

The first ethical issue involved in any kind of research with human subjects is informed consent. We are all familiar with hideous examples of medical research done without people's consent, for example, the Tuskegee study of black men on the effects of untreated syphilis.[4] It might seem as though social research, in comparison to clinical or medical research, is relatively harmless. Nonetheless, ethnography does carry certain risks. People's stories, particularly their faith stories, are personal and often highly valued. Certain stories can carry identity in a potent way. If we are less than honest in our efforts to "get" people's stories, or if we tell these stories recklessly, we may inflict emotional or spiritual harm. All ethnographers, and particularly pastoral leaders, do well to remember the first principle of medical ethics: "First, do no harm." It is our moral and legal responsibility to deal honorably with people and their stories.[5]

Power Dynamics and Relational Boundaries in Pastoral Care and Counseling (Nashville: Abingdon Press, 1995).

3. For an explanation of justice as right relationship, see Carter Heyward, *The Redemption of God: A Theology of Mutual Relation* (Washington, D.C.: University Press of America, 1982).

4. See *www.tuskegee.edu/Global/Story.asp?s=1207598*.

5. See Tom L. Beauchamp and James F. Childress, *Principles of Biomedical Ethics*, 5th ed. (New York: Oxford University Press, 2001) for a discussion of the four principles of medical ethics: Non-maleficence, Beneficence, Autonomy, and Justice. While ethics for the practice of medicine do not transfer seamlessly to ethics for pastoral research, the principle of non-maleficence is a basic tenet of

The ethical standard of informed consent begins with asking permission to conduct a study. Our "research partners" need to know that they have a choice, that their participation is voluntary. This means that we must respect people's right to choose whether or not they wish to participate. Individuals may be reluctant to participate for any number of reasons. They may have secrets or personal matters that they do not want to share. They may be reluctant out of concern for the privacy of family members. In the event that someone declines, researchers should not apply any pressure to participate. Even repeating the invitation or expressing one's disappointment when a person declines could be a subtle form of manipulation, especially in the context of a pastoral relationship, as we shall see below. Coercion, however subtle, is not appropriate.

Similarly, an organization may decline to be studied for a variety of reasons. Members of a congregation or other group may be reluctant to authorize such projects because they feel that their group's story has been misconstrued in the past. When an ethnographer asks for permission to study a faith group or a religious practice, and the answer given is "no," this refusal must be accepted. This happened to David Mellott, when, as a graduate student, he set out to study the religious practices of a group of Catholic religious known as the Penitente Brotherhood in Arroyo Seco, New Mexico. Mellott had long been interested in this group; he was planning to tape interviews with a broad sample of the members and participants in the religious rituals that the group performs. Early on, Mellott learned that the group's rules of secrecy would not allow the members to participate in interviews without official permission from their governing body. When Mellott's requests for official permission were met with silence, he faced a conundrum that was both ethical and practical. He realized that if he tried to persuade members of the group to give him interviews, these members might end up violating

---

ethical codes for ministry as well as for social research. For a discussion of this principle in relation to ministry, see Bush, *Gentle Shepherding*, 19–43. For a discussion of this principle vis-à-vis the American Anthropological Association's Code of Ethics, see Madison, *Critical Ethnography*, 110–25.

their vows of secrecy and/or compromising their standing in the group. Therefore, Mellott decided against doing research in this way. He was, at first, disappointed that his plan for a full-scale ethnography could not be undertaken. Yet this is what caring relationships require of us: that we sometimes hold back on our wishes in light of the needs of the other persons involved.

What can we do when we don't have permission or access to interview a group of subjects? As in any relationship, sometimes there is room for negotiation; sometimes there is another way of approaching a study that doesn't carry such high risks of hurting the people involved. In his case, Mellott decided to reshape his study, accepting the group's restrictions. Fortunately, Mellott was able to find one man whom he could interview. This man was a group member, catechist, and archivist who had been speaking and writing publicly about the group's history for many years. This group historian had experience and savvy in talking about the Brotherhood; he knew how to protect the group from unwanted publicity and he knew how to maintain the boundaries around secret matters. Mellott revised his research plan and focused it on a combination of documentary research and extensive interviews with this one key figure.

While this change involved some disappointment for the researcher, eventually Mellott came to see that his change of plans also had some ethnographic benefits. Through this more personal approach, Mellott was able to gain what he calls "a deeper look" at the group's religious practices by coming to appreciate this one member's religious experience. This man's experience became a lens through which Mellott could glimpse a theological appreciation of the Pentinentes.[6] For Mellott, the very process of the ethnographic encounter became a moment of *"primary theology."*[7] Entering into ethical relationships with research

---

6. David Mellott, "Ethnography as Theology: Encountering the Penitentes of Arroyo Seco, New Mexico" (Ph.D. dissertation, Graduate Division of Religion, Emory University, 2005), 19–23.

7. Ibid., 140, emphasis in the original. Mellott takes the term "primary theology" from Aidan Kavanagh, *On Liturgical Theology: The Hale Memorial Lectures of Seabury-Western Theological Seminary, 1981* (Collegeville, Minn.:

partners involves respecting their freedom and their religious commitments. Research relationships formed in this way may yield surprising depth and insight.

In seeking informed consent, pastoral leaders have the added challenge of avoiding the abuse of their clerical authority by co-ercing people into participation. The line between inviting people to participate and coercing them can be blurry, especially in congregations or organizations with top-down power structures. When congregants are in the habit of doing whatever their pas-tor says, or even merely respecting their pastor's position, they may automatically assume that it is their religious obligation to comply with their leader's request for participation in a study. It is incumbent upon the pastoral leader to emphasize the participants' freedom of choice.

Even in religious groups that are run more democratically, religious leaders possess a degree of psychological power and in-fluence in the group. Members naturally want to be in the good graces of their pastor or rabbi. They may be afraid that saying no would harm their good standing in this relationship, or that they might be passed over for leadership roles, or that their pastoral needs might get short shrift if they turn down this request. There-fore, pastoral researchers must take extra care to avoid even the subtlest forms of manipulation. They must be completely clear with themselves and with the people they serve that informed consent involves real choice. If a pastoral researcher feels resent-ment toward those who decline, this feeling has to be recognized and managed, and not expressed as any kind of reproach. This

---

Liturgical Press, 1984). Basing his argument on the words of Prosper of Aqui-tane, a disciple of Augustine, *lex supplicandi legem statuat credendi*: the law of praying constitutes the law of believing, Kavanagh understands liturgical wor-ship as primary Christian theology. Mellott expands this understanding and claims that actually being in relationship with God, in worship and in other ways as well, such as by feeding the hungry or loving our neighbor, constitutes primary theology, rather than secondary theology, here understood as thinking about God. Mellott suggests that ethnographers who recognize and treat re-search participants as primary theologians enter into a spiritual practice — an act of primary theology — as well (Mellott, "Ethnography as Theology," 5–13).

is what informed consent requires: the genuine freedom to say "yes" or "no," without recrimination.

Thus far, we have focused on the "consent" part of informed consent. It is equally important to attend to the duty to inform potential research partners about the nature of the research you are asking to conduct and the particular details of their participation in it. This may seem straightforward at first, involving a simple written permission form to be signed before an interview. However, informed consent turns out to be a bit more complicated. It involves conveying three basic kinds of information to participants: information about you and your study, information about the research process itself and any known risks or benefits to the participants, and information about what you intend do with the data you collect and the narrative you construct.

If you are using written consent forms, begin by indicating, in writing, your name, contact information, and your affiliation with the school, hospital, clergy association, or other peer group that you will be working with. Bring two copies of the consent form to an interview, so that you can leave one with your research participant. Both copies should be signed and dated. Include the name of the supervisor overseeing your research, and his or her contact information as well. This supervisor might be a teacher of ethnography, a facilitator of a peer group, a director of chaplaincy at a hospital, or a professional colleague who has agreed to review your research. Include a brief explanation of the purpose of the study and explain the particular question that you hope to explore.

The second kind of information to disclose for informed consent is a description of the actual research process and the voluntary nature of it. If you are doing interviews, explain approximately how long the interview will take, where the interview will be held, and whether and how you will be making any written, electronic, or photographic record of the interview. Clarify that the participant has the right to stop the interview if at any time during the process he or she feels distress or wishes to withdraw for any reason. Also list any of the possible risks and benefits of the research to the participant.

The third set of particulars that must be disclosed regards what will happen to the stories and data that are shared with you. If you are planning to write a book, for example, or if you think that you may some day decide to publish an article derived from this research, the people being interviewed need to know that publication may result. (It is much easier to get this permission at the time of the initial research than later to try to track down individuals with whom you worked years before.) Your plans for publication may affect an individual's willingness to participate, or they may inform that participation, so that the individual refrains from sharing a story that might be embarrassing if it were printed. If you are planning to share your results with the group, participants need to know this as well. To the degree that you know the form your presentation will take, explain this. If you cannot fully anticipate how you will share the material, describe some of the possible ways you might present your findings. Additionally, explain how you intend to store your notes, photographs, or recordings (in a locked safe, for example), who will have access to them (such as you and your transcribing service), and whether these records will be kept or destroyed when your research is concluded. Think these things through as thoroughly as possible, because you will be bound by the written agreements you make with your research partners.

When I did my research in San Pedro, my consent forms for taped interviews included a promise of anonymity to the participants. Later, I was invited by an oral historian at the University of California Los Angeles to deposit my interview tapes into their oral history archive. Because I had promised anonymity, and the people's names were recorded on the tapes, I could not share the tapes. In this case, I suspect that certain individuals might have actually preferred that their names were used and their stories preserved at the archive. If I had anticipated this possible use of the tapes, I could have given individual participants a choice in this matter and clearly specified it on the consent forms. When constructing your plans and forms, bear in mind that some individuals may wish to be known and remembered by name and credited for their contributions.

For an example of a generic written consent form, see Figure 2 on pages 96 and 97. Note that this is a sample form that will have to be adapted to suit the particular design of your research project.

Confidentiality and Anonymity

As in other forms of ministry, issues of confidentiality and anonymity are enormously important to the conduct of ethnography. First, it must be said that not all studies require confidentiality or anonymity. For example, you may be doing a developmental study of the founding principles of a congregation. As part of this study, you may decide to interview congregational elders in order to hear their stories and preserve their memories. This kind of study might involve interviews that lean in the direction of oral history. In this case, participants may be willing and in fact delighted to have a chance to get their stories recorded for posterity. As long as the participants are fully informed and give their consent, it is perfectly acceptable to use their real names. The key is to be clear about this issue at that time that people consider giving their consent.

In other studies, you may determine that confidentiality or anonymity would help protect the privacy of your research partners. In this case, clearly distinguish between confidentiality and anonymity on your consent forms. I have often had students in my ethnography courses hand in drafts of their consent forms that promise complete confidentiality. This leads me to ask, "So what are you going to write about?" If you promise interviewees complete confidentiality, then you can't use their stories in your writing at all!

In practice, there are degrees of confidentiality that you can offer. One common approach is to agree to keep the research partner's name confidential. In this case, what you are really offering is anonymity. If you take this approach, you will be using the surveys, stories, and statistics that your research partners share with you, as well as the statistics that you develop from your data, without identifying individuals by name. You will need to identify the interview data in some way, either with a number or a pseudonym, in order to allow readers to track your sources and follow the line of your reasoning in your ethnographic writing.

Sometimes researchers opt to use pseudonyms in order to support the narrative flow of the writing. One way to offer research partners a bit of control in this matter is to allow them to choose their own pseudonyms. Then they will know when you are referring to them, but other readers (hopefully) will not. Pseudonyms offer participants a level of privacy and control.

Still, be aware that this isn't a perfect solution. If you are interviewing people in a community, members of that community know each other and know at least some parts of each other's stories. If you write about these stories, perhaps quoting some portions of your interviews, even with the use of pseudonyms, many insiders will know who is who. This limits the anonymity of the participants. In light of this reality, caution your participants in advance that others in the group who know them well may be able to recognize their stories.

Additionally, you may decide to keep anonymous the name of the organization that you are studying. A troubled church, for example, might not wish to have its name identified in any publications. Using a pseudonym and a vague description of the church's locale — "somewhere in the Midwest," for example — offers the group a degree of privacy. Still, this is not a foolproof strategy. Members of the group may talk openly to outsiders about the study, thereby giving away the identity that you have tried to protect. If you write up your story, for example, in a denominational journal, members of the denomination may recognize the details of the story and be able to figure out the congregation's identity. If you are trying to guard the group's identity, be careful about citing public documents, such as newspaper articles, even in your footnotes, because readers might look them up and discover the group's identity.

In *Being There,* the comparative study of two seminaries that I referred to earlier, the names of the seminaries and the individuals described — presidents, students, deans, and faculty — were

Figure 2. Sample Consent Form for Interviews
Informed Consent

Introduction: My name is _____, and I am a student at _____ conducting an ethnographic study for a course on ethnography and ministry. My telephone number is: _____. My professor (or research supervisor) is _____ and his/her phone number is _____. You may contact either of us at any time if you have questions about this study.

Purpose: The purpose of this research is to study the practice of _____ at (*name of congregation or agency*). I am trying to learn more about _____.

Procedure: If you consent, you will be asked several questions in an oral interview that will take place (*where*). I will make an audiotape recording of the interview.

Time required: The interview will take approximately 1–2 hours of your time.

Voluntary participation: Your participation in this study is completely voluntary. If you choose to participate, you may still refuse to answer any question that you do not wish to answer. You may also withdraw from the study at any time.

Risks: There are no known risks associated with this interview. However, it is possible that you might feel distress in the course of the conversation. If this happens, please inform me promptly.

Benefits: While there is no guaranteed benefit, it is possible that you will enjoy sharing your answers to these questions or that you will find the conversation meaningful. This study is intended to benefit the congregation (or hospital, school, etc.) by enlivening our discourse on the theology and practice of _____.

Confidentiality/Anonymity: Your name will be kept confidential in all of the reporting and/or writing related to this study. I will be the only person present for the interview and the only person who listens to the tapes. When I write the ethnography, I will use pseudonyms — made up names — for all participants, unless you specify in writing that you wish to be identified by name.

If you wish to choose your own pseudonym for the study, please indicate the first name you would like me to use for you here: _____ .

Sharing the results: I plan to construct an ethnography — a written account of what I learn — based on these interviews together with my reading and historical research. This ethnography will be submitted to my professor (or research supervisor) at the end of the term.

I also plan to share what I learn from this study with the congregation (hospital or ecclesiastical board). Portions of the ethnography may be printed and made available to the members.

Publication: There is the possibility that I will publish this study or refer to it in published writing in the future. In this event, I will continue to use pseudonyms (as described above) and I may alter some identifying details in order to further protect your anonymity.

Before you sign:

By signing below, you are agreeing to an audiotaped interview for this research study. Be sure that any questions you may have are answered to your satisfaction. If you agree to participate in this study, a copy of this document will be given to you.

Participant's signature: _____ **Date:** _____
Print Name: _____

Researcher's signature: _____ **Date:** _____
Print Name: _____

all changed.[8] However, it is really not too hard for readers who are familiar with theological schools in North America to ascertain the names of the schools involved. This is both because word travels — the folks at the two schools knew they were being interviewed and could not be prevented from talking about it — and because certain identifying characteristics of the schools tend to narrow down the possibilities.

It can be difficult to protect the identity of a person or a group. In light of this reality, ethnographers sometimes opt to alter or disguise some of the identifying details in a story. For example, a researcher might alter a person's occupation or physical characteristics in a narrative, if these details are not directly related to the question being explored. If you think you might decide to take the tack of altering some identifying information in order to protect a person's or a group's identity, explain this possibility to your research participants at the time that you request consent.[9] Additionally, in the introduction to the written ethnography explain that you are altering identifying details. The practice of altering details points to the way that different ethical values sometimes have to be weighed against each other in social research. The values of truth telling and historical accuracy compete with the value of protecting privacy. Thoughtful reflection on these competing values is needed throughout the planning, research, writing, and presentation phases of the work.

Hammersley and Atkinson remind us that the goal of ethnographic research is to produce knowledge. This implies an ethical duty to tell the truth.[10] However, this goal and duty may collide with other goals and duties. Pastoral sensitivity may lead us to hold back some information from the narrative that we eventually write. This is not the same thing as lying outright.

---

8. Carroll et al., *Being There*.

9. You will not necessarily know which details you will need to alter in advance. If a participant is concerned about this, you can offer to consult with the participant about these changes prior to the publication or presentation of your findings.

10. Hammersley and Atkinson, *Ethnography*, 286.

Nevertheless, the ethical advisability of hiding parts of our findings is not always clear-cut. If we learn of a nefarious activity going on in the group, should we keep it secret? For example, if through your research, you learn that the group's treasurer is "cooking the books," should you keep this secret? It could be argued that doing so would actually be a form of collusion in the wrongdoing, harming the institution. Such ethical quandaries require us to make difficult judgments, weighing one ethical good against another on a case-by-case basis.

If you encounter an ethical dilemma of this magnitude, I would suggest working through it with a trusted supervisor or colleague. Joseph Bush Jr. offers a helpful exercise for reflection on the ethical issues related to confidentiality in ministry.[11] This exercise suggests many helpful questions that ethnographers would want to consider when ethical duties have to be weighed against each other.

In less extreme cases, one practice of reflection that Hammersley and Atkinson suggest is to consider the values and feelings of those being studied. If we suspect that some information shared may prove embarrassing or harmful to an individual or a group, we must respect and consider this possibility. Any questionable information that is not crucial to the research should be omitted from the written ethnography. For example, if you are studying prayer practices in a retirement home, and a resident shares a personal story about a painful divorce, should you include this story in your writing? It could be that the story seems only tangentially related to your research question. You conclude that it could be hurtful to the woman to include this story and decide to omit it. Alternatively, if there were some compelling research reason to include the story, you could go back to the resident and explicitly ask her how she feels about your use of it, and abide by her wishes. If a research participant dies while you are still writing, you will have to make a judgment call on the details in question. When in doubt, I believe it is wise to err in the direction of caution and avoiding harm.

---

11. Bush, *Gentle Shepherding*, 125–26.

As is evident already, the matter of obtaining informed consent for interviews is not always simple or straightforward. Further complications and ethical concerns arise in special situations such as when interviewing minors, interviewing across cultural boundaries, or interviewing with vulnerable populations, such as persons with stigmatizing illnesses. Other groups that are commonly considered vulnerable include whistleblowers, prisoners, those with physically or mentally disabling conditions, those at risk of losing their livelihood from participation in your study, or those who are not able to fend for themselves in society. In these cases, more care must be taken to avoid compromising the participants' rights and safety. Highly specific and carefully crafted consent forms and research protocols are needed.[12]

While some of these specific situations can be anticipated during the research planning phase — for example, the need for obtaining parental consent as well as participant consent when interviewing youth — complicating factors are frequently discovered during the conduct of the research. It is perhaps for this reason that the American Anthropological Association's code of ethics states that the process of obtaining informed consent for ethnography may be considered "continuous and incremental."[13] Ethical dilemmas that demand our attention arise throughout all stages of the work.

The challenge of obtaining informed consent for participant observation is even more complex. For example, perhaps you want to study the use of a worship space. You may seek and receive the consent of the pastor or the group governing board of the congregation. But what about the people you are observing

---

12. Many universities have Institutional Review Board websites that provide good sample consent forms for studies involving specific populations. See, for a good example, the University of Virginia website at *www.virginia.edu/vprgs//irb/sbs_help_consent.html*. The "IRB Forum" is a helpful site with links to many other university IRB websites. See *www.irbforum.org/links/links.php?category=4*.

13. American Anthropological Association Statement on Ethnography and Institutional Review Boards, p. 2. *www.aaanet.org/stmts/irb.htm*, accessed June 20, 2007.

in the worship space? How would you gain their consent without disturbing their worship? Do you need it?

When studying a congregation or school or agency, it may not be possible to obtain written permission from every single person involved. However, there are many ways to inform people about who you are and what you are doing in their midst. For example, with permission from congregational leaders you may put a notice in a group newsletter or on a public bulletin board or a website. For this purpose, construct a summary that includes the three basic kinds of information related to informed consent: first, your name, institution, and contact information; second, your research purpose and methods, any risks or benefits that you anticipate, along with the clear statement that participation is voluntary; and third, your plans for publishing or sharing your results. Make copies of this summary, post them, and distribute them liberally throughout the community. Another helpful tactic in the effort to inform people of your presence is to wear a badge that identifies you as researcher. Additionally, consider requesting permission to speak publicly to groups within the organization, disclosing all of the pertinent facts.

If you are using surveys as the primary research method, include your basic summary of information on the survey instrument and on a separate sheet of paper or e-mail message that participants can keep after they return the survey to you. Indicate in writing that by completing the survey participants are granting their permission for you to use this material in your study. Making signatures optional is one way of offering anonymity. Be careful, though, to allow participants the option of identifying themselves if you are planning any follow-up interviews. Once anonymous surveys are turned in, there is no way to go back and ask clarifying questions.

If it is your own congregation or agency that you are studying, it is important to let the people you serve know when you are wearing your ethnographer's hat and when you are not. Of course, there will be times when your roles overlap. For example, gazing out over a congregation during worship, your newly trained ethnographer's eye will pick up certain things that you had not noticed before, such as where people are sitting and how they are grouped. Noticing social groupings within the congregation might be considered both an ethnographic and pastoral function, because it is a pastoral duty to attend to the life of the community. In view of this inevitable overlap, you will need to communicate with the congregation as openly as possible about the ways in which your research fulfills or augments your pastoral leadership.

Research conducted within the context of one's ministry carries some special risks as well potential benefits. If you as a pastor or rabbi are interviewing a member of your congregation or a resident at the nursing home where you serve as chaplain, and the individual begins to discuss sensitive personal material, you must clarify what is happening. If you are not certain about what is happening, query your research partner: "We seem to be getting into some private material here; would you like me to stop the interview now so that we can talk about this as a pastoral matter? Perhaps we can finish the questions at another time." If the congregant asks you to turn off the tape recorder or wants to tell you something "off the record," you must comply. Your pastoral duty to care for the emotional and spiritual well-being of the participants does not stop during research; it is made more complex.

These matters can get muddy. We do not want to exclude all of the deep and honest stories that people tell from our ethnographic writing, especially since one of our goals is to help people give voice to their deepest wisdom. We do not want to stop people from talking to us "on the record" any time they show emotion. At the same time, the ethical duty to do no harm trumps the desire to write a good story.[14] Even when we have obtained informed

---

14. This is perhaps one way in which the ethics of pastoral ethnography differ from those of journalism. In the Society for Professional Journalists' Code of Ethics, truth, accuracy, and credibility are noted as the primary standard: "Seek truth and report it." Respect for human subjects is noted next under "Minimize harm." The tension between these two duties is present in both disciplines. In pastoral ethnography, as we have seen, particular cases might require us to make difficult judgments. In my view, the duty to do no harm takes precedence over

consent, we must exercise discretion.[15] The integrity of a research relationship is finally more important than the writing. Even if we can't write about everything that a congregant shares, the experience of the interview may be an important one. If handled in a trustworthy way, the research experience could become a turning point, leading to a more open and honest pastoral relationship. Of course the reverse is also true. If ethical safeguards are not followed, the research experience could result in broken trust and lasting harm to the relationship.

The Use of the Self in Pastoral Ethnography

During the time that I was engaged in my research in San Pedro, it happened that I was also taking clinical training for pastoral counseling.[16] On the surface, these seemed to be two very disparate practices — conducting social research and offering pastoral counseling. Yet it struck me that there were some similarities in these two endeavors. Both involved caring relationships, though with different purposes and procedures involved. Both endeavors required that I think carefully about my role in the relationships.

When I looked back at this dual experience and began to write about it, it occurred to me that practicing reflexivity in ethnography is analogous to a key practice involved in pastoral counseling that involves the use of the self.[17] The technical term for this is "counter-transference." Attending to counter-transference involves the pastoral counselor's thoughtful awareness of her

---

other duties in pastoral ethnography, as it does in medical ethics. See the ethics webpage of the Society for Professional Journalists at *www.spj.org/ethics.asp*. Click on "Code of Ethics." Accessed March 11, 2008.

15. Along these lines, also remember the bounds and limits of what has been shared in the interview when writing the ethnography. You are not free to use all of your prior knowledge of a person's life or story in your ethnographic writing.

16. The training took place at the Christian Counseling Service in Redlands, California.

17. Mary Clark Moschella, "Food, Faith, and Formation: A Case Study on the Use of Ethnography in Pastoral Theology and Care," *Journal of Pastoral Theology* 12, no. 1 (January 2002): 77.

own emotional responses to the parishioner or client. These responses often yield helpful information about the counselor, the relationship, and the care-seeker. Pastoral counselors are trained to "delve into our own subjective experience of the counseling relationship"[18] in order to advance diagnostic and therapeutic goals.

Pamela Cooper-White, a psychotherapist and pastoral theologian, offers an excellent explanation of counter-transference and the history of ideas about its use.[19] She argues eloquently for a "totalist" approach to counter-transference in pastoral care and counseling. This approach requires a comprehensive process of introspection on the part of the pastoral counselor or caregiver:

> The more we are able to tune in to our own inner perceptions and to reflect on these in a thoughtful way, the more sensitively we will also be able to tune in to the nuances of the helpee's own feelings, wishes, and experiences.[20]

The insight gained from this introspective work, in turn, will enhance the pastoral counselor's accuracy and effectiveness in choosing appropriate treatments and modes of response to congregants or clients. This is an "intersubjective" approach that attends to the shared meaning that emerges between the two people.[21]

Analogously, the practice of reflexivity in ethnography involves the use of the self as a medium through which knowledge about the research partners and their religious practices can be gained. For this reason, ethnographers usually keep a journal in which they jot down not only their observations about the people whom they are studying, but also the ethnographer's personal responses

---

18. Pamela Cooper-White, *Shared Wisdom: The Use of the Self in Pastoral Care and Counseling* (Minneapolis: Fortress Press, 2004), vii.

19. Ibid., 9–34.

20. Ibid., 12.

21. Cooper-White, *Shared Wisdom*, 56. Cooper-White defines "intersubjectivity" as "a complex inter-relation between self and other that generates patterns of meaning-making and also influences the quality of the healing that evolves in the relationship over time," 6.

to what he is seeing, hearing, or experiencing on site (see chapter 5).[22] When these responses are recorded, researchers can go back to them later and try to understand what was transpiring during the ethnographic encounter. Upon reflection, researchers may be able to achieve a deeper and more genuine understanding of the ethnographic encounter, their own role in it, and the "shared wisdom" that may emerge from it.

Karen McCarthy Brown's pivotal work *Mama Lola* exemplifies a way in which an ethnographer's experience can become the medium through which interactions in the setting can be better understood. Brown bases her research upon extensive conversations and a developing friendship with one person — "Mama Lola" — also known as Alourdes. Brown terms her work "an intimate spiritual biography."[23] Through years of spending time with Alourdes, observing and participating in rituals, hearing stories, and participating in Vodou practices, Brown is able to open up an understanding of the practice of Vodou in a Haitian immigrant community in Brooklyn, New York. Brown's careful attention to herself in this research relationship yields considerable insight into Alourdes's religious practices.

For example, as part of her research, Brown traveled with Alourdes to visit the town of Gros Morne, a family homestead in rural Haiti.[24] The people in this community were excruciatingly poor. Upon the two women's arrival, Alourdes's old friends and family members began cooking a festive meal with the food Alourdes had brought as a gift. As the cooking smells wafted through the air and more folks were drawn into the gathering, Alourdes suddenly announced that she could not possibly eat before bathing. The cooking was halted and the group took time to give Alourdes an elaborate bath. Brown, the researcher, was frankly annoyed; she thought Alourdes was acting like a "Queen Bee," absorbing gifts and attention from these folks who were

---

22. This journal must, of course, be kept confidential, in accordance with your consent agreements.

23. Karen McCarthy Brown, *Mama Lola: A Vodou Priestess in Brooklyn* (Berkeley and Los Angeles: University of California Press, 1991) ix.

24. Ibid., 174–77.

so poor. In Brown's words, "Empathy failed me and judgment intruded."[25]

Later, as she reflected on the visit, Brown was able to see something more going on there between Alourdes and her friends and family in Haiti. Brown realized that she had been witnessing a practice of reciprocity. By receiving the gift of the elaborate bath, Alourdes had allowed her friends and relatives to practice reciprocity. She had asked them to give her something, instead of merely receiving the extravagant charity of a goat to roast, money, and the other gifts she had brought. The importance of reciprocity in the values of the group became more and more evident to Brown as she pursued her study. But Brown couldn't see this practice until she took the time later to query and explore her own feelings of resentment toward Alourdes.[26]

Not every ethnographer need take Brown's highly personal approach to social research. Yet we cannot escape the need for reflexivity in research, nor the ethical demand for self-awareness. We need to take time to reflect on what bothers us, causes us to judge, or otherwise captures our attention. We do this not only in order to be able to recognize our biases and blind spots, but also so that we can learn something more about the interactions that we witness and in which we take part.

This might be called a "totalist" approach to reflexivity, analogous to the totalist approach to counter-transference in pastoral relationships.[27] Our approach is "total" in the sense that it encompasses all of the researcher's responses to the ethnographic experience and considers them valuable to the research and to the theology and ministry at hand. Some of a researcher's responses reflect personal biases or what is called "our own stuff," in the lingo of Clinical Pastoral Education. This "stuff" is comprised of personal issues or distortions that we need to become aware of and eventually resolve in order to clear the way for genuine and open interpersonal engagement.

25. Ibid., 177.

26. Ibid. See also Spickard, Landres, and McGuire, *Personal Knowledge and Beyond*.

27. Cooper-White, *Shared Wisdom*, 24.

At other times, our responses constitute a great source of information about the practices we are studying or about the relationships we are developing. Every time we are moved by the research or the relationships that are developing, we need not view the experience as problematic or as a detriment to the research. Rather, our responses — such as curiosity, excitement, or resentment — may be clues that we need to pay more careful attention to what is transpiring. We do well to record and examine our responses particularly carefully in such circumstances because they may be a sign of new insight or shared wisdom that is about to break forth, the truth that arises between us in relationship.

This kind of thorough self-reflection might seem daunting. How can we work our way through it? Certainly, individually we can set aside time to reflect on our experiences of the research, relying on the notes we jot down along the way. But how exactly do you "interrogate your sources" when you are one of the sources?

Pamela Cooper-White provides a detailed pastoral method for such reflection that she recommends for pastoral caregivers who are trying to understand and work with counter-transference. Her method includes the counselor's practice of self-care, centering prayer, reflecting on one's own issues or "buttons" that the relationship may be "pushing," examining the shared wisdom that might be emerging from the encounter, and reflecting theologically in a way that involves free-association with biblical stories or spiritual images that resonate with the case.[28] This method holds promise as a resource that can be adapted for pastoral researchers engaging in the work of reflexivity.[29] Such practices of introspection help us stay clear and genuinely present in ethnographic pastoral relationships.

---

28. Ibid. See pages 80–81 for a summary of this pastoral method.

29. Ibid., 74–79. The specific practice of theological reflection that Cooper-White recommends holds particularly intriguing possibilities for writing pastoral ethnography. See chapter 8.

Accountability Groups

Beyond reflecting individually on self-awareness in pastoral research, an ethical "commitment to authenticity and integrity and faithfulness"[30] in pastoral relationships requires us to have some kind of a community of accountability with whom we can discuss reflexivity. Just as those who offer pastoral counseling need to consult with peer groups or supervisors in order to achieve greater clarity about counter-transference, those who practice ethnography need to consult with colleagues and supervisors in order to process research experiences and to choose healthy and genuinely helpful responses to research partners.[31]

We need such practices of accountability because there is a power differential inherent in research relationships.[32] The author of ethnography exerts the power to tell his or her story of an encounter with a group. While we make efforts to use this power justly — such as through seeking informed consent — we cannot avoid the power and responsibility that come from the very practices of studying, recording, analyzing, interpreting, and writing ethnography. We must try, to the best of our abilities, to use this power as "power with" the people and not as "power over" the group. Throughout the research process, there are opportunities to consult with the people who are "stakeholders" in the group. Even at the point of site entry, when exploring our initial questions, we can invite the ideas and insights of group members. We can ask them what needs to be studied and why.

Another way to exercise "power with" the people is to be careful about the theories we bring to bear on the data we gather. We should strive to avoid reading a kind of unity or consensus

---

30. Ibid., 59–60.

31. Eileen Campbell-Reed presented a fascinating table, "An Analogy of Two Learning Processes," which stemmed from her experience of graduate training in pastoral psychotherapy and in social research at the same time. She helpfully compared numerous aspects of learning the two practices. Eileen Campbell-Reed, "Epistemological Issues," unpublished paper presented to the study group on Religious Practices and Commitment at the annual meeting of the Society for Pastoral Theology, Atlanta, June 19, 2004.

32. For a good discussion of power and vulnerability in research, see Swinton and Mowat, *Practical Theology and Qualitative Research*, 64–65.

into a group, in order to support our interpretations. We must be aware that our interpretations could influence the ways in which the people begin to see themselves.[33] (In chapter 7 we will address some strategies for keeping these tendencies in check.) Narrative leadership is a potent form of leadership; its power derives from the authenticity of shared stories and the ring of truth that will sound in the telling of a corporate story. It is therefore incumbent upon pastoral ethnographers to recognize this power, and to attempt to use it appropriately, honestly, and with humility as well as transparency. To put it in biblical language, a pastoral ethnographer is involved in "speaking the truth in love" (Eph. 4:15).

The story shared must include the ethnographer's own story of engagement, encounter, and new learning. There is an intersubjective element in this process that is similar to what Elaine Lawless has called "reciprocal ethnography."[34] Pastoral ethnographers who are working for transformation and hope must be open to being transformed, moved by the persons and stories that they encounter.

This challenging work requires input and oversight, whether it is from your ethnography class, clergy group, or a direct supervisor. Consultation with research colleagues begins in the design phase, continues as you move through the actual research, and then extends into the work of analyzing, writing, and sharing ethnographic accounts. These are all highly interpretive activities; in order to achieve the greatest possible level of clarity, honesty, and care in relationships, we need the wisdom of colleagues and others who can help us discern the most ethical paths to take.

---

33. See Tanner, *Theories of Culture*. Tanner states that anthropologists often miss "the power dimension of meaning. How situations and the actors in them are understood makes a difference in what it is those actors can conceive of doing," 47.

34. See Elaine J. Lawless, *Holy Women, Wholly Women: Sharing Ministries through Life Stories and Reciprocal Ethnography* (Philadelphia: University of Pennsylvania Press, 1993), 60–61.

Institutional Review Boards

Another important practice of ethical accountability involves the submission of research plans to authorized groups known as Human Subjects Panels or Institutional Review Boards (IRBs). These panels are groups of people who examine research plans in order to give careful attention to the rights and protection of human research subjects. The purpose of these panels is to protect research institutions and individual scholars from violating laws and international treaties that protect the human rights of research subjects. These boards may approve your plan, reject it, or, more typically, ask you to make certain clarifications or revisions in order to ensure, to the greatest extent possible, the rights and safety of research participants.

Institutional review is legally required for most ethnographic research conducted at universities, research centers, and schools in the United States. This is explained in a set of regulations known as the "Common Rule" or the "Federal Policy for the Protection of Human Subjects."[35] It is not clear that every small-scale ethnographic research project falls under the Common Rule. The review board is primarily necessary for those who plan to publish their research. Schools that receive federal funds in any form, such as student loans, are required to have review boards and policies in place if faculty and graduate students are publishing research that involves human subjects. This would logically include doctor of philosophy dissertations and doctor of ministry theses as well as other studies that may be published in articles or books. As more theological schools in the United States are adopting ethnographic methods of study, many are moving into compliance with the Common Rule by setting up Institutional Review Boards or Human Subjects Panels.

---

35. For a fuller understanding of federal regulations, consult the following: Title 45–Public Welfare Department of Health and Human Services, Part 46–Protection of Human Services, found at *www.hhs.gov/ohrp/* under "regulations." For a discussion of how these guidelines apply to ethnography, see the American Anthropological Association Statement on Ethnography and Institutional Review Boards, *http://aaanet.org/stmts/irb.*

If your institution has an ethical review board, you may be required to submit a research proposal and receive approval before you begin your research. Teaching hospitals will almost certainly have their own review boards, so if you are doing research in the context of a hospital chaplaincy, you will be required to submit your protocol for approval before beginning your research. Each review board will have a slightly different application, but the basic items covered on the application will be similar to those shown in Figure 3 on the following page. Even if your institution does not yet have such a review board, and even if you are not planning to publish your work, it may be helpful to complete such a proposal and submit it to your supervisor, instructor, or research peers for review. This process can help you gain ethical clarity about your research plan and procedures.

Much of the basic information covered in these applications overlaps with the work you will have already done in constructing your consent forms. IRB applications usually require some additional detail. Explain your research plans with as much specificity as possible, paying attention to the precision of your language. This procedure will help you carefully think through the possible and likely effects of your research on your research partners. While it may seem to be a burden to go through this application process, this process could offer you guidance that helps protect you from violating the law. It could also save both you and your research partners from the experience of harm or broken trust.

Institutional Review Boards commonly require researchers to revise their protocols if the panel members identify a need for more detailed planning or clearer explanations of what you will do to protect your research participants. Try to anticipate IRB members' concerns by thinking through these matters in advance and sharing your protocol with your class or peer group ahead of time. When in doubt, err in the direction of providing more detail than you think might be needed. Specify how many surveys, interviews, or forums you are planning to use. Estimate the length of time for each activity. Offer detailed plans for safely storing your data — such as in a locked filing cabinet — and state the

Figure 3. Institutional Review Board Application: Research Protocol

1. **List your name, contact information, and the name of the institution, course, or project to which your research is related. List the names and contact information for your advisors to this project.**

2. **Explain the nature and purpose of this research.**
   What do you hope to learn and why?

3. **Describe your research methods and procedures.**
   Be specific. Indicate the length of time involved and the place where you plan to conduct interviews or observation. Explain how you will select or recruit participants, and how you plan to make and keep records of your research. Specify your intentions for the use of visual records, such as photographs and videotapes.

4. **Attach a copy of the survey instrument or a list of the questions that you intend to ask potential participants.**
   If these questions are not completely settled, submit your tentative plans.

5. **Describe your relationship to the potential participants.**
   Are you their pastor or rabbi? Are you their chaplain or a field education intern?

6. **Discuss any potential benefits for the participants in your study.**
   What is the good that you hope will result from this study? What benefits, if any, will accrue to the participants?

7. **Discuss any potential risks to the participants in your study.**
   Are any of your participants members of vulnerable groups (such as children, persons with stigmatizing illnesses, whistleblowers, prisoners, persons with physically or mentally disabling conditions, etc.)? Explain the measures that you will take to provide for their privacy. Explain how you will respond if a participant has adverse effects as a result of your study.

8. **Explain the policies and procedures that you will use to insure the confidentiality or anonymity of your participants.**
   Will you use pseudonyms or a numerical coding system? Are there any factors other than names that might identify your research subjects? If so, what will you do to insure anonymity? How will your data be stored? How long will the data be kept?

9. **Include a copy of any consent forms that you are planning to use.**
   The language used on these forms should be clear, simple, and straightforward, not laden with technical jargon.

10. **What will happen to the final report of your research? Do you plan to share a summary with the community or congregation? What form will this representation take, and what media will you use? List any possible venues in which you might publish this work now or in the future.**

length of time you intend to keep the data, when and if you will destroy it, and so on.

Think through the section on risks and benefits carefully. Even if you think there are no possible risks to participants, try to imagine some possible contingencies that might cause harm or emotional distress. Indicate your plans to try to prevent or mitigate this possible harm. Similarly, elaborate on all of the potential benefits of the research. Review boards weigh risks and benefits. Explain the potential contribution to knowledge or practice that the research will make, along with any potential benefits to the participants for which you can make a good case.

Finally, in regard to research review panels, pay attention to timing. The sooner your plan is approved, the sooner you can begin your research. Try to find out when the panel will be meeting in advance, and get your proposal in so that it will be reviewed in a timely manner.

Summary

The ethical issues and practices of accountability that we have looked at in this chapter are complex and sometimes vexing. Nevertheless, the effort that you put into this aspect of the process will serve you and your research participants well. The ethical care you take in planning, conducting, writing, and sharing your ethnography will matter a great deal in the eventual outcome of your work. In fact, this kind of ethical care taking *is* a large part of the work of pastoral ethnography. As you attend to these issues, you are helping to bring about caring and responsible relationships in your community. On the journey that is ethnography, strive to take the "high road" of justice and integrity in research relationships.

For Further Study

Brown, Karen McCarthy. *Mama Lola: A Vodou Priestess in Brooklyn*. Berkeley and Los Angeles: University of California Press, 1991, chapter 6.

Bush, Joseph E. *Gentle Shepherding: Pastoral Ethics and Leadership.* St. Louis: Chalice Press, 2006, chapters 3 and 6.

Cooper-White, Pamela. *Shared Wisdom: The Use of the Self in Pastoral Care and Counseling.* Minneapolis: Fortress Press, 2004, chapters 1 and 4.

Hammersley, Martyn, and Paul Atkinson, *Ethnography: Principles in Practice.* 2nd ed. New York: Routledge, 1995, chapter 10.

– F I V E –

Keeping Track of the Journey

Notes from the Field

Don't get me right, I'm just asking.

— YOGI BERRA

Now that you have your plans and permissions in hand, you are ready to start your actual journey to the field. As you enter the research field, you will need to be prepared to record your observations in thorough and accurate detail — to get them right. Pastorally, you can think of this recording work as a way of remembering the people and their faith-in-action, a form of caring that focuses on gaining increased understanding.[1] Though making notes and tapes and coding and organizing records can become tedious, these tasks are essential for keeping track of the journey. The careful, consistent effort that you exert in recording your observations and experiences will improve the precision and accuracy of your data and help refresh your memory when you try to recall and understand your experiences at a later date. With precise records, you will be able to analyze your findings rigorously and then to compose a reliable, descriptive ethnographic narrative. The care you take in this part of the practice is an expression of regard and respect in the research relationship. The classic approaches to recording field observations include: taking field notes, keeping a research journal, making audio or video recordings, and taking pictures. Additionally, this work involves collecting or making copies of key written documents related to

---

1. See John Patton's description of remembering as a central task in pastoral care. Patton, *Pastoral Care in Context,* 15–36.

115

the life of the group. You will need to choose the approaches that best suit your pastoral and ethnographic goals, your consent agreements, and your practical resources, such as time and money. In this chapter we will explore the use of these various kinds of records and also address ways of organizing and keeping track of the data you collect.

What to Watch For

First, though, begin to anticipate what you will be observing and recording. At a busy event, where should you train your gaze? All descriptions are selective and partial. Though you cannot be objective, you can strive to create a full and credible account.[2] In order to achieve a fair and dependable understanding of what is happening at a given event, start out with a broad view. Watch for the forest first; then have a look at the trees.

When you arrive at the scene of an event you are studying, strive to take it all in. As if you were using a wide-angle camera lens, try to get a broad view of what is going on, one that includes as much as possible in the picture. Use all of your senses. Notice smells and sounds and textures and styles. Some aspects of the event may not seem important initially, but later, as analytic ideas develop out of your experiences, these aspects may take on greater significance. Because you cannot judge the significance of each aspect in advance, starting out with a wide angle and recording as much detail as possible serves the process well. Take note of what strikes you, whether it be the colorful clothing of the person in front of you, the different languages that you hear spoken at the gathering, or the light streaming through the windows and falling upon a group of children in a corner of the room. As you move through your research, you will find yourself concentrating — zooming in — on one or more particular foci. A carefully

---

2. For further understanding of the issues of credibility, confirmability, and dependability, see David Erlandson, Edward L. Harris, Barbara Skipper, and Steve D. Allen, *Doing Naturalistic Inquiry: A Guide to Methods* (Newbury Park, Calif.: SAGE Publications, 1993), 33–35.

described record of the broader social scene will serve as a backdrop for your more focused study. Additionally, you might find that some of the stray details you recorded are actually germane to your research question.

A few of the most basic subjects to observe at any event include: people, actions, interactions, contexts, and material evidence. As an example, consider observing a church council or governing board meeting. A focus on *people* would include attention to who is present at this meeting. Notice their gender, ethnicity, race, age, differing physical abilities, and other social factors. Are these the power brokers of the congregation? Are they longtime members or newcomers? Do you know anything about their socioeconomic status? Also, consider who is absent from the meeting. Are there any subgroups of the congregation that are not represented at the table?

Also focus on *actions*. This involves noticing what the purpose and agenda of the meeting are, and what the main activities of the group include. Are there set procedures for what happens at the meeting? Do the people sit in a circle and say a prayer before or after the meeting? Record what people do and what they say. Note carefully any official actions or votes the group takes and the content of its discussions.

To observe *interactions,* focus on the interpersonal process that unfolds rather than the content or the agenda. Who leads the group and what is his or her leadership style? Does spirituality enter into the discussion or the conduct of the meeting, or do you have a sense that it is "all business" here? Who speaks up and who is quiet? How does the group deal with conflict? Do people express themselves directly or do you sense that the group's communication style is indirect? Perhaps some individuals are clear and forceful, while others are quiet and apparently passive. Notice interruptions as well, such as if someone should come to the door to request financial help from the group. How is this handled?

Paying attention to *context* involves recognizing how people may act differently in the council meeting as compared to other settings — such as in the kitchen, preparing refreshments for the meeting, or chatting in the parking lot afterward. Consider the differences between people's behavior in this meeting and their behavior during a worship service. How do the unspoken rules change? What are the particular norms in this context?

A focus on the *material* aspects of the meeting might include noting features of the physical space, art, and artifacts in use at the meeting.[3] Notice aesthetic styles. Look at mundane things such as the way that people dress. If refreshments are shared, describe the food. Consider the material decisions people are making, involving finances, buildings, or environmental concerns.

As you can imagine, there is a great deal to notice all at once. A helpful sidebar providing an observational protocol is found in *Studying Congregations*.[4] Using this list can help you make sure your observations and records cover the range of important factors, which includes demographics. In part because of the sheer bulk of all of this information, researchers need to jot down notes or make recordings in order to be able to reconstruct their observations and experiences at a later time.

Field Notes

The venerable practice of taking down field notes is indispensable to the work of ethnography. Invest in a small and sturdy notebook to carry around with you on your ethnographic journey. As the saying goes, Don't leave home without it! Record in this notebook the date, time, place, and purpose of your research event *before* you enter the scene. Start the process of note taking as soon as possible during or after the event.

Obviously, note taking can be disruptive in some situations. Exercise sensitivity and discretion, especially when you are observing a formal religious practice or ritual. Even if note taking is

---

3. On the symbolism of church art and architecture, see Colleen McDannell, *Material Christianity: Religion and Popular Culture in America* (New Haven: Yale University Press, 1995); and R. Kevin Seasoltz, *A Sense of the Sacred: Theological Foundations of Christian Architecture and Art* (New York: Continuum International, 2005).

4. Ammerman et al., *Studying Congregations*, 200–201.

not disruptive, overzealous writing can compromise your ability to take in or experience the social setting in its fullness. Hammersley and Atkinson suggest the strategy of jotting down brief notes whenever possible. Using key or colorful phrases will help jog the memory when you try to reconstruct speech and events later.[5] For example, imagine that you observe an intense and protracted argument over professional salaries in the organization. A phrase such as "tearful debate" might be more descriptive and memorable than "discussion." You might also jot down the key issue that people were arguing over, trying to use their own terms. If an employee is referred to as an "overpaid loudmouth" or a "humble servant," jot down these phrases. Also make a note about people's tone and nonverbal communications when that is possible.

Jotting brief notes works well if, as soon as possible after the event, you take the time to write up a more comprehensive description. You may need to do this on a laptop in your car in the parking lot after the event or late at night when you get home. Do not underestimate the time that you will need to write up your notes. The longer you wait, the more uncertain and possibly inaccurate your memory will be.

Don't make the mistake I made by scheduling two interviews in quick succession. When the first interview ran longer than expected, I had to rush to leave it, saying hasty goodbyes, and then make apologies for arriving late at the second interview. I had no time to write up my notes in between. Later that night, I had to work hard to fill in my notes, as the two interview experiences tended to blur together in my memory. Of course, when it comes to public events, you cannot control their timing. You may have to rush from one event to the next. You can, however, strive to find pockets of time for filling out your notes as soon as possible.

When taking notes, try to render speech verbatim, rather than summarizing it. Students of Clinical Pastoral Education may remember their struggles to write accurate verbatim reports of their first hospital visits. Verbatim reports are difficult to write because

---

5. Hammersley and Atkinson, *Ethnography*, 178.

they require us to listen carefully and remember as accurately as possible the specific words of a pastoral conversation as well as the facial expressions and body language observed. Striving to recall exact language is important in ethnography as well. Particular terminology, such as slang, is important because it may carry local meanings. Summarizing involves an interpretive leap that may blunt the particular force or meaning of speech. Similarly, strive to describe nonverbal behavior as accurately as possible, rather than analyzing it at first. As with speech, descriptions should be concrete and particular rather than broad and sweeping.

Try to avoid assigning too much meaning to the events you witness at this early stage of note taking. Instead, specify the features of the event as fully and completely as possible. This is more difficult than you might think. Concentrate on observing, listening, and paying attention to what transpires.

At the same time, our own thoughts and feelings about what we are seeing are important. While striving to be thorough and rigorous in recording events, we may realize that we are being swept up in the singing of a hymn at a worship service, for example. Or we may be put off or distressed by the theological viewpoint that we are hearing put forth in a sermon. These responses are also a kind of data to record. The trick is to separate the two kinds of data, as much as possible, in the note taking process.

The Fieldwork Journal

Somewhere in your notes — whether spiral bound or electronic — your private thoughts and feelings about your observations should be recorded. Ethnographers often keep a *fieldwork journal* for this purpose. There are different ways to approach this journaling work. One involves keeping all of your notes — first jottings, comprehensively filled out notes, and your private responses — in the same notebook and creating a separate column for your private responses. So, for example, you might have a running description of an event on the left side of your notebook in column one, and a running description of the ideas and emotions that the material evokes in you on the right side in column two. Alternatively, you might carry around a small notebook just for brief jottings at events, and then use a separate larger book or electronic file in which you record both comprehensive, filled-out notes and your emerging theories and emotional responses to the events in separate sections. Either way, you will need to record all of these kinds of notes, making a good effort to distinguish between your observations and responses.

Figure 4 on the following page offers an example of a portion of a student ethnographer's fieldwork journal, which she kept in electronic form.[6] Notice how helpful it is to see the field notes and the journal notes side by side. When Jessica went back to analyze her data later, she could recall her early interpretations easily, and yet keep them separate from her more "raw" data. In the process of interpreting her findings she looked at the material in several different ways. Her initial impressions informed her analysis because they conveyed her *tacit* knowledge.[7]

Tacit knowledge is unspoken but implied understanding that comes across in human encounters. People may suddenly look sad or embarrassed. Or they behave politely but seem to distance themselves. While understanding body language and facial expressions involves subjective interpretation, it is still imperative to try to read nonverbal communication and record our impressions. When you jot down these sorts of impressions, be as specific as possible about what you saw and what that suggested to you. When you go back and write up these notes, you can elaborate on your interpretations.

As shown in Figure 4, Jessica noted identifying details in the upper left column before she began the interview. Then she used the left column to record her observations of the participant's living room, reflecting on the objects in the space and the style that the décor suggested to her. Jessica notes the prominence of the

---

6. "Jessica," unpublished journal notes, used by permission. The names and some identifying details have been altered to protect the privacy of the persons involved in the study.

7. Hammersley and Atkinson, *Ethnography*, 185.

Figure 4. A Sample Fieldwork Journal

Interview with Abigail S. — 9/20/05	Personal responses
Date: 9/20/05 Presbyterian retirement home, greater D.C. area, 7:30 p.m. Gender: Female Race: Caucasian Age: 80 **Details about the interview context** — Abigail is a longtime member of St. Paul. She is on my Learning Partners team and has served on the Committee on Preparation for Ministry (CPM) of the presbytery for a long time. She is a career educator. She taught and then worked for a long time as supervisor of foreign languages in county public schools. After retiring, she earned her Master of Theological Studies degree from a nearby divinity school. She now teaches Sunday school classes at area churches on contract. The interview was at her apartment at a Presbyterian retirement community. She met me downstairs in the lobby and helped me find parking. She had moved her car out to a further away visitors' parking lot so I could have her spot in the garage. She then had me drop her off at her car afterward. Her apartment was small but warm. She has bookshelves filled with theology and Bible books built in and a corner desk unit that was well organized and ran the width of the apartment. Clearly her study was as important as her social area. It took up a third of the space. The other third was taken up by her dining room table and china cabinet. Her apartment was organized and decorated with very feminine white, light blue, and pink. Her decorating style was that of her generation. She had her china displayed in a cabinet although she admitted she doesn't have meals there. She was very concerned about my comfort in taking notes and wanted to get me something hard to write on. I told her I was fine. She sat adjacent to me on the sofa. I told her that I had read the written history of St. Paul. She said, good, she was going to give me a copy. We discussed the consent form. She signed it and I began the interview with the following preliminary questions. **When did you join St. Paul?** 1970. **What attracted you to St. Paul?** She had been a part of another Presbyterian church in D.C. for a number of years. That church was closing. She had moved out to this suburb. She went into a bookstore at a nearby mall and found Alice Miller's book *The God Squad*, which was about the cutting edge youth activity that was happening at SP. She was fascinated by the book. SP was involved with civil rights and other issues important to her, so she joined.	*The way her apartment was decorated reminded me of my grandmother, who is eighty-nine and has severe dementia. She decorated with the same colors. Abigail had a glass blue bird on her coffee table that my grandmother also had. I felt welcome and at home. I found myself forgetting how old Abigail was. She kept talking about growing up in the Depression and said things like "after the war." She is only a few years younger than both my grandmothers. I was struck by how different she was from them, both in her life choices and in how active she had been and is. My grandmothers were both homemakers and focused on family. I feel proud to know her. It felt like a gift to talk to her. I will also say that I felt like I was talking to a colleague. She never condescended to me. She talked with me as a colleague and a caring mentor, as a peer. This made me feel very respected.*

study space and the display of china, which Abigail admits she does not use. This is a good example of noting some of the material cultural features of the space. Jessica describes the process of settling in for the interview, fills in some background and demographic information, describes her use of informed consent forms, and then records her questions and Abigail's answers. In these notes, Jessica describes Abigail's responses, rather than attempting to record all of her words verbatim. Nevertheless, Abigail's answers are recorded in great detail. In the column on the right, Jessica adds her personal responses to the situation, which in this case were very positive. She describes how she was reminded of her grandmother and experienced a feeling of being treated with respect.

Keep up with recording your private responses to your field notes as you go. Think of this part of it as a kind of travel diary. Take time to sort out what you find moving or hopeful or troubling about an event. Your private responses and ideas may or may not reflect accurate understandings of what you have just observed. In recording these faithfully, however, you will be keeping a journal of your ethnographic travels and your emerging interpretations of the people, their faith practices, and yourself in relation to them.

This comprehensive record of your notes and your reflective explorations will be critically important to your analysis, interpretation, and writing. The ability to trace your sources and explain the logic of your reasoning will lend credence and dependability to your conclusions.[8] Furthermore, this record of your honest responses will help you in your ongoing work on self-awareness, counter-transference, and reflexivity, which are necessary for ethical clarity in pastoral research relationships (see chapter 4).

Audio Recording

Audio recording is a tool that can be used to enhance the precision and extent of data collection. Ethnographers often make audio

---

8. Erlandson et al., *Doing Naturalistic Inquiry*, 34–35.

recordings of qualitative interviews. There are pros and cons to consider in deciding whether or not to use this technology. One important caution to consider is that, as noted in chapter 4, you do need explicit permission to tape interviews. In some cases, ethical considerations may lead you to conclude that the privacy and confidentiality needs of members of a vulnerable population preclude taping interviews. For example, if you were studying the religious practices of victims of domestic violence, your concern for the safety of the participants could weigh against recording the interviews. If the perpetrators of the violence were to find out about the recordings, or by some accident gain access to them, the participants in the study could be at risk of further harm.

Furthermore, some potential research partners in any group may decline because they do not want to be taped. If this happens, a disadvantage to taping is that it could reduce your pool of participants. Another possible disadvantage to audiotaping is that it could inhibit the rapport and spontaneity of the interview. Seeing the taping device turned on, a person might become anxious and guarded. You too might be distracted, especially in the event that your equipment malfunctions. The depth and honesty of the conversation might be challenged by both parties' felt sense that this is going "on the record."

The major advantage of audio recording is that you will get an accurate record of the speech, intonation, and rhythm of the interview. Your records will be much more thorough, concrete, and exact than if you relied solely on notes. If your taping equipment is working well, you will be free to focus on the conversation itself, and not worried about taking down every word. You can minimize the interference of the digital or cassette recorder by moving it slightly away from the direct line of vision between you and your interviewee(s).

Another way of looking at the issue of distraction, particularly for ministers who have dual roles in relationship to research participants, is that the presence of a tape recorder can be a helpful reminder of the purpose of the interview. Both you and your congregant may benefit from this cue to stay focused on the research questions and to avoid slipping into your other roles or digressing onto other topics. This sense of limits can function to protect the parishioner from revealing personal information unintentionally in the interview.

If you decide to use audiotape, bear in mind that the tape will not provide a record of the entire experience. For example, your visual impressions of the conversation — facial expressions, gestures, body language — will not be picked up on the tape. Descriptions of the visual environment, such as the person's home or other setting should also be noted, along with other contextual details, such as time of day and what has taken place just prior to the interview, and so on. Therefore, even if you make audiotapes, you will still need to take notes, including jottings and comprehensive logs as well as journal responses that are written up later.

In my own work with interviews, I have found tape recording to be very helpful. Even with the tape recorder rolling, I still take notes throughout the interview, because this helps me think through what is being said, slow down the conversation a bit, and figure out what I want to say next. When a portion of the interview seems critically important, such as when emphasis or emotion is expressed, I indicate this with a star in my notes next to the particular question that elicited this response. Later, using my notes, it becomes easier to locate the portions of the tape that I may wish to review.

Along these lines, I suggest taking notes directly onto a printed copy of the interview questions while you are conducting the interview. Bring a hard copy of your list of questions that is dated and coded with an interview number or pseudonym in advance. Before you print this copy, insert extra space between the questions, so that you can take notes on the page in the space following each question. Attach some extra blank pages to the hard copy for extra notes. This copy will help later when you are navigating your way through the recording.

As you can see, the practical and technical aspects of tape recording require careful consideration and planning. Take into consideration the cost of recording and possibly transcribing tapes. Quality equipment, whether purchased or borrowed, is vital. If you are depending on a tape and later you discover that the recording device malfunctioned, the sound was muffled by extraneous noise, or the batteries ran out half way through the interview, you will be sorely disappointed. My students have found that efforts to go back and redo an interview rarely yield satisfactory results.

Consider the probable length of each interview when buying tapes or digital cards. Label tapes promptly with names, numbers, and dates. Because electrical outlets are not always nearby, keep extra sets of fresh batteries on hand for your recording device. Practice with your device ahead of time, so that you are familiar with its capacities and its quirks. At the start of each interview, do a quick test to make sure that the device is picking up the voices of all of the participants in the interview.[9]

During the interview, as you jot down your notes, record as much nonverbal information about the interview as possible. Include a description of the setting, the actions and interactions you observe and are part of, and any circumstances that may interfere with or alter your conversation. When you later fill in your notes and your journal, describe your overall impressions and the tacit understandings that you took away from the interview experience. Then, as soon as it is reasonably possible, listen to the tape in its entirety. Take more notes as the tape jogs your memory and your thoughts. Include in brackets your description of the nonverbal elements of each communication, for example: [weeping quietly] or [face reddens].

Transcription is another matter to consider if you decide to tape interviews. Complete transcriptions represent a kind of gold standard for thorough analysis of what was said. (Of course, the researcher would still need to add in bracketed descriptions of the gestures and nonverbal expressions, as noted above.) Having complete, electronic transcriptions stored on a hard drive also gives you the option of using software tools to help sort, retrieve,

---

9. In accordance with your research protocol, if you are interviewing someone who does not read the language that you are using, you may also use the tape to record verbal permission for the interview in the presence of an interpreter.

and analyze the material. Many of these functions can be accomplished with basic word processing tools such as "search" commands; several specialized software programs designed for ethnography are also available. These tools can help identify patterns of word usage and help you do various kinds of coding and indexing.[10]

If you decide to transcribe your interviews, a transcription machine, operated with a foot-pedal, can help you replay the conversation at your own pace as you type it up. Most university libraries own transcription machines and some allow patrons to borrow them. If you wish to have full transcriptions of your interviews, but do not have time to transcribe them yourself, professional transcription services are also available. These services usually charge at a per page rate; you can use them if your confidentiality agreements do not preclude allowing another person to hear the tapes.

As you can imagine, transcribing interviews takes a great deal of time, energy, and sometimes money. Depending on your research goals, it may not be necessary to transcribe every word of every interview. For example, if your interviews are broad ranging and you gradually determine that you wish to focus your ethnographic reflections on one part of the conversations that you have recorded, you might wish to transcribe just this part of each interview. You would still listen to the interview in its entirety, because clues to meanings may be embedded in other parts of the conversation. You might, however, not need verbatim records of everything said. Another less labor-intensive approach would be to rely primarily upon your notes from the interviews, marking important sections as you listen to the tapes, and then transcribing only the parts of the interviews that you wish to quote directly. Of course any direct quotes should be transcribed exactly.

For smaller, first-time ethnography projects, it may not be practical to try to transcribe interviews extensively. Nevertheless, it can be an enlightening learning experience or assignment for students to transcribe one interview completely. You may find that

---

10. Hammersley and Atkinson, *Ethnography*, 196–203.

you learn a great deal more about a conversation — the words, the pauses, the expressions of emotion — through the process of careful moment-by-moment reflection on every audible detail.

Visual Records

In addition to written and oral records of your research, you may wish to obtain or create visual records of your ethnographic journey. The use of visual records such as videotapes and photographs is an area of increasing interest in ethnography in general and in studies of religious practices in particular. Due to rapid developments in media technology, the possibilities for making and using visual records in ethnographic studies are multiplying. If full and adequate permissions are obtained, photographic records can be used both for purposes of data collection and for representation. Visual data can bring a sense of immediacy and evocative power to ethnographic narratives.[11]

The decision to use visual media in pastoral ethnography should be related to the particular focus of your research question. What is the likelihood that the time, effort, and expense involved in using these media will help you learn or express something significant about your social setting? If, for example, you are studying the importance of stained-glass windows to a group's worship experience, visual records of the windows are germane to the question. Photos may aid you in your analysis and they would likely enhance your ethnographic writing and presentation of your research results. Pictures will help the reader understand your interpretation of a social setting; likewise, some readers may look at the photos and form different impressions and perhaps contest your view of the group. Presenting visual records along with your writing provides the reader with greater access to the

---

11. See Sarah Pink's foundational text *Doing Visual Ethnography: Images, Media, and Representation in Research*, 2nd ed. (Thousand Oaks, Calif.: SAGE Publications, 2007), 4–17. While academic approaches to ethnography and the study of religion have long favored words over images, this is starting to change as scholars are recognizing the validity of visual records as "texts" that contribute to historical narratives.

data, gives your argument greater transparency, and thus tends to increase the range of knowledge and interpretation that can be gleaned from your study.

There are times when visual recordings of any kind may be irrelevant or inappropriate. For example, if you were probing a sensitive question about a church's recent experience of a deposed pastor's ethical misconduct, it is difficult to imagine a possible use of photography. Taking photos would likely not help you answer your research question, and it could be counterproductive in terms of your relationships with the people, especially if they are experiencing feelings of shame or anger about the situation.

While the use of visual records has great potential to enrich data collection and representation, these media also heighten the need for pastoral and ethical safeguards in your research procedures. In deciding about the use of visual records, think ahead to the form that your ethnography will take and the ways in which you hope to present or share it later. Your IRB application and your informed consent agreements should specify these plans. Give special consideration to the possibility of doing harm, especially when visual records involve images of people, and even more when these people are members of vulnerable populations such as children or socially ostracized groups.[12] Members of these groups may be at risk for violence if their pictures identify them or their whereabouts. The privacy and safety of research partners is of first importance.

Still Photography

The meaning and function of visual environments in religious experience, theology, and practice comprise an area of exploration that is wide open for study. Much rich detail can be made available for analysis by taking or collecting photographs for careful examination. Certainly, when working with the material cultural aspects of religious practice, photographs of religious art, architecture, artifacts, and landscapes are germane.

---

12. Pink, *Doing Visual Ethnography,* 49–61.

Material cultural studies examines the meaning that physical objects, architecture, and landscapes hold for people. A photograph of a built environment — such as a synagogue — by itself would not necessarily tell us what it means to the members. On the other hand, if interviews with the members reveal some of the meanings that the people ascribe to this sacred space, then it is worth taking a closer look at the space. Photographs may help you see the space more fully and thus aid your analysis and understanding of how the people see and interpret their built environment.[13]

Collecting and displaying photographs may be particularly helpful if you are a creating a timeline or documenting a major change in the life of a group. If, for example, a building is being demolished and rebuilt, photographs that document the process could be very helpful to the group. Because visual environments are so central to religious life, they become precious and important to people. If a couple has been married in a sanctuary, for example, had their children baptized or Bar or Bat Mitzvahed there, and experienced their parents' funerals there, the demolition of this building will be painful. Taking photographs can help memorialize the loss of sacred space. Displaying the photographs may also prove beneficial as people go through the process of letting go and moving forward into a new space.

If you are creating a timeline as part of a historical study, collecting old photographs can help you document the story and jog people's memories. Likewise, photographs of local, national, or world events, juxtaposed near photographs of the congregation's history, can help the group see its stories in relation to its social historical contexts.[14]

The practical matters involved in taking photographs are similar to those identified in relation to other technologies. Digital

13. See McDannell, *Material Christianity*, 2–16. This explanation of the importance of material dimensions of Christianity can be extended to include other religions; thus this example of a Jewish congregation. See also T. J. Gorringe, *A Theology of the Built Environment: Justice, Empowerment, Redemption* (Cambridge: Cambridge University Press, 2002).

14. Ammerman et al., *Studying Congregations*, 209–10.

photography is the most versatile and inexpensive approach. Of course, the quality of your equipment and your facility in working with digital images will have an impact on the results. Remember to identify and date the photos electronically as soon as possible after you take them. Also, because taking pictures is a selective activity and not a mere collection of visual facts, it is crucial that you write up thorough notes, describing the context of your photography and noting the interconnections between your photographs and your other interactions and observations. Did the participants seem eager for you to see and photograph a particular painting in their home, for example? Did they tell you a long story about how the painting was passed down from their grandparents' generation? Keep the stories with the photographs as you go along.

Not all participants in interviews or events might welcome the presence and use of a camera. The issue of consent is complex: permission to take photographs does not necessarily imply consent to publish them in any form. Clarify the possible uses of photographs in advance, as much as is possible, to avoid harm or misunderstandings. If your plans for photographs change or evolve, check back with your research participants to inform them and get their permission before proceeding with your plans.

Videography

Until recently, video has been an underutilized tool in ethnography. Video is a tool that has the potential to be used for both data collection and for ethnographic representation.[15] A case in which you might use video recordings for representation is in the example noted previously of interviewing congregational elders who want to tell their stories of the founding of the church or synagogue. They may indeed grant permission, understanding that the video recordings will become a part of the congregation's historical archive. Videography has enormous potential as a medium for creating records and for enriching conversations with research

---

15. Pink, *Doing Visual Ethnography*, 96, 168.

participants. Video camcorders with open screens can be set up off to the side of an event or an interview and no longer need be hand-held in front of the researcher's face. Camcorders can also be used with external microphones that allow you to play back footage "in the field," so that your research partners can view a segment with you and offer their interpretations.[16]

The ethics of videotaping are complicated by the vibrant and convincing nature of the medium. Documentaries, for example, allow researchers to present their interpretation of a situation in a powerful and persuasive form. You don't want to make a beautiful and compelling film that misinterprets or disempowers the people.

Researcher D. Soyini Madison tells the story of watching a highly touted documentary at a film festival. The documentary addressed women's human rights in Ghana. Madison had lived in Ghana and worked with and learned from some of the numerous indigenous human rights groups in the rural areas. This film, which won the highest honor at the festival, depicts the story of one woman alone in her struggle for human rights in Ghana. The woman sought asylum and found it in the safe haven of the United States. Madison points out how the documentary, while beautifully telling one woman's story, "erased the local human rights activists and their work," in Ghana.[17] Madison indicates that she believes the filmmaker had good intentions, but nevertheless ended up presenting a skewed view of this part of Africa.

When using a medium as rich and evocative as videography, it becomes especially critical to avoid creating portraits that blatantly or subtly contribute to negative views of the "other." You can help avoid doing this by collaborating with your research participants, sharing your "authorial" power as power with, rather than power over, the people involved, as discussed in chapter 4. You can also try to avoid this form of harm by continuing to

16. Ibid., 97.
17. Madison, *Critical Ethnography*, 1–5.

think reflexively about your purposes and your way of framing the research.[18]

There are some other significant ethical issues to take into consideration before deciding to videotape. Once a recording is made, it is always possible that someone other than the researcher will see it. Again, consideration of the social location and vulnerabilities of the research participants is needed. For example, videos of children that reveal their homes or neighborhoods or identities might fall into the wrong hands. What are the potential benefits and risks of this form of recording? How will you safeguard the tapes once they are made? Carefully adhere to the procedures that are spelled out in your research proposal.

In the case of interviews, some of the same disadvantages that apply to audio recording also come into play with video. It may be difficult to gain consent for videotaping and to establish trust in an interview when the camera is running. Issues of participants' safety and privacy are heightened, as we have noted. Videotaping is technically challenging and good equipment is expensive. If you decide to videotape, pay attention to the quality of your equipment and the placement of the microphone, and remember to do some test runs before you launch into the interview proper. Also, though video adds visual information to your records, it does not completely alleviate the need to take notes. Videotapes record selective data in need of identification and contextualization.

Still, the advantages of gaining a visual record of a conversation are significant. I remember when I was being trained as a pastoral counselor how helpful it was to analyze tapes of my early counseling sessions. (This was done with the informed consent of clients who knew that I was in training.) Often I could see on the tape some of the facial expressions and body language of the counselee that were lost on me during the session. I could gain a much deeper understanding of what the counselee was saying and feeling by watching the video, even before my supervisors and peer review colleagues offered feedback on what *they* saw

18. Ibid., 4.

happening in the session. Moreover, I could see *myself* in the session and gain a greater understanding of how my words and movements were coming across to the client.

Similarly, in ethnography, having a video record that includes both the researcher and the interviewee affords the researcher opportunities to see oneself in action in the field. Watching yourself in an interview video can help you in the ongoing work of reflexivity. Also, if your consent agreements allow it, you can garner more impressions and analysis of an interview by screening it with your research peers. Colleagues or supervisors might notice different aspects of the interview, points you may have missed. Colleagues may be able to give you helpful feedback on your performance as an interviewer as well, which could help you do better next time, or at least add to the depth and clarity of your analysis of the recorded interview.

A more common use of video in ethnography is for taping large-scale public events. The camera may be less obtrusive in this type of setting, and the payoff in terms of information gathered considerable. The flow and pattern and emotional tone of a ritual event, for example, can be picked up on tape. Later you can replay the tape numerous times, perhaps with some of your participants, reviewing the parts that are particularly dramatic or puzzling. Bear in mind, however, that video recordings, like documentary films, are selective and partial records. They do not tell the whole story. You may be busy recording one side the room, and completely miss something more significant taking place on the other side.

Obtaining informed consent for videotaping a public event is a complicated endeavor. You may gain official permission to videotape from a group's governing board; nevertheless, each person who attends the event may not know that you are taping. Some people may duck when they see you, as wedding-goers often do when a videographer works a reception. At public events you cannot possibly get each individual person's permission to tape. It could be argued that in public gatherings, people have less of an expectation of privacy. (If you can feel the wind on your face, it is said in law enforcement, your privacy rights are diminished).

Yet pastoral ethics still require that you make an effort to inform the group when you are observing. You can do this by wearing a badge when you are researching, and also by keeping printed information about your research on hand, so that those who ask you about it can be informed. If someone does make clear to you that he or she does not wish to be filmed, you must respect this decision.

There is an additional research issue to be considered in deciding to use videography. This is the trade-off between creating a filmed record and being fully present at the event. For example, if you are taping a moving event such as a procession, you have to carry the camera around with you. You might be trading some of your capacity to participate in the gathering by staying behind the camera. It is a little bit like going on a vacation and being preoccupied with taking pictures. While you are gaining a vibrant record, you may also be losing some of the experiential learning that comes from involvement in ritual events and related social interactions. In the context of a dinner, for example, if you stay behind the camera the whole evening, you won't get to taste the food. Use videotape judiciously, so that you don't miss out on the flavors of things.

Printed Documents

It has been pointed out that because ethnography was once conceived as "the investigation of essentially oral cultures," or the study of exotic but illiterate societies, there has been a traditional bias in favor of the spoken word over the written.[19] This bias perhaps no longer makes sense in the literate environments in which most pastoral ethnographies will be conducted. Printed material found in worship bulletins, temple newsletters, sermon copies, church websites, religious school curricula, congregational histories, hymnbooks, and bulletin boards harbor rich caches of information about particular social settings. Much of this material can be copied, printed, or borrowed and culled for data.

---

19. Hammersley and Atkinson, *Ethnography*, 157.

Newspaper clippings, found in libraries or historical societies' archives, may also be valuable to your research.

While we can't assume that written accounts of a group's story are more historically reliable than spoken ones, we shouldn't assume that they are less reliable either. Written materials generated by insiders in the community, such as group histories, biographies, autobiographies, diaries, letters, and minutes from meetings are of particular interest. This is not because we can expect them to be completely accurate, but because they may reveal a great deal of insight into their authors' worldviews, vocabularies, and preoccupations.

Literature, too, can be an important documentary source. What are the books that people in this group read and perhaps study together? If the group prizes the study of scripture, to which books and passages do they most frequently refer? Is there a scripture verse that you hear quoted over and over again? If there are certain novels or devotional books that you hear people talking about frequently, read these as a source of information about the issues, ideas, and theologies that the people routinely draw from. Take notes on these sources, and record your personal responses to what you read in the column or section of your journal that you have delineated for this purpose.

Another class of reading material that is pertinent to your study might be called "secondary sources." For example, if you are studying a mostly white congregation that is trying to achieve a stated ideal of becoming multicultural, it would be helpful to do some research on other congregations who have attempted similar changes. Reading some similar stories and taking notes on key questions and issues that were raised in the reading can help you clarify and begin to analyze the data you are collecting in your setting. Similarly, theological and pastoral theological literature related to this topic may be of service to you as you do the ongoing work of theological reflection on what you are learning. Take notes on this reading along the way, and record your thoughts about how it intersects with the actual practices that you are observing.

Organizing and Storing Data

After a few days in the field, the data you collect may start to get bulky. Before you find yourself tripping over piles of videotape and searching frustratedly for that copy of last week's meeting agenda, plan a way to organize these materials. Consider how you will file, store, and retrieve your data both manually and electronically.

Material from interviews can be alphabetized according to interviewees' names, or it might be numbered chronologically, according to the order in which you conducted the interviews, or both. Consider various ways to "code the record."[20] This means that you begin to code or index your gathered data by marking the record directly. For example, you can jot down some key features of an interview directly in the top right margin of your notes. Or you may color-code cassette tapes with Post-it tabs or dots.

The identification of categories for sorting is a key component of the process of analysis.[21] Early on in the process, you will not yet know all of the categories by which you will wish to sort records. As you go along, you will start to form ideas about the pertinent topics or features of the material that you want to flag. If, for example, you were conducting a study of congregants' responses to a newly added worship service, the age of respondents would likely be one category for sorting. You may want to label your records with differently colored dots that represent particular age groups, or you may just want to put the age number in a circle at the top corner of each item. In addition to age, you might also identify and mark other significant factors in your survey.

When I was conducting interviews on the devotional practices of Italian immigrants in San Pedro, California, I began to hear stories about fishing accidents and the loss of life at sea. I had not anticipated these stories, so it wasn't until I was about halfway through the interviews that I started asking people directly about such accidents. Combing back over my packets of interview notes,

---

20. Ibid., 195.
21. Ibid.

I then coded the records of all of the interviews that contained a reference to at least one serious accident in their family story. Counting them up, I saw that the number was significant; this led me to do more historical research on public records of accidents at sea and to consider this topic as an important piece of a larger story.

This illustrates the gradual and ongoing nature of the process of analysis and the way in which some simple manual coding can help you keep track of the frequency with which particular factors or topics come up. You can expect to organize and reorganize your materials several times along the way. The key is to begin with a storage system that will allow you to sort and retrieve information easily and to begin to pick out patterns and interrelationships within and between the various categories.

Documentary evidence can add up rapidly. Devise a system for filing it that will help you sort and retrieve the information most pertinent to your research question. For example, if you are telling a developmental story (according to Mason's taxonomy), you may want to store your written materials according to a historical chronology. If you are covering a ten-year period in the organization's history, you might create a separate file for each year. You could put copies of newspaper clippings and other documentary evidence in each folder. These can be stored in hanging files in the type of cardboard boxes that attorneys routinely use to store large quantities of pages.

The manual storage of video or audiotapes and disks is also important. If you have promised to keep these materials confidential, do not leave them lying around your home or office. Store them in a lockable safe or filing cabinet. To some extent, these records can also be coded directly with labels.

Electronic storage and filing is now commonplace for ethnographers. New software is rapidly developing for coding and retrieving data. Weigh the costs of time and energy these tools require against the potential benefits they provide for your particular study. This we will discuss further in chapter 7, where we address analysis and interpretation. For now, in the data collection phase, there are two critical points to remember regarding electronic records. First, back up your files. Second, protect confidential files by limiting access to them.

Reflexivity and Recording Practices

In a film entitled *The Blinking Madonna and Other Miracles*, educational videographer Beth Harrington reflects on her role in her research work. In this film Harrington intentionally moves herself out of a (relatively) safe position behind the camera, where she does her usual work of filming religious rituals, and into the more vulnerable position of becoming the subject of her film. In this offbeat and entertaining piece, Harrington tells her own story of growing up Catholic in Boston, the granddaughter of Irish and Italian immigrants. Her colorful stories of Catholic school life along with her footage of national and world events during her youth allow the viewer to understand some of the cultural influences on Harrington's childhood and youth. The author/director probes the impact of this upbringing upon her professional work and her personal choice to live in Boston's "Little Italy," making videotapes of the local religious processions known as *Feste*. Harrington depicts the story of when one of her videotapes of an annual procession captures an image of a statue of Mary, the Madonna, apparently blinking into the camera. The tape becomes public in the North End community, and eventually the local news media pick up on this story of a "miracle," a blinking Madonna. As word travels and people come to see the statue, Harrington finds herself in the middle of a controversy.

This video is a kind of memoir that portrays the complicated interactions between a researcher and the people and subjects she chose to study. The piece illustrates how the recording practices used in ethnographic study can open up more questions, both professional and personal, than we might expect. The film exemplifies the wisdom of being willing to turn the camera, or the research questions, onto ourselves.

The Blinking Madonna is suggestive of the richness and unpredictable nature of the research journey. Pastoral researchers cannot know in advance where the journey will take us, personally and spiritually. Even a recording process and the relationships formed through it can be the occasion for growth and transformation.

For Further Study

Hammersley, Martyn, and Paul Atkinson, *Ethnography: Principles in Practice*. 2nd ed. New York: Routledge, 1995, chapter 7.

Harrington, Beth. *The Blinking Madonna and Other Miracles*. Videorecording. Hohokus, N.J.: New Day Films, 1997.

Pink, Sarah. *Doing Visual Ethnography*, 2nd ed. Thousand Oaks, Calif.: SAGE Publications, 2007, parts 1 and 2.

- S I X -

Ears to Hear

Pastoral Listening in the Field

It was impossible to get a conversation going; everybody was talking too much.   — YOGI BERRA

Pastoral ethnography is, at its heart, a listening practice. At this point on the ethnographic journey, you will be going out into the field, following your research plans, observing and listening, trying to take it all in, and making thorough records. All of these efforts and activities serve the purpose of making you a more care-full listener to both the individual stories and the corporate stories of the people. Most people long to be heard. The aim of pastoral listening in ethnography is that the speakers and the group become empowered, "heard to speech"[1] that is authentic, honest, and transformative. In order to hear the deeper stories, pastoral ethnographers must "listen" with all their senses, for what is communicated in words, tone of voice, silences, gestures, and actions.

Religious leaders are often socialized to be better at speaking than at listening. It is understandable that preachers want to preach, teach, and lead with their voices and their carefully honed understandings of scripture and theology. Members of congregations often look to clergy for expertise in these matters, expecting spiritual wisdom. While the role of the religious expert is daunting in one way — you have to be sure you know your stuff — it is appealing in another: being the resident religious expert gives

---

1. Morton, *The Journey Is Home,* 205.

141

you a kind of status and a feeling of control. One downside of accepting this role, however, is that it may lead to what Yogi Berra called "talking too much."

By contrast, consider the story that theologian Nelle Morton told of a workshop participant who, after sitting silently for most of a weekend, haltingly began to speak. "I hurt," she said. "I hurt all over." The woman touched herself in various places and slowly told her story to an attentive circle of listeners. The group simply sat and listened intently, without saying a word, as the woman spoke from a place deep inside. When she was through speaking, the woman began to weep with relief and expressed gratitude. "You heard me," she said. "You heard me all the way." She then added, "I have a strange feeling you heard me before I started. You heard me to my own story. You heard me to my own speech."[2]

What is striking in this story is the way in which the group listened, paid attention, without interrupting, in order to hear the woman "all the way." This level of listening is rare; when it happens, it is almost always experienced as a gift.[3] So often we can't stand to hear deep or difficult stories. We rush in to speak: to tell our competing tale or, in the role of religious expert, to offer help or advice.

Listening is difficult because it requires us to give up the role of expert, and become a learner again. In his wonderful little book on pastoral listening, James Dittes talks about giving up the concern with our own "performance and prowess" as one of the "ascetic renunciations" that is necessary in order to be fully present to a parishioner.[4] The act of letting go of the status and control that come with being an expert is difficult. Dittes compares it to floating.[5] Do you remember the first time you tried to float in a swimming pool or pond? It can be a frightening

2. Ibid.

3. See Robert Brizee, *The Gift of Listening* (St. Louis: Chalice Press, 1993).

4. James E. Dittes, *Pastoral Counseling: The Basics* (Louisville: Westminster John Knox Press, 1999), 64–74.

5. Ibid., 79.

moment: there is that uncertainty of wondering whether the water will hold you.

Ethnographic listening also requires some floating, some willingness to tolerate the uncertainty of letting go and seeing what happens. When you really start to listen, people will know. They will start to speak more openly as soon as you communicate that you can stand to hear the truth. This kind of listening is not really hard, but it does take practice. It is like floating: as you stop being an expert, you start really being there; suspended, you listen, watch, perceive, take in the context of the interaction, and perhaps begin to sense the currents of group life.

Ethnographic listening involves suspending judgment and going for fuller understanding instead. Staying curious, probing for clarity, and allowing the stories to be told — these are the conscious intentions that we adopt. Our job is to notice as much nuance as possible, and to help a person magnify his story, make it larger, clearer, and more available to the teller. The plot thickens, the mystery unfolds, and we witness a story in progress. We hear what is beautiful, agreeable, and pleasing. We listen also for "the contradictory, the unpleasant, the negative."[6] We try not to censor the difficult details of the story, but to accept them without fear.

In interviews or focus groups, such deep stories are shared. On surveys, too, where people can be anonymous, they write in their reasons for being and proclaim their longings for God. It is amazing how much people will share with you, especially if you ask as one who is a fellow sojourner in the life of faith rather than as an expert trying to prove a point. Queries that are simple and humble yield thoughtful replies; they also support the emergence of authentic speech and developing voice.

The work of creating a space in which new and honest speech can emerge in a community is theologically crucial. In this chapter we will talk about *how* to do this work, but not until we pause to consider *why* we must do it. Researching religious practices will likely bring many new voices and versions of the people's stories into your hearing. Hearing so many stories may be confusing or

---

6. Brizee, *The Gift of Listening*, 44.

perplexing. It takes a good deal of courage to listen, especially at the level of supporting someone to new and authentic speech. Why is this work of listening so important? Where is God in it?

A Pastoral Theology of Listening and Speaking

The pastoral duty to listen was artfully described by Dietrich Bonhoeffer, who wrote in *Life Together:*

> The first service that one owes to others in the fellowship consists in listening to them. Just as love of God begins with listening to His Word, so the beginning of love for the brethren is learning to listen to them.... Christians, especially ministers, often think that they must always contribute something when they are in the company of others, that this is the one service they have to render. They forget that listening can be a greater service than speaking.[7]

Listening is indeed a great service, a primary duty of love; it brings honor and recognition to the speaker. Listening gives another the chance to experience his or her inner knowing. Listening can be a means of grace, as it brings forth stories through which people make sense of their lives and become aware of the larger reality.

Narrative theologians claim that storytelling is the primary way in which human beings structure and understand their experience of life.[8] The stories we tell express our beliefs about God, the world, and our place in it. Our stories may suggest the futures that we hope for or imagine. Herbert Anderson and Edward Foley write, "Stories are privileged and imaginative acts of self-interpretation."[9] Inviting someone to tell her story is a

---

7. Dietrich Bonhoeffer, *Life Together,* trans. John Doberstein (San Francisco: Harper and Row, 1954), 97.

8. This key idea builds upon the influential essay of philosopher Steven Crites, "The Narrative Quality of Experience," *Journal of the American Academy of Religion* 39, no. 3 (September 1971): 291–311.

9. Herbert Anderson and Edward Foley, *Mighty Stories, Dangerous Rituals: Weaving Together the Human and the Divine* (San Francisco: Jossey-Bass, 1998), 5.

way of calling forth her power to imagine or to "compose" her own life.[10]

When we invite someone to describe a religious practice, we are inviting this kind of privileged self-interpretation with a specific focus on faith-in-action. Often this involves listening to the ways in which someone brings his or her personal or group stories together with biblical stories or theological interpretations. Anderson and Foley refer to this process as one of "weaving together the human and the divine."[11] Inviting a congregant to tell his own faith stories empowers him to name his experiences of the divine, in his own words. This honors the speaker and invites him or her to enter into a theological conversation, free to express his or her own thoughts about God, rather than merely receiving the ideas of experts.

As Anderson and Foley indicate, stories can conceal or reveal.[12] In ethnographic listening, we strive to create a safe space for honest reflection in which new connections can be forged. If we suspect that someone is lying, we have to pay attention to that. We may be able to probe a bit, to find out why there is a need for pretense. We may need to say something to signal that we are there to learn and not to judge. At the same time, in our journals and analysis we can puzzle over why there might be a need to conceal, distort, or fabricate information in this group.

In ethnographic listening, we strive to make room for all kinds of stories — stories that comfort and affirm us and our congregations or organizations and stories that challenge us or move us to see the contradictions and problems in the community. When we ask a question, we must bear witness to the answer that is given, however surprising, moving, or disturbing it may be.

Biblical stories, like personal stories, hold the power to comfort or disturb. Anderson and Foley call these stories "mythic" and "parabolic" narratives.[13] Mythic stories are hopeful ones. They

---

10. Mary Catherine Bateson, *Composing a Life* (New York: Plume, 1989).

11. Anderson and Foley, *Mighty Stories, Dangerous Rituals*, 36–54.

12. Ibid., 9–12.

13. These authors are building on the work of John Dominic Crossan, *The Dark Interval: Towards a Theology of Story* (Niles, Ill.: Argus, 1975), 51–57, cited in Anderson and Foley, *Mighty Stories, Dangerous Rituals*, 13–14.

resolve contradictions and comfort us by suggesting that mediation and reconciliation are possible.[14] Parabolic stories are more
challenging and unsettling; they keep us from getting too comfortable with our current narratives. Biblical stories, like human
stories, are complex and intriguing, open to many possible interpretations, and have a lot of "loose ends." Some are gritty and
edgy, full of ambiguity and contradictions. These disruptive stories are important, lest we oversimplify and miss the hard truths
of the prophets or of the parables of Jesus. Such stories challenge
us to take in the reality and complexity of human life; they do
not always end happily ever after.

Just as we need comforting stories to give us hope, we need
these disruptive stories to awaken us to uncomfortable truths. As
Anderson and Foley put it, "Myth may give stability to our story,
but parables are agents of change and sometimes disruption."[15]
Heather Walton points out that we also need testimony from outside our faith traditions to challenge our theologies. She points
to the literary work of Elie Wiesel, Ettie Hillesum, and other
survivors of holocausts whose writings bear witness to human
suffering of such a magnitude that no theology is left unchal-
lenged.[16] Uncomfortable or parabolic stories hold the potential
to reveal the presence of God in the midst of human struggle and
ambiguity, which defy and potentially invigorate our theologies.[17]

Similarly, in ethnographic listening, we need to hear the full
range of experiences that people in the group may describe. We
may also want to include "outsiders" in our studies, to help learn
more about the impact and impressions that the group is leaving
beyond its doors. We want to understand, rather than censor,
the disruptive narratives. They may hold within them the seeds
of change: the clarity of understanding that present arrangements

---

14. Anderson and Foley, *Mighty Stories, Dangerous Rituals*, 13.
15. Ibid., 14.
16. Graham et al., *Theological Reflection* (London: SCM, 2005), 71–72.
17. The biblical witness of Job and the lament traditions also function in this
way. See Kathleen D. Billman and Daniel L. Migliore, *Rachel's Cry: Prayer of
Lament and Rebirth of Hope* (Cleveland: United Church Press, 1999).

are hurtful or untenable, or the anger that rises over injustice that finally pushes us far enough to cause us to take action.

Challenges and Tensions

Of course, we cannot be too sanguine about the benefits of constructing theological narratives. While the telling of stories may lead to relief and healing for some, there are some tragedies and traumas that require different kinds of responses and care.[18] Pastoral ethnographers need to be able to hear the difference, to see when their participant-congregants are struggling and need some form of counseling, aid, or safe haven. Moreover, pastoral ethnographers must recognize that not every story shared with them can be repeated or woven into a larger narrative without risking harm or embarrassment to the teller.

As noted earlier, there is a particular tension in using ethnography as a pastoral practice, which has to do with managing the dual roles of minister and researcher. This tension can be felt in the field, in the midst of ethnographic listening to individuals or groups. If you sense that your interviews or procedures are leading your participants in the direction of making significant personal revelations that go beyond the scope of the study, pause and take stock. Discernment is needed. You may need to acknowledge the tension of your dual roles and discuss what you think is happening with your participant-congregant. Clarify the role that you are in at the moment, and tell your research partners if you sense that things are shifting.

While we want to encourage open and honest sharing, we do not want to turn interviews into pastoral psychotherapy sessions. We want to put forward a feeling of acceptance and welcome and express a willingness to really be there, without judging, for the purpose of learning. If a real crisis is shared with you in the midst of an interview, you might need to intervene and call this to the attention of the participant. Perhaps he or she will have a suggestion as to how to proceed. You might offer to turn off the

---

18. Ibid., 73.

tape recorder and finish the interview some other time. Then in your pastoral role, you can proceed to listen to the story of crisis and decide how best to care for the person as his or her pastor. This might include making a referral for further care if you think it is needed.[19]

The point is to stay clear about your role and avoid any mis-understandings about when you are conducting research. Keeping this role distinction is difficult when you are a pastoral leader, because a participant-congregant may casually mention that he thought about the interview and has more to add. It is up to you to clarify the boundaries of the research relationship. In a situa-tion like this, you might say, "Okay. Let me get my notebook so that I can add what you are saying to your interview record."

This clarity about the research process is important for ethical reasons. The person being interviewed is in a vulnerable position, sharing stories in the context of a trusting relationship. The dual role of pastor-researcher heightens the congregant's vulnerability in the relationship. The congregant might freely answer questions or offer information of a personal nature, without guarding his or her privacy, because the authority of the clerical office is a deeply felt conviction for some congregants (as well as some pastors), and the interview setting does not completely erase this power arrangement. Similarly, the usual assumption of confidentiality in pastoral conversations could also influence the congregant's willingness to speak openly and relax boundaries in the inter-view, even though this is a research conversation. Recognizing both the pastoral needs and the privacy rights of the congregant-participant requires pastoral ethnographers to keep clear about the boundaries of each role and the distinct duty of confidentiality in pastoral matters.[20]

Still, be aware that every deep story shared is not necessarily going to precipitate ending the interview or intervening in some way. You may learn that someone is in a crisis of sorts and is

19. See Swinton and Mowat, *Practical Theology and Qualitative Research*, 64–66.

20. See Doehring, *Taking Care*.

managing to cope fairly well. In this case, your interview may be the catalyst for that person to share something that he might not have bothered to tell you if you hadn't asked a certain question. In a case like this, the ethnographic conversation can serve the role of enhancing the pastoral bond. The person may really be glad for the chance to tell you, not because he wants "help," but because it is a comfort to be known and understood.

Handle sensitive material with care, and check for clarity if you are not sure whether a person wants a part of his story to be kept confidential or not. Some people are proud of their difficult stories — such as stories of overcoming poverty or alcoholism — and want to proclaim them, while others might consider this kind of story highly embarrassing and want it to be treated in a strictly confidential manner. When in doubt, stop and ask. This way of tending to the complexity of your dual roles will help both you and the people do the important work of building reliable and clear relationships.

As in the practice of any form of ministry, there may be times when your work touches you at a level that surprises or upsets you. If, for example, you feel that you are becoming defensive or unable to listen carefully, this is a clue that something is troubling you. If you start to sense that you are in some way "in over your head," take note of this. It may suggest the need to consult with a colleague, supervisor, or therapist. Practice the same self-care strategies that help you stay balanced and spiritually centered in the ministry.[21] Pay attention to yourself as you do the work of listening, and keep writing about your experience in the reflections section of your ethnographer's journal.

The complexity of using ethnographic listening as a pastoral practice should not deter pastoral leaders from the work of careful listening to the stories of the people. The practice of constructing and sharing faith narratives helps create community and nurture commitment. The act of listening as a person or a

---

21. See Margaret Zipse Kornfeld, "Tending Yourself," in *Cultivating Wholeness: A Guide to Care and Counseling in Faith Communities* (New York: Continuum International, 2005), 281–305. Note her annotated bibliography of related resources on self-care and boundaries in the ministry, 304–5.

group describes their faith practices is fundamentally a theological act. Such a speaking and listening event can be the beginning or inkling — the spark of awareness — of God's presence for both the teller and the hearer. Tom Frank, speaking out of his Christian theology, puts it this way: "When we ask what exactly is the Christian way, we must turn and face one another."[22] In turning to face each other, we listen, hear, and see a divinely inflected story unfold. God is there in that person, in her doubt as well as in her faith, in the ambiguous and the painful experiences as well as in the joyful and the beautiful moments; God is present in the hope and the courage that go into composing a life.[23]

Who May Speak?

The power of ethnographic listening derives from the power to speak. Theologian Rebecca Chopp suggests that language "can birth new meanings, new discourses, new signifying practices."[24] The power to speak is no small matter; it cannot be taken for granted that everyone shares this power. In congregations and in groups, as in the wider society, the power to speak is not evenly distributed. Some sit silently at the margins of shared life, assuming that they have little to say that is of value to the group. Others speak boldly and confidently, perhaps unaware that their confidence and power to speak are privileges not shared by all.

In congregations as in the wider society, the dynamics of social power and economic privilege often dictate who may speak. An employer's voice trumps an employee's; a landlord's voice, a tenant's; and in many arenas, such as in U.S. national politics, social factors such as class, gender, and race still influence the selection of leaders empowered to speak on behalf of the people. The kind of "emancipatory transformation" that Chopp describes requires

---

22. Frank, *The Soul of the Congregation*, 35.
23. The phrase "composing a life" alludes to Mary Catherine Bateson, *Composing a Life* (New York: Grove Press, 1989).
24. Rebecca Chopp, *The Power to Speak: Feminism, Language, God* (New York: Crossroad, 1989), 14.

listening to those whose voices are not well heard, and supporting marginalized persons in gaining the power to speak.[25]

The practice of pastoral ethnography can challenge or disrupt tacit power arrangements that privilege some voices and quiet others. One way for researchers to do this is by choosing research questions that intentionally probe such injustices. Another strategy is to select research participants whose lives are in some way marginalized to take part in the study. Of course, ethical care must be taken when interviewing members of vulnerable groups, especially when it comes to representing ethnographic learning to others. Certain groups maintain silence for their protection, as noted in chapter 4. We do not want to do harm, nor do we want to speak for others. Rather, we want to support the emergence of new voices, new discourses, and new practices.

The power to speak, to tell one's own story, is integrally related to the power to change. This is one of the key insights that authors such as Paulo Freire have taught us.[26] This was also a principle of civil rights activist Ella Baker's famed teaching and organizing, which some referred to as "mothering." One of Baker's better known "daughters," singer Bernice Reagon of Sweet Honey in the Rock, says of Baker: "She also led by the way she listened and questioned. In her presence you got the feeling that what you felt inside made sense and could be offered up to the group for discussion as policy or strategy."[27] In ethnographic listening, we want to emulate this empowering approach to listening as a key component in pastoral leadership by taking seriously the voices and the insights of the people we are called to serve.

One way to practice empowering or even subversive pastoral ethnography is by intentionally creating opportunities for the less visible or powerful members of society to speak and to be heard.

---

25. Ibid., 71–98.

26. Paulo Freire, *Pedagogy of the Oppressed*, 30th anniversary edition, trans. Myra Bergman Ramos (New York: Continuum International, 2000).

27. Bernice Johnson Reagon and Sweet Honey in the Rock, *We Who Believe in Freedom* (New York: Doubleday, 1993), 21–22, cited in Mary Field Belenky, Lynne A. Bond, and Jacqueline S. Weinstock, *A Tradition That Has No Name: Nurturing the Development of People, Families, and Communities* (New York: Basic, 1997), 177.

In your work in the field, it is important to notice the quiet people, those who seem to be at the periphery of power and influence. Such folks may be pleased to be noticed, even if they do not have a great deal of confidence that their words will matter. By inviting folks from the sidelines to talk with you, you are already beginning to challenge their undervalued status.

A student of ethnography named "In Sun" focused her ethnographic research project on the experiences of the wives of Korean students in a freestanding denominational seminary in North America.[28] Just in her choice of research partners, In Sun challenged several assumptions about whose voice matters. To begin with, international students often experience marginalization in North American schools because of their language difficulties and their experience of "culture shock." By focusing on these students' wives, In Sun chose a group of research partners whose social experience is of double or triple marginalization — by virtue of being women of color, by virtue of being newcomers to this country, coping with the barriers of language and cultural displacement, and by virtue of being pastors' wives, whose status and role are often sharply proscribed. In Sun's study began to challenge their marginalization by moving these women to the center of the discussion, letting them know that their experience and their stories matter.

The power to change is integrally related to the power to speak to and for the world. This connection remains mysterious at some level. The process of naming one's current situation and worldview may give rise to deeper knowing and the longing for change. The power of sacred stories and symbols, intersecting with our particular human stories, challenges our ways of thinking and being and makes room for the imagination of new, alternative visions and actions.

Still, you may be wondering, how does this process work? What forms of listening can truly empower, especially in the case of those persons and groups who are not accustomed to speaking,

---

28. "In Sun," "A Study of Korean Students' Wives," unpublished paper, June 6, 2007, used by permission.

those who do not even know that they have something of value to say? How can your ethnographic listening help move someone from silence to speech?

From Silence to Speech

Some years ago, a group of social researchers set out to study the development of voice.[29] They wanted to explore the movement from silence to speech in individuals' lives and in families and communities. The researchers tried to find one of the most isolated and marginalized groups of people they could in their initial work on what they termed the "Listening Partners Project." The first group that they chose to work with was a group of poor white women, who were mothers of small children, living isolated lives in rural Vermont, not far from the Canadian border.[30] The purpose of the research was to examine and understand, but also to help facilitate, the women's "development of self, voice, and mind" in the movement from silence to speech. In this, their research can be called "an action research program."[31]

This fascinating story describes a research program that involved 120 isolated women in small listening groups that met for three hours, once a week, for eight months. This study is interesting in many ways, particularly in that it shows how extreme poverty made it difficult for the women to get to their weekly group meetings in a consistent way. The researchers had their own learning curve as they discovered the difficult conditions of the women's lives that seemed to conspire to keep the women isolated.[32]

In spite of these difficulties, the study clearly sparked dramatic changes in the women's ways of knowing, speaking, and living.

---

29. This research was first described in Mary Field Belenky, Blythe Clinchy, Nancy Goldenberger, and Jill Tarule, *Women's Ways of Knowing: The Development of Self, Voice, and Mind* (New York: Basic Books, 1986).
30. Mary Field Belenky et al., *A Tradition That Has No Name*, 4.
31. Ibid., 100.
32. Ibid., 106–12.

Many women in the study started out almost unable to speak, answering even simple questions with "I don't know," or "I don't like to think about things. I don't expect anything to change."[33] They seemed to be extremely passive, experiencing life as something that just happened to them. In a profound way, they were "silenced."

Over the eight months, as these women participated in the listening groups, they slowly started to express confidence in themselves and to reflect carefully upon the decisions that they were making for their lives and for their children's lives. One woman summed it up when she said she was "developing a voice."[34] Over time, the women came to talk about themselves and their lives in a different way. Somehow in the process of listening to themselves and to each other, they had become more confident and capable, more thoughtful and more determined in the ways that they managed their lives. Later follow-up research, a year or more after the project had ended, indicated that the women had made even greater strides in their thinking and decision-making skills in the time that had passed since the project ended.

One of the most interesting aspects of this study for our purposes is a set of procedures that the researchers used in the listening groups. At a certain point in the eight-month program, a researcher interviewed each individual woman in the group with her peers sitting around her listening. Each woman was "given the floor" for an entire session and asked to tell her story. The sessions were audiotaped. After each session, the woman had the choice of either taking the tape and the tape recorder home with her, so that she could listen to it and write out her story, or she could have the tape professionally transcribed and a copy of the transcription given to her so that she could read, edit, and revise it as she wished in the creation of her own story. Each woman then brought her story back to the group and read it aloud. Other members of the group were encouraged to say what they liked

33. Ibid., 4–5.
34. Ibid., 7.

about the story and to ask questions that helped draw out the author.

The women's power to tell their own stories developed slowly, in the context of small groups of avid listening partners who shared similar circumstances, such as the constraints of poverty, the inability to speak up to authoritarian husbands, or the challenge of raising small children with or without a partner. As the women heard similarities in each other's stories, they seemed to gather strength.

The experience of reading or hearing one's own words seemed to be a key factor in the participants' progress in developing the powers of voice, identity, and mind. Some women reported that they were surprised when they heard themselves speaking on the tape or read their own words, because they hadn't thought that they were smart enough to speak so well. The process of growth for these women began when, in the presence of an encouraging community, they heard their own words.

While there is much more wisdom to mine in this research study, for now let us consider the importance of inviting a person, particularly a person who is in some way marginalized, to hear herself or himself speak. There is a power that comes through speaking, through hearing one's own voice and having others listen and bear witness to one's story, with all its problems and possibilities. This is the kind of listening and speaking process that we want to tap into with pastoral ethnography. This kind of listening is a form of empowering love, a gift of time and kind regard, that leaders can both practice and nurture in faith communities.

Example: Struggling between "Self" and *Samonim*

When In Sun, the Korean student ethnographer mentioned earlier, undertook her study with the wives of Korean seminary students, she began with semi-structured individual interviews. She asked the participants simple questions about their lives in America, their joys and sorrows, their faith practices, and their understandings of God's help in their lives.[35] In these interviews, conducted in Korean, In Sun heard unique but similar stories: stories of moving from Korea to America, stories of missing loved ones back home, and stories of life in the seminary dormitories. Various joys and struggles were shared. When the women spoke of God's presence in their lives, In Sun invited them to be more specific. In response, one woman offered a biblical passage that she felt spoke to her situation: "The human mind plans the way, but the LORD directs the steps" (Prov. 16:9). Through her careful listening and gentle questioning, In Sun invited the women to enlarge upon their faith stories. In the process of bringing their faith to speech, the women were deepening their spiritual lives.

One of the important themes that emerged for most of the women in the group was the struggle to maintain a sense of self during this time when they were pouring all of their resources into their husbands' educations. Many of these women had put their own professional development (which they had begun in Korea) on hold in order to support their husbands' educations and, in some cases, to focus on raising their children full time. The women described experiences at their husbands' internship congregations that seemed to reinscribe a sense of lesser status. One woman in the research group reported that she was regularly expected to baby-sit for all the church children, which meant she could not even attend worship. Other stories recounted more ways in which the women in the research group were often dismissed or rendered invisible, not only in their husbands' internship churches, but also on the seminary campus, where they were often expected to cook for Korean student functions and rarely even acknowledged for doing this. The women spoke of feeling that they were not valued as individuals, but only as women who fulfilled the role of pastor's wife, or *samonim*.

Some months later, In Sun undertook the process of sharing her research results back with the participant group (see chapter 9).

35. "In Sun" had first gone through the careful practice of obtaining informed consent, letting the women know in advance that she intended to share her research results with the group later.

She invited the women to her home for this time of sharing. She served both Korean and American foods in an effort to reflect the hybridity of the women's cultural experience. Through creating this pleasant event, In Sun was welcoming and honoring her research partners, offering them the kind of respect and care that they did not always receive in other parts of their lives.

Once they had gathered, In Sun began by sharing some of her own story. In this act of reciprocity, she revealed something of herself and her role in the research. She acknowledged her social location as a Korean woman who was in some ways like the women in the group, having moved to this country some years ago and endured a similar experience of dislocation, but who was in other ways different, in that she was a single seminary student and not a pastor's wife. In Sun was thus entering into the dialogue, allowing herself to be vulnerable, reciprocating some of the trust that her research partners had offered to her.

In Sun then proceeded to share one of the broad story lines that she had heard in her research. By doing this, in essence, she was giving the women a chance to hear their own words. This is what she said:

> I told them of my observations of the way students' wives are called on campus. I saw many times that many Korean students called the students' wives *samonim,* which means "pastor's wife," rather than calling them by name.... The unknown women are not recognized by their name, even though they usually cooked for Korean students' meetings such as the new school beginning party and the graduate celebration party.[36]

After lifting up this theme of how the women were not addressed or "called" by their own names, In Sun opened the floor, inviting the women to share further. In the group, the women continued to share their stories, narrating their struggles to balance their lives as mothers, wives, pastors' wives, and housewives, while deferring their own professional careers. One

---

36. "In Sun," "A Study of Korean Students' Wives," June 6, 2007, 15.

woman expressed a desire "to take off the mask of pastor's wife and live in my own world." In Sun then invited more theological reflection on this struggle.

In Sun's research engendered the growth of voice and community among this group of women, even as it touched her and enabled her to grow closer to them. In Sun also witnessed some changes in the lives of the group that appear to be related to her research. She learned at the sharing event that three of the women had recently taken on a rigorous program of study to learn English and were meeting with great success. In Sun also noted at the next Korean student campus-wide event that the women did not do the cooking. Instead, the men had ordered the food and some of them also served it.

The most touching story of change was told by a woman who, after her interview with In Sun, must have told her husband about how she was feeling disregarded at his church where it had been assumed that she would care for the children during worship. Her husband had taken it upon himself to hold a meeting at his church, where he told the congregation that his wife missed being able to worship because she was expected to care for the children all the time. He then asked for volunteers to take a turn baby-sitting so that she would not be confined to the nursery. His request was met with great support; the women of the church all volunteered to take a turn in the nursery, and the woman who was the student-pastor's wife was freed to sing in the church choir, using her special gift of voice.[37]

This is just a small part of the story, but it demonstrates the way in which the power to speak can be supported and encouraged through ethnographic listening. When these women were given a chance to tell their stories, make sense of their faith, and hear their stories and their faith stories echoed back to them in the group, some things began to shift. The low status that comes with the role of student's wife and pastor's wife was challenged, and in the careful listening and gentle sharing processes that followed, a space was opened up for spiritual and interpersonal growth.

37. Ibid., 20.

Of course, this experience did not solve all of the challenges in these women's lives. Likewise, it cannot be claimed that this ethnographic project dismantled sexism in their lives. Even in the last example, where the student pastor asked for volunteers in the nursery and the volunteers came forward, it is fair to point out that the volunteers were all women. The church did not suddenly decide that childcare should be the shared responsibility of both men and women. It could be argued from this example that ethnographic listening does not really effect social change.

The links between personal voice and interpersonal change and social transformation are often subtle, slowly evolving, and complex, rather than sudden and obvious. We will explore this interplay further in chapter 10. Still, in this example, it appears that In Sun's research sparked some new awareness in the women's lives and in their roles in community. Perhaps the women were heard into speech. The questions that In Sun offered, in the spirit of care and connection, became a gift of grace to these women, offering them the occasion to reflect on their lives, their value in God's sight, and their callings or vocations. When the women heard their own voices and their own prayers reflected back through In Sun's perceptive presentation, they received nurture, affirmation, and encouragement. Through this experience they found ways to communicate their needs to the larger communities to which they belong — their families, their churches, and their campus home. They also found ways to help themselves improve their lives, such as through singing and studying English, which can be viewed as additional forms of developing voice. We do not know where these women's stories will go next, but we can infer that the power to speak and the grace of being heard are gifts that can support the women in the work of composing their lives.

Deep Story Listening: How to Do This

Ethnography involves listening or watching as people express or enact their faith through stories, interactions, and rituals. As people share their stories with you, try to listen for the recurrent themes, metaphors, and meanings. In the example above, In Sun was able to observe key interactions in the group and in the community and connect them to the common theme of tension between self and *samonim*. Such common themes do not always emerge, and sometimes they are not immediately apparent. Careful listening can alert you to themes at the different levels at which people tell their stories.

The work of John Savage can assist us as we try to discern story levels and themes.[38] Savage describes four levels of story telling and listening. The first level is a story from long ago, a "once upon a time" recollection of something in the past. You may find that interview questions that recall a group's past help start the story-telling process. In the case described above, stories of life back in Korea could be considered long ago stories. The second level of story also involves the past, but it includes the expression of feelings, which may be directly described or just expressed through a feeling tone that you can pick up in the voice. In the case above, if a participant spoke of her life back home in Korea with emotion, In Sun could "tune into" this. The third level of story is one that describes the present. Recent or current stories are often told at the level of feelings, so you will be able to see or feel the expressions of joy, anger, or sorrow that accompany the story. In Sun heard several stories describing the current situations of her participants where emotion was expressed, such as the stories of heartfelt prayer and searching described above. The final level of story is when someone starts to understand a deeper meaning of his life story while talking about it in your presence. This is the "aha" moment that we often hope for when we share our lives with others.[39] In Sun observed such moments and in them was able to decipher some key themes in the women's stories. In Sun also experienced deeper meanings in her own life story as a result of her deep story listening and heartfelt appreciation for her

38. John Savage, *Listening and Caring Skills: A Guide for Groups and Leaders* (Nashville: Abingdon Press, 1996).

39. Ibid., 79–81.

research participants. She describes her own growth and theirs as a kind of resurrection, recalling one of the deepest themes in the Christian story.[40]

In pastoral ethnography, storytelling happens at all of these different levels. One level isn't better than another. As an ethnographer, try to notice which level is being used. At any level of storytelling, be patient. If a person repeats something, stay with it a little longer. If you hear a theme, try repeating it or checking back with the person to see if you are comprehending his meaning. If you don't understand a word someone is using, or if a person seems not to understand your usage of words, stop and ask for clarification. It is more important to hear a person well than to cover all of your questions. Clarity is necessary before any of the deep understanding can unfold.

For example, when Terry, a Protestant chaplain, was interviewing some of the Catholic residents of a retirement community, she gradually realized that the Catholics were using certain terms differently than the way she did. She was asking them about their experiences of viewing a crèche, which one woman said was "on the altar." Terry assumed this meant that the crèche was on the altar table. She was then shown pictures of the crèche, where it looked to Terry as if the crèche were under, not on, the altar. Terry realized that while she as a Protestant understood "altar" to mean "altar table," the Catholics were using "altar" to refer to the entire space up in the front of the sanctuary, which Protestants usually call the "chancel." Terry discovered similar confusion over the terms "crèche" and "nativity scene." As Terry so aptly puts it, "What you think you know, may not be what it is."[41] When you are confused about people's meanings, it makes sense to check back with them and see whether you are perceiving their meanings correctly or not. If you have the wrong idea, participants can correct you and no harm is done.

---

40. "In Sun," "A Study of Korean Students' Wives," 26–34.
41. Terry-Thomas Primer, "Catholics and the Creche," March 18, 2005, 11–12.

Similarly, when thinking about the deeper levels and tacit meanings of stories, you can offer a "story check."[42] After listening a long while, sometimes an idea or image comes to you about the larger meaning of what you have heard. This may feel like a hunch or a guess. It is helpful if you can stop and ask, in essence, whether you are getting an accurate impression.

Making a story check is a bit more sensitive than just asking for clarification about word usage. Savage recommends a kind of three-step formula for going about this story check. Begin with a stem, something tentative-sounding like, "I'm wondering whether your story suggests that..." or, "It sounds as if..." After the stem, name the story piece, theme, or metaphor that you think sums it up in some way. Then the third step is to add another question, also very tentative, such as, "Could this be true?"

So, for example, imagine a man telling you a long tale about a congregation's history, recalling the glory days of overflowing pews and parking lots, and bemoaning that "things here just aren't what they used to be." What would you be thinking? Would you surmise that the person is nostalgic? Or would you get the feeling that the person is crabby and critical and doesn't like your sermons? Would you suspect that there is something lost or missing in the congregation for this person? How would you check out your impressions? Following Savage's formula, you might say something like this:

Stem: "Correct me if I'm wrong, but I have the sense that..."

Name the story: "you've experienced a lot of loss here in this congregation..."

Question: "Could that be true?"

If the person responds affirmatively, you could ask him to say more about what has been lost, to name or describe it more fully.

---

42. Savage, *Listening and Caring Skills,* 98–100.

If he responds negatively, and says, "No, that's not it," keep listening. No harm is done. You can withdraw your guess and gently ask the person to help you understand.

Maybe the man in this vignette was really talking about himself, and feeling that *he* isn't "what he used to be." This would be a metaphoric meaning, a level of meaning you might not perceive the first time a story is told. This possible meaning might not strike you until later, when you are writing up your notes or your journal reflections.

Deep story listening requires the patience to listen to a long story, perhaps more than once, and the ability to tolerate the emotions the story elicits. If the man is telling you a hard truth, for example, that he feels out of touch with the congregation, or that he doesn't like your preaching, or that he feels he is slipping away with age, you need to listen attentively and bear witness to that experience. Remember that any time someone is being honest with you, he is really honoring you and expressing a certain level of trust. If you can tell yourself to hang in there and listen, you will learn something important about this man's way of understanding his life and his congregation.

You don't have to agree with someone in order to acknowledge his experience, emotions, or point of view. Savage teaches a skill he calls "negative inquiry," whereby leaders learn to ask their critics to tell them *more* about what it is they don't like.[43] This is not an exercise in self-flagellation. As the critic shares more specific information, you, the leader, will better understand how this person perceives you. You might be able to use this information to improve your work. Alternatively, you may realize that the disgruntled person is really just trying to get your attention. When you give a person who is annoyed or upset a chance to speak and treat his or her ideas with respect, you are creating a small bridge upon which you both can stand in the relationship.[44]

---

43. Ibid., 63–74.
44. Of course, in an extreme case, if a participant were to demonstrate threatening levels of rage or other behavior suggesting psychopathology, it would be wise to stop the interview and call for emergency help. See Kornfeld, *Cultivating Wholeness*, 297–300.

Similarly, when someone is telling you a positive story about what he loves about the congregation or about your sermons, do not nod with embarrassment and skip to the next question. You are not "fishing for compliments" if you ask him to say more about that. Ask for specific information about what he likes, so that both of you can learn more about his experience. Linger over whatever is good and wholesome and hopeful.[45]

Questions and careful listening should not be overly focused on problems or pathology. A person may strongly need to tell you a story about her personal achievements or about a feeling of deep joy. Bring reverence and curiosity to such moments of expression. Honor the disclosure by probing for greater clarity. As the action-researchers in the Listening Partners project found, taking the time to dwell on emerging strengths can actually support growth and development. In Sun found this to be true in her research, as the women in the group reflected on their unfolding stories over time. Marveling at the experience of growth and new life helps it take root and grow.

Positive revelations about congregational life can also help you grow and expand as a leader. There is a whole school of leadership training called "appreciative inquiry," which is based on the power of focusing conversations on what is good about an organization, what is working, and what positive wishes and hopes people have for the future.[46] As a pastoral ethnographer interested in transformative growth, it is important to learn about what is working well and moving the faith community forward. The information gleaned from this can help you and the people discern a hopeful and holistic direction for the future chapters of your shared life.

---

45. "Finally, beloved, whatever is true, whatever is honorable, whatever is just, whatever is pure, whatever is pleasing, whatever is commendable, if there is any excellence and if there is anything worthy of praise, think about these things" (Phil. 4:8).

46. For a theologically oriented description of the practice of "appreciative inquiry" in congregations, see Mark Lau Branson, *Memories, Hopes, and Conversations: Appreciative Inquiry and Congregational Change* (Herndon, Va.: Alban Institute, 2004).

Summary

In listening to stories, strive to take an open posture, an attitude of interest in whatever is offered. We want to give people the space to name their experiences, theologies, and practices in their own words. This storytelling may include an appreciation for the wonder and beauty of the earth, the goodness of God's love, the friendliness of the group, the support of the community. Likewise, we want to make space for the sharing of conflicts and contradictions, doubts, wounds, or worries. In ethnographic story listening, it doesn't matter whether you "get" all the levels of meaning quickly, in the first moment of hearing. In your notes and in your journaling, begin to puzzle over stories and allow them to work on you a bit. You can request a second interview if you think you need further clarification. There will also be opportunities later, through sharing events, to bring your insights and hunches back into a broader conversation.

Terry-Thomas Primer, the Protestant chaplain who came to understand her Catholic residents better through her study of their uses of the crèche, describes the story listening and reflection process as a kind of spiral. She writes:

> This project has given me a new way of exploring the religious landscape at my community. . . . What I find helpful is the spiral of learning implied in the concept of reflexivity. Puzzlement over what is different, unusual, or perhaps disturbing, leads to investigation thereby increasing the opportunities for knowledge and inviting more interactions. The questions, if asked sensitively, strengthen the bonds between congregation and pastor.[47]

Ethnographic listening, puzzlement, and investigation for new knowledge can indeed serve the pastoral relationship, by increasing the depth of storytelling and the clarity of understanding in interpersonal interactions.

When we attempt to support a person or group's power to speak, we cannot know or predict the outcome. Frightening as

---

47. Primer, "Catholics and the Crèche," 13.

this may be, we know that listening is a pastoral duty. To the extent that we can listen to the people, trusting that genuine speech will emerge, we can support the empowerment of the people. Empowered research partners and group members are likely to become more creative and committed partners in the shared faith and praxis of the congregation.

To the extent that we make efforts to include the quieter characters, the members who are in some way marginalized, we can support "emancipatory transformation" within the group through this pastoral practice. Attentive listening to "the least of these" — those whose social power is more limited than others' — can help us understand and begin to redress inequalities within the group. This practice also helps us gain a broader picture of the faith practices in this setting, a larger collage of viewpoints, memories, and meanings. In it all we strive to hear the truth of the stories being shared and inviting our research partners into liberative and life-giving speech.

For Further Study

Anderson, Herbert, and Edward Foley. *Mighty Stories, Dangerous Rituals: Weaving Together the Human and the Divine.* San Francisco: Jossey-Bass, 1998, chapters 1 and 2.

Belenky, Mary Field, Lynne A. Bond, and Jacqueline S. Weinstock. *A Tradition That Has No Name: Nurturing the Development of People, Families, and Communities.* New York: Basic Books, 1997, chapters 3–6.

Chopp, Rebecca S. *The Power to Speak: Feminism, Language, God.* New York: Crossroad, 1989.

Savage, John. *Listening and Caring Skills: A Guide for Groups and Leaders.* Nashville: Abingdon Press, 1996, chapters 6 and 8.

SEVEN

Organizing Data

Methods for Analysis

If you come to a fork in the road, take it.
— YOGI BERRA

The spiral-like learning process of ethnographic inquiry does not lend itself to simple, step-by-step instructions. To the contrary, by this point, you may be feeling mired in stories, observations, documents, and pictures, and wondering what to do with it all. As your records pile up, your system of organizing may need attention. At the same time, you may be reflecting back upon your original research question and wondering whether the data you are accumulating are going to help you find any answers. Some of this uncertainty cannot be avoided. The discovery of complications in fact may be a sign that you are really paying attention: you are discovering a more complex social setting than the one you expected to find. Though it is not possible or desirable to erase all of this uncertainty at this point in the process, you can manage the complexity by choosing suitable methods of organizing and analyzing your data.

How do you start the process of "reading" your data and identifying categories for analysis? Somehow this mountain of cassette tapes, DVDs, CD-Rs, printed documents, and photographs has to be sorted through, divided up, and organized in such a way that you can work with it. You need to be able to manipulate pieces of your findings, move them around, much as you would pieces of a large puzzle. You will want to group pieces — just as you might group puzzle pieces by their color or by putting all the straight edged pieces together to create the puzzle's outer frame

167

first. Looking at your data, your pile of pieces, how do you get started? The best guides suggest that you must begin by familiarizing yourself with all of the pieces you have collected over time. This process is sometimes called immersion.

Immersion

The metaphor of immersion has been used to describe ethnography itself. First-hand experience is a key strategy in ethnography: the researcher's presence and participation in a setting serve to generate knowledge. Immersion can also be a metaphor for the approach you take to your data. Tempting as it may be to try to impose order upon chaos, do not rush into categorizing your data too firmly too quickly. First, review what you have. Listen to the stories on your tapes. Read and reread your field notes and your journal entries. Go through your documentary evidence — those newsletters or agendas that you hastily picked up after a group meeting. Get a feel for the data, their content and scope. As Jennifer Mason puts it, "read them, look at them, study them, listen to them, think about them and their process of production, sleep with them under your pillow if you think it will help."[1] At the same time you are doing this, think about your research questions and the intellectual puzzle that you are trying to put together.

Immerse yourself in it all. This takes an investment of time, but it is one that will pay off in several ways. First, you are going to be reviewing all of the data you have collected and not relying solely on your recent impressions or your distant memories. This will increase the breadth of your understanding of your social setting; it will help you pay sustained attention to the larger picture. As you hold all of this material in your consciousness (as well as in your unconsciousness, if it's under your pillow), new connections between the pieces will begin to suggest themselves to you. You might notice the frequent use of a particular phrase in nine of your ten interviews. Or you might suddenly see that a

---

1. Mason, *Qualitative Researching*, 159.

shift in membership corresponds to a historical event that your participants narrated.

Second, immersing yourself in your data will lead you around the spiral path toward revisiting your original intellectual puzzle. You can start to assess whether the data you have collected is of the appropriate type and sufficient amount to actually help you answer your research questions. You may decide that you are right on track, zeroing in on helpful explanations and understandings of your original query. Alternatively, you may realize that the data are vibrant and interesting, but that they illuminate a question slightly different from the one you were asking at first. If this happens, you may decide to revise or sharpen your research question, so that you can continue to probe this new and unexpected turn in the data set. Still another possibility is that in going through your data you will realize that your research methods are not really helping you put together your puzzle. You may decide to stick with your original question but devise new methods or forms of research that will help you get closer to the understanding you are seeking. For example, you might decide that in order to answer your question you need to add follow-up interviews, asking different questions, or including different individuals or groups in your sample. In this case, you would need to revise your research plan and, depending on the magnitude of the changes, you might also need to resubmit the plan for ethical review.[2] Immersion in the data while rethinking your questions helps you to see where you have come so far and to determine your next steps.

Slices and Bags

After you have become familiar with your data, while some of these alternatives are swirling around in your mind, you can start the process of sorting the data into categories or groups. Mason

---

2. Consult with your research peers, supervisor, or a member of the IRB if you are unclear as to whether the new research you propose to add is substantially different from your original plan in nature or scope, so that it requires further IRB review.

describes the initial grouping of material as putting the data into loose "bags" or "slices," and treating these as "unfinished resources," that can be examined in order to help you see themes in your data set.[3]

Organizing your data involves putting them into forms that you can work with, move around, compare, and contrast. There are several different ways to approach this, practically and intellectually. While, practically speaking, you might be organizing materials into cardboard boxes or electronic files, there is also a component to this sorting that is more challenging intellectually. The challenge is to decide how you want to "slice" the data, so that your scheme of organization will help you think through your questions. For example, if you are trying to understand why certain members of an organization seem more active and engaged than others, one of your tasks would be deciding how you are going to measure the levels of activity and commitment. If you sort through the group of surveys, for example, and pile all the surveys of high worship attendance members together in one box and decide to focus on these surveys, you might be ignoring the surveys of some of the most committed members in terms of financial giving or participation in ministry programs. Ideally, you could come up with a system that would allow you to sort and re-sort the surveys according to several different categories and then be able to make associations across categories. The categories that you choose to focus on and your ability to move the data around will become important to the arguments that you construct and the larger story you tell in your ethnographic writing.

How do you come up with the categories or bags by which you organize your data? There are different schools of thought on this. One school, known as grounded theory, claims that you should allow the data themselves to suggest the categories or groups. As you begin to go through the data and read them, detecting patterns in interview answers, for example, or rules in ritual practices, you can tag the data according to "what is

---

3. Mason, *Qualitative Researching*, 159.

there." Eventually, you construct a theory that is "grounded" in the data.[4] This involves inductive reasoning.

Another school of thinking suggests that you begin with your questions and some kind of theory, theology, or hypothesis. You then derive categories for organizing the data from your theory. This involves a more deductive form of reasoning, where you ask a question, offer a theory or a hunch — a hypothesis — and then line up the data in such a way as to test the theory. If your research question is a *predictive puzzle,* you will likely be using this approach to help you select the important factors in your analysis. These will be the basis for the ways you divide up your data.

Most pastoral ethnography involves a combination of inductive and deductive reasoning, which is sometimes called abductive reasoning. Participant observation tends to lend itself to this kind of back and forth: your experience of a social setting works on you while you are working on understanding it. The data you collect and absorb through experiencing the setting will suggest bags and slices, while at the same time your questions and deductive reasoning may produce more ideas about how to sort or measure your data.[5] While all ethnography does not necessarily go so far as to create or a test a theory,[6] it is necessary nevertheless to be aware of the form or forms of reasoning that you employ in your analysis. This will help insure that the story you eventually tell in your written ethnography will be logically consistent with your data. Your reasoning process should be as transparent and coherent to your readers as possible.

Ways of Reading

As you go about identifying potential slices and bags, also try to clarify the way in which you intend to read your data. Mason

---

4. An excellent resource for developing grounded theory is Anselm Strauss and Juliet Corbin, *Basics of Qualitative Research: Techniques and Procedures for Developing Grounded Theory,* 2nd ed. (Thousand Oaks, Calif.: SAGE Publications, 1998).

5. Mason, *Qualitative Researching,* 181.

6. See Swinton and Mowat, *Practical Theology and Qualitative Research,* 46–49.

points out that there are at least three ways in which you may wish to read the data: literally, interpretively, or reflexively.[7] If, for example, you are considering a group of interviews, which you have listened to and transcribed or noted carefully, the categories that you use to index the material in the transcribed conversations will vary depending upon the way you wish to read the data.

A *literal* reading of a recorded conversation might involve coding particular vocabulary, forms of speech, pauses, interruptions, and so forth. This would be useful for conversation analysis or discourse analysis, two specific forms of analyzing the way that people communicate and use language. These technical approaches have their own sets of conventions for indexing, analysis, and theory building.[8] If you wanted to study the data in this literal way, these are the kinds of categories you would need to identify for organizing them.

By contrast, *interpretive* readings of a conversation involve sorting the data for implied or inferred meanings. In this case you are attempting to "read through or beyond" the words shared.[9] This could overlap with but extend a literal description, in the direction of more interpretation. In order to do this, you would need different categories to organize the data. For example, you might want to identify rules or norms implied by the things that people say, or certain doctrines or ideas about God that people express in a roundabout way. This is a more likely approach to reading the data for pastoral ethnographers who are concerned with context and culture. With this approach to taped interview data, you would try to think of categories that name the tacit meanings you see in the data.

Reading the material *reflexively* would involve concentrating on your own comments and influence in the interviews. For pastoral ethnography, this is one of the critical ways of reading data because we often want to plumb the "shared wisdom" that

7. Ibid., 148.
8. Ibid., 57–58.
9. Ibid., 149.

emerges through the ethnographic encounter. In reflexive reading, your responses become one of the subjects of your research. For this kind of analysis, you need to find categories in which to group your responses to your research participants and experiences. These may be found in the recorded conversation and in your ethnographic journal, where you recorded your private responses. These responses might be grouped as, for example, supportive, surprised, shocked, amused, annoyed, and so on.

Most beginning-level pastoral ethnographies will involve all three types of reading, with emphasis on the interpretive and reflexive. Though the literal words and their local meanings are important (as we saw in chapter 6), we are usually interested in broader forms of understanding as well, including cultural understandings. So we will be looking for categories or slices that help sort implied rules, meanings, functions, properties, and dimensions of the religious practices we study. We will also need to sort and study the phrases, attitudes, expressed ideas, and emotions of participants, as well as our own personal responses to the people and practices we encounter in the research experience.

Tagging or Coding

Once you have decided on a few loose groupings of your data, categories that seem central to your questions, find ways to tag or code them so that you can rearrange the material and look for patterns and interrelationships between different pieces of the puzzle. This coding may be done manually or electronically, as noted in chapter 5.

If you are working manually, for example, with written transcriptions or notes, you might want to tag any portions of conversations that refer back to a certain topic, say "community." Then you could line up all of these comments next to each other to see how the comments of various individuals compare to each other. By doing this, you would be better able to discover certain *properties* and *dimensions* of the local discourse on community. For example, if almost everyone sampled says they love this congregation because of the community they find there, you would be discovering something about the quality of the community as experienced by the persons you interviewed. This is a quality or *property* of the sample group's experience of community that you find in your data. If you then decide that you want to test the *dimensions* of this feeling about the quality of community, you might decide to spiral back and add some more research, in order to question the experience of a larger sample of members. Moreover, you might want to question a different sample of people, such as visitors rather than members, in order to learn about their experiences of community in this setting.

Of course, you could use electronic sorting to help you with this. Word searches can help you find instances of the literal use of the term "community." Yet in order to read the data interpretively, you would also need to go through the transcripts and "tag" sections that tacitly discuss community life, even if other words are being used, such as "hospitality" or "caring." Whether you are working manually or electronically, you have to read your data interpretively yourself. Software can help you code, sort, and identify patterns and dimensions in your data. However, you must do the careful reading for implied ideas so that you can program in your index terms. You cannot avoid the careful thinking that goes into the tasks of reading of data for tacit meanings and identifying the categories you will use in your analysis.

There are software products that can help you organize data and detect patterns in it.[10] If you are involved in a large-scale project and have a great deal of text to read and manage, some of these programs may be helpful. Similarly, if you are using multiple forms of data, including digital imagery and text, some products can hyperlink the different forms of data together. For more basic research projects, it may not be necessary to invest in this kind of software.

---

10. For more information about specific software products, both free and commercial, visit the website of the American Anthropological Association, "Anthropology Resources on the Internet Web Page," at *www.stanford.edu/ ~davidf/ethnography.html.*

Charts and Graphs

Particularly if you are a visual learner, charts or graphs can help you "see" aspects of your data in a more efficient and comprehensive way. If we continue with the example of organizing data from structured qualitative interviews, we can see how this works. Suppose you have gone through your transcripts or notes and done the necessary interpretive reading and highlighted the main points of each respondent's answers to four of your questions. Using a simple grid from any word-processing program, you can list your four questions on the left side of the grid, and then list your respondents' names (or pseudonyms) across the top of the grid. You can then insert the main points of each respondent's answers into the appropriate boxes on the grid. See Figure 5 on the following page.

These grids are expandable, so you can paste direct quotations into each box. You can also note the emotional tone of responses near each answer. Once the grid is filled in, you will be able to spot similarities and differences in the answers people give. My students have often used color-coding to highlight the similar answers, which then can be spotted not only across the row of question one, for example, but all through the grid. In this way, for example, if an issue present in question one of one interview is highlighted in yellow, and the same matter comes up in answer to question four in another interview and is highlighted in yellow, the researcher can see both the similarities and the differences in the ways each respondent brings up the issue. When color-coding, you can code the typeface itself or, after printing the grid and studying it, highlight portions of the text with markers as you make these connections. In lieu of color-coding, in Figure 5 I have used different print styles to identify similarities in responses.

In using a grid like this, you can add codes for identifying demographic information, which may help you analyze patterns more fully. For example, you might use printed symbols or color-coded stick-on dots to indicate each respondent's age, income level, gender, or race to see if these factors seem to be correlated to the respondents' answers. This kind of system could help you

Figure 5. A Sample Grid for Interview Data Organization

	Respondent 1	Respondent 2	Respondent 3	Respondent 4
Question 1 How do you practice your faith?	*Prayer* **Worship** Good works	Donations to good causes Yoga	***Political activism*** *Prayer* I *pray* as I **march for peace**	**Worship** I keep religion separate from politics
Question 2 How often do you do this?	I *pray* every day	I give to the <u>church</u> and to the Salvation Army	Two weekends out of four I am out there ***marching against this war***	I go to **worship** every week and I *pray* every day
Question 3 Do you prefer to practice your faith alone or in community?	I *pray* in the PRIVACY of my room	I prefer to be ALONE	Alone I can't effect change; only in a group can my actions make a difference	I like the support and <u>friendship of the congregation</u>
Question 4 Who is in your primary faith community?	<u>My church friends</u>	The birds and the trees	The folks in my ***moveon.org*** group	My family My church

Key to repeated themes: *Italic* = *Prayer*
Bold = **Worship**
Bold italic = ***Political activism***
<u>Underline</u> = <u>Church</u>
SMALL CAPS = PRIVACY

see, for example, that women list prayer more than men do in this sample, or that the youth and seniors seem to practice political activism more than middle-aged respondents in your sample. Creating grids like this gives you a way to view large amounts of material all at once, and note some of the interrelationships between and among various pieces of data. You could also use cross-tabulation of the data in a computer program for producing charts and graphs that show this kind of cross-referencing.

Graphs or timelines can be helpful for categorizing your data according to *time*. If you are working on a developmental puzzle, seeking to understand how a certain idea or practice developed over time, you might try plotting your group's history along a chronological line from left to right. Timelines can also help you see your group's history in relationship to larger historical events and issues. If you plot a group's history across the top of a time line, the community's history below it, and national and world events along the line below that, you can see the interplay of issues and events. Seeing the larger picture of neighborhood and historical events can often help you gain a better appreciation of the context of your group's life.[11]

Time is also an important issue in interviewing. What someone says in an interview one day is likely to depend upon how he or she was feeling that day and on what else was going on in that person's life. This is perhaps best illustrated by the example of student life. Students at a university who are interviewed in September, at the start of a school year, may speak very differently than they would in May, at year's end. In fact, a comparative study built on interviews or surveys of students at key intervals in their education would be quite interesting. In this case, time would be one of the key axes of comparison, and graphs could help chart the data for comparison.

Thematic Analysis: Finding the Stars in the Sky

As you sort through your data and examine it from various angles, certain key themes may suggest themselves to you. Swinton and Mowat reference the work of Max Van Manen, who defines *themes* as structures of experience and compares them to knots or stars of meaning. Themes are "like knots in the webs of our experience, around which certain lived experiences are thus spun and thus lived through as meaningful wholes. Themes are

---

11. For more information on the creation and uses of timelines, see Ammerman et al., *Studying Congregations,* 43–46, 209–10.

the stars that make up the universe of meaning we live through."[12] Certainly many pastoral ethnographers will want to recognize and understand these themes that are like stars in the sky of meaning.

How do you identify themes in an interview, for example? The immersion process helps you begin to notice some of the key elements in a person's story. Importantly, this work of identifying themes may go a little beyond the interviewee's current way of explaining or interpreting his or her own life. When you identify themes, you are noting what you see at a deeper level. This is akin to the deep-story listening process described in chapter 6. The researcher may see or hear some aspect of the story of which the teller is not yet fully aware. Sometimes a key word in the story strikes the researcher as having a deeper or metaphoric meaning. The researcher may recognize this as a theme because it is repeated frequently, or because it succinctly names a star or a knot of meaning that the researcher sees in the interviewee's story.

The themes we pick up at first are really guesses and need to be checked in some way for authenticity. Swinton and Mowat offer a fine example of the process of thematic analysis in a research study of personal experience that focused on depression and spirituality.[13] The researchers' analysis of interview data began with a process of immersion, in which the researchers moved back and forth between studying individual words and sentences (literal chunks of text) and the larger narrative and context of the interviews. The researchers found that themes that appeared to "incorporate something of the essence of depression and the role of spirituality in living with it" gradually emerged into their awareness.[14]

---

12. Max Van Manen, *Researching Lived Experience: Human Science for an Action Sensitive Pedagogy* (New York: State University of New York Press, 1990), 90, cited in Swinton and Mowat, *Practical Theology and Qualitative Research*, 118.

13. See Swinton and Mowat, *Practical Theology and Qualitative Research*, chapter 4, 101–32. The authors call their method "hermeneutic phenomenology," an approach philosophically grounded in the work of Hans Georg Gadamer and his "hermeneutical circle." See especially 105–16.

14. Ibid., 118.

The researchers tested these themes in several ways. First, the themes were collected and analyzed using a software program called MARTIN, which is designed to help facilitate analysis rather than create theory.[15] The themes were grouped together and the researchers reflected upon them dialogically, going back and forth between the themes (the parts) and the whole story. Then, using these reflections, the researchers wrote up "thematized narratives" for each of the persons interviewed. These narratives were then given to other researchers to be checked for authenticity, which was defined as coherence between the data and the thematized narratives. These thematized narratives were also given back to the research participants themselves, so that they could read, comment upon, and validate the narratives. The research participants thus actively participated in shaping the data.[16] All of this preceded the final phase of narrative construction.

This example is helpful in many ways. First, it demonstrates a disciplined process of identifying themes or stars in the sky in each interview and studying them in relationship to the larger story. Second, it shows how the writing process becomes a part of the analytic process when dealing with a study of experience. It was only in writing up the thematized narratives that the researchers found words to describe the themes adequately. Third, this example demonstrates a way of working with research peers to have them vet your reasoning and with research participants so that they really do become partners, sharing in the *author*ity of the narrative. This move helps address the ethical questions that are heightened when studying the personal experience of a vulnerable population, such as persons who suffer from depression. Finally, this research study suggests a liberative benefit of the research for the participants, who *all* commented upon how the thematic narratives given to them for validation made them aware of some aspects of their experience that they had not fully recognized before.[17]

---

15. Ibid., 117.
16. Ibid., 119.
17. Ibid., 118.

While your initial research project may not be as extensive or as rigorous as this one, there is still much to learn from this example. This research illustrates a process of analysis that helps us gain access to the themes, symbolic meanings, and the *habitus* (see chapter 2) or worlds of meaning that transpire in religious practices.

Analyzing Documentary Sources

In addition to looking at the texts of your research notes and your transcribed interviews, you will also be immersing yourself in the documentary resources that you have collected. Both primary and secondary resources can be considered in your analysis (see chapter 5). If you have collected documentary evidence such as newspaper clippings, sermon or speech texts, and newsletter articles, scan it all thoroughly. What seems useful and most directly related to your study questions? If the organization you are studying has good historical archives, take a look at what is there. Familiarize yourself with the range of archival material available. "Read around" in it as much as you can, sampling the different kinds of extant records, looking for resources that shed light on your research questions or on the themes that you have extrapolated from other forms of research, such as interviews.

If the sheer amount of paper is overwhelming, you must make some practical decisions about what you will use and how you will analyze it. One method is to select a single source, such as the annual meeting minutes, and limit your investigation to these minutes, reading them thoroughly in order to try to absorb the culture, norms, and themes of group life. This is a legitimate approach, as long as you realize its limitations. For example, there is much in the *habitus* of group life that goes unspoken in the official minutes of the meetings: there are assumptions that are so clear to the group that no one bothers to write them down; also, there are usually some areas of conflict or events that the group intentionally decides to leave out of its official stories. Studying the minutes can give you some basic knowledge about the group;

for example, it can help you document the group's official actions in relation to a religious practice. As long as you treat this as only one limited piece of the puzzle, this historical record could be useful to you.

Nancy Ammerman and her colleagues provide guidelines for a systematic way to study a congregation's documentary archives. They offer a particularly helpful chart on "document content analysis" for those who want to do a rigorous examination of a congregation's history.[18] They also offer extremely helpful guidelines for obtaining and using census data.[19] This resource will be helpful even to those who are studying organizations other than congregations, who want to understand the make-up of a particular population. Additionally, these authors offer a helpful sidebar on "Methods of Analysis" that can help pastoral researchers move through complex organizing, ordering, and analyzing processes.[20]

As your research focus sharpens, consider as well the secondary documents and related literature that you have collected. One way of increasing your understanding of a religious practice in your local setting is to compare it to something similar in another setting, or to relate your local findings to a larger reality.[21] How does your case compare with studies of similar organizations in the community or in different locales? Do your findings match up with or challenge the wider denomination's theology or practices? Secondary reading can help you see your group's practices in light of wider customs, patterns, and possibilities.

Analyzing Material Evidence

Along with interview data and documentary sources, you may also need to analyze material evidence such as artifacts, landscapes, places, architecture, and spaces. You may have photographs of some of these, and written descriptions along with

---

18. Ammerman et al., *Studying Congregations*, 211.
19. Ibid., 213–17.
20. Ibid., 236.
21. Ibid.

vivid memories of others. Immerse yourself in these, scanning for details, surprises, or patterns.

As you look at all of your material evidence, how do you derive understanding from it? Colleen McDannell has helpfully laid out a process for analyzing material evidence that involves three phases: description, analysis, and interpretation. The first stage, *description,* involves noting the design, style, production, and patronage of things, with great specificity and attention to detail.[22] It may help to begin writing out careful descriptions of this evidence. Ask questions of the material evidence, such as, What is this building made of? Who donated the money to build it? What is the visual impact of walking into this space?

Drawing or obtaining simple diagrams or maps of material evidence can help you notice the properties and dimensions of objects, spaces, and places. If, for example, you are studying a group's use of a particular worship space, sketching out a simple map or acquiring the building plans drawn to scale can help you understand the features of the space more clearly. Looking at the layout of a sanctuary, you will be able to grasp such things as relationships of crèche to altar, or the distance between the access ramp and the seating for dis/abled persons. Similarly, neighborhood maps are tremendously helpful in understanding an organization's place and role in a community. Such diagrams and maps will also be useful later, when you are constructing your ethnographic narrative, because they will help the reader see the spatial layouts, distances, and proximities that you describe.

McDannell's second stage, *analysis,* involves looking at the way material objects or environments function in the life of the group. This includes understanding the "manifest functions" that are "intended and recognized by the participants in the culture."[23] These understood functions include the ways in which a particular article fits into the group's conventional theology, ritual, or

22. Colleen McDannell, "Interpreting Things: Material Culture Studies and American Religion" *Religion* 21 (1991): 371–87.
23. For an explanation of manifest functions, see Robert K. Merton, *Social Theory and Social Structure,* rev. ed. (Glencoe, Ill.: Free Press, 1975), 19–84.

ethics.[24] Additionally, you need to explore a range of popular functions of the evidence that may or may not be consistent with the intended or clerically sanctioned uses. If, for example, a choir loft is full of paid soloists who read the Sunday paper during worship in between performances, this probably represents an unintended and unsanctioned use of the space. In a case like this, try to note or discern all of the uses of a space, those that seem explicitly religious and orthodox and those that seem to be at odds with conventions or with spoken theologies. There can be more than one meaning, purpose, or use of a sacred space operating simultaneously.

The third and final phase that McDannell describes is called *interpretation*. This involves the researcher examining the symbolic functions of things, looking for intrinsic meanings that may go way beyond the avowed purpose of the article or the environment.[25] This form of analysis is somewhat akin to looking for themes or listening for the deeper meanings of stories. For example, if there is a large and prominently place stained-glass window depicting a picture of Jesus in the garden, it may have been donated for the avowed purpose of enhancing the worship experience to the glory of God. The window may actually function in this way for some individuals in the church. At the same time, you cannot help but notice that this is a picture of a white Jesus in a predominantly African American congregation. You start to wonder: isn't this window symbolically functioning to reenforce the idea that God is white, or that white skin is better, more holy than dark skin? Is a covert message that God supports the white society and its values being communicated? You can see that at the level of *interpretation,* the researcher's own ideas are brought into the analytical process more consciously and fully. It is also at the level of interpretation that the pastoral researcher might begin to wonder about liberating praxis in this setting.

---

24. McDannell, "Interpreting Things," 376.
25. Robert Merton refers to these as "latent functions." Merton, *Social Theory and Social Structure,* 36, cited in McDannell, "Interpreting Things," 367.

How might the congregation decide to alter its worship practices or space, so that a different message might be communicated?

In addition to this progressive form of analyzing material evidence, you might also try sorting photos and objects into some of the same categories and themes you identified in your textual data. Notice the congruencies and disparities between these different kinds of evidence. For example, if a main theme of the interviews seems to be a group's hospitality, but the material evidence reveals locked doors, poor signage, and no offerings of food or drink to newcomers, this suggests a disparity, a disconnect between ideas and practices. The group's practices do not appear to "speak" the people's stated values. This is an interesting point to ponder. Comparing different kinds of evidence against each other in this way is called *triangulation*.

Triangulation

According to Hammersley and Atkinson, the term "triangulation" derives from an analogy with navigation and surveying.[26] In locating your position on a map, you can get a more accurate reading if you can take your bearings in relation to two different landmarks, rather than one. You can imagine the three lines of a triangle mapping your position in relation to two others. In ethnography, similarly, if you take your meanings from one piece of data alone, you may not be able to get accurate "bearings" from it; you may misinterpret. If you look at two or more pieces of data related to the same phenomenon, you are likely to get a better reading. This does not guarantee that you are comprehending the phenomenon correctly, but it increases your chances of grasping the situation.

You can use triangulation in order to sharpen your analysis of various phenomena in your social setting. There are several different types of triangulation that you can use. The first is comparing data from different kinds of sources, such as in the

---

26. Hammersley and Atkinson, *Ethnography*, 231.

example above, where data from observations and study of material evidence are held up against the themes you find in interviews. Another example would be looking at newspaper accounts of a certain historical event (documentary evidence) alongside insider accounts from your research partners. Generally speaking, you will gain a fuller picture when you have at least two different sources. Another variation on this method is comparing several informants' accounts of the same data against each other. These practices can also help you check for the accuracy of the historical details of the stories you hear. If you discover contradictions or dissonance between and among your various sources, keep digging. This might suggest that something is at stake in the contested accounts.

Still another form of triangulation involves comparing the accounts of two or more different researchers. In *Being There*, the comparative study described in chapter 3, two researchers went to each theological school.[27] When two researchers study the same setting, they can meet to compare impressions and accounts, checking their inferences against each other's, and perhaps finding interesting contradictions and contingencies in their understandings of the data.

One more form of triangulation is called *respondent validation*. When the researchers in the thematic study of depression and spirituality (described above) shared their thematized narratives with their research participants, they were using respondent validation. Careful listening and story checks (described in chapter 6) also constitute a form of respondent validation. The main idea here is that you offer your understandings and your take on an interview or an event back to the research participants to see whether they find your analysis to be accurate and appropriate.

There are advantages and limitations to using respondent validation. One advantage is that you are allowing your research partners to co-author their own story. Ethically, this would seem advisable. There is less risk of causing harm or embarrassment to someone if you give him or her some control over the writing.

---

27. Carroll et al., *Being There*.

From a pastoral theological perspective as well, the goal of supporting emerging voices rather than speaking for participants is supported through the use of respondent validation. In terms of sharing power — exercising power *with* the people rather than power *over* them — this approach would seem well suited to pastoral ethnography.

Moreover, in light of the goal of producing knowledge, respondent validation may be helpful. Participants who are involved in the events you are documenting may have further knowledge of the context that they will share with you when they have a chance to see the way in which you are construing and possibly misconstruing their story. They may not be able to know, in advance, which crucial pieces of information you are missing in order to fully understand the data.[28]

The main limitation of respondent validation is that "we cannot assume that anyone is a privileged commentator on his or her own actions, in the sense that the truth of their account is guaranteed."[29] Research participants might have false information, or they might not be fully aware of all of the implications of their social interactions. Sometimes you, as a researcher, can see parts of the story that individual participants, from their vantage points, cannot see. Further, we know that people do sometimes lie or misrepresent themselves to researchers in order to influence the creation of a more favorable or flattering account. Here I think it is helpful to realize that doing ethnography is not the same thing as writing a person's or a group's autobiography. You as the researcher have a perspective to offer the group. If a participant disagrees with you, this is interesting and important information that may help you rethink your interpretations. Consider this feedback as data. It is not necessarily the case, however, that you are always wrong. Sometimes an accurate picture, held up like a mirror, provokes a strong reaction. From a pastoral perspective, this reaction is best handled as an opportunity for dialogue.

---

28. Hammersley and Atkinson, *Ethnography*, 228.
29. Ibid., 229.

Depending upon the nature of your study, it may not be necessary to seek respondent validation before you write your ethnography. In fact, the process of pastoral ethnography that I am putting forth in this book has a form of respondent validation built into it, though this "reflecting back" comes at a later stage in the journey. This is the *sharing event,* in which you present your ethnography or a part of it in some shape or form to your research participants. This part of the process will be explained in chapter 9. For now, let's look at an example of a student's ethnographic project that brings some of these various forms of analysis together in a coherent way.

Example: Putting It All Together

Eleanor is a researcher who studied the interrelationships among the residents of a denominationally based Protestant retirement home, where she served as chaplain. Eleanor was particularly interested in the interactions, or lack thereof, between residents in the "Assisted Living" section of the home and those in the "Nursing Care" section. The first group of residents was in generally better health and able to function more independently than the second group; those in the nursing section of the home had more acute illnesses and infirmities and needed more care. From her perspective as a Christian chaplain who valued caring relationships in community, Eleanor found it troubling that so little interaction seemed to be occurring between members of the two groups who lived in this home.

Eleanor was particularly troubled that even when two residents appeared to be close friends, if one of them was moved from assisted living to nursing care, the connection between them seemed to fade. Eleanor wondered what was preventing the residents in assisted living from walking down the hall to visit their friends and neighbors in nursing care.

Through her interviews, Eleanor learned that moving around without falling was a great challenge for most of the residents of the home. As Eleanor listened more carefully to her residents, she heard themes of vulnerability and concern for physical safety; the fear of falling in particular was noteworthy. Through observation and her own experience, she could see how easy it was to fall over someone else's walker, particularly in a crowded situation like waiting in line at the entrance to the dining hall. Doing the work of reflexivity, Eleanor realized that if she herself, young and agile, could almost fall over a walker during a worship service, then perhaps the residents' reluctance to simply "walk down the hall" to the other section of the home to visit a friend involved a reasonable concern over the risk of falling.

In analyzing her data, Eleanor used several tools. First, she decided to draw a map of the facility. This diagram showed the ways in which the residents' lives in the two sections of the building sometimes intersected and sometimes did not. In this case, the home had two separate dining rooms; this was one feature of the building and the administration of programs that tended to reinforce the separation of the groups. Some of this separation had to do with the practical matters related to care and the mobility of residents. Eleanor also noticed from her map that the physical structure of the home did not lend itself to easy maneuvering, especially for someone using a walker or wheelchair. There were corners to negotiate, elevators to ride, and heavy doors to be opened. There was also the possibility of getting lost, particularly for persons who were not familiar with the layout of the other side of the building or for persons experiencing cognitive decline.

When Eleanor could actually see all of this on the map, her understanding and empathy for the residents increased. She found herself judging them less and wondering how she and the administration of the home might try to reduce the physical and programmatic obstacles to community building.

In this example, we see how different forms of analysis can work together to help the ethnographer get a clearer view of what is happening in a setting. Observing large group meetings such as mealtimes and worship services gave Eleanor a chance to see the residents' movement patterns through the building, the obstacles, and their extent. Constructing the diagram helped Eleanor "see" how hard it could be for residents to navigate through unfamiliar territory, especially with their various dis/abilities and illnesses.

The interviews allowed Eleanor to find out more about the residents' experience of their lives in this setting. She also discovered that there were, in her words, "acts of kindness between residents that I do not always see."[30]

In this case, Eleanor did not change her theological commitment to the value of community building, which she understands as a central value in Christian life. Eleanor did experience a shift, however, as she came to appreciate the fears and challenges of living in either side of the home as the participants shared their stories. Eleanor developed more empathy, which enabled her to share, in a spirit of "journeying together across rough waters,"[31] an encouraging word about the value of the mutual care and connection that residents did enjoy, rather than blaming them for a lack of faithful practice. Eleanor began to think of ways to create or support community within the structure of the home's weekly worship service, such as by opening up a time for the residents to share their joys and concerns, or by inviting particular residents to serve as greeters. Eleanor then reflected on her ministry setting in light of some of the secondary literature she had been reading. She found both theological foundations and practical suggestions for encouraging community building among persons with dis/abilities in books by Harold Wilke and Nancy Eiesland.[32] Eleanor made good use of multiple sources and data sets as she analyzed her research questions and her reflexive role in the study. Eleanor did not use respondent validation to check her analysis early on in this case. Later, when she shared some of her findings with the residents through a sermon, she passed out forms on which residents could offer written feedback and thereby share

30. "Eleanor," Title Anonymous, unpublished paper, Wesley Theological Seminary, April 20, 2007, 29.

31. Ibid.

32. These books include Harold H. Wilke, *Creating the Caring Congregation: Guidelines for Ministering with the Handicapped* (Nashville: Abingdon Press, 1980); and Nancy L. Eiesland, *The Disabled God: Toward a Liberatory Theology of Disability* (Nashville: Abingdon Press, 1994). See also Nancy L. Eiesland and Don E. Saliers, eds., *Human Disability and the Service of God* (Nashville: Abingdon Press, 1998).

in the continuing conversation about caring relationships in the community of residents living in both sections of the home.

Summary

The process of organizing and analyzing data is a gradual one that is ongoing throughout each research journey. As you work your way through your data using the methods described in this chapter, you will discover that you are gradually moving from seeing things at face value, toward more complex understandings of your setting, and finally toward understanding some of the deeper or more significant social dynamics of the setting and your own role in these. You will be unearthing "the familiar in the apparently strange" and perhaps "the strange in the familiar" as well.[33] Pay attention to what surprises you, what moves you, what catches you off-guard. Stay open to your own creativity as you think about deeper meanings. Additionally, test your creative hunches against the data. Through this process you are seeking to assemble a puzzle that adds understanding and insight to your knowledge about the group.

As we saw in the case of writing thematized narratives, sometimes our grasp of the deeper issues is not fully realized until we begin to write about it. The writing process taps into our memories and creativity in a unique way. In the next chapter, we will explore the writing of ethnography as a pastoral practice.

For Further Study

Hammersley, Martyn, and Paul Atkinson, *Ethnography: Principles in Practice.* 2nd ed. New York: Routledge, 1995, chapter 8.
Mason, Jennifer. *Qualitative Researching,* 2nd ed. Thousand Oaks, Calif.: SAGE Publications, 2005, chapters 8 and 9.
Swinton, John, and Harriet Mowat. *Practical Theology and Qualitative Research*. London: SCM Press, 2006. See especially chapter 4.

---

33. Hammersley and Atkinson, *Ethnography,* 207.

- E I G H T -

Writing It Up

Composing the Story

Baseball is 90 percent mental and the other half is physical.
— YOGI BERRA

There comes a point in the journey of pastoral ethnography when it is time to start writing it up. This point ought to come sooner rather than later. My use of the phrase, "writing it up," may seem to imply that the task of writing ethnography is a simple or mechanical activity.[1] In reality, writing pastoral ethnography involves rigorous rational thinking as well as a more receptive kind of reflection on the language, themes, and theological hunches that "bubble up" in the mind. Playing off of Yogi Berra's famous baseball mathematics, we could say that writing ethnography is ninety percent mental rigor and the other half is inspiration.

Still, let us not make the writing process sound too mysterious. The act of sitting down and starting to write is, for many, the hardest part. We do not need another excuse to postpone getting started, because we are waiting around for the muse. It is better to simply begin, reminding ourselves that the first draft is not the final product. Rather, writing is a discovery process that unfolds over time. Once we show up at the desk and start to write, inspiration often arrives. Even when we feel uninspired, it is a good idea to keep trying to write something. If this fails, come back to the desk (or any other place set aside for writing) the next day,

---

1. Hammersley and Atkinson, *Ethnography*, 240.

191

ready to try again. This discipline creates an opening for inspiration. It is like putting a welcome sign out for our creative energy and trusting that it will come in and pay us a visit.

Though individuals' cognitive processes do vary, the usual source of inspiration for writing ethnography is the experiential learning that occurs through engagement in all of the various phases of research. This experiential learning stays with the researcher, accumulating in the form of hunches and insights, which then get examined and interrogated through the work of analysis. The activity of writing taps into all of this accumulated experience and cognitive work. The ethnographer gradually discovers words that can represent the social world in which she has been immersed.

Getting Ready to Write

One way to deal with the resistance that inevitably accompanies the work of writing is to read widely. This practice also helps you understand the form and structure of writing ethnography. Reading a variety of ethnographic and congregational studies can help you see a range of models and approaches to the use of theory and structure in this form of writing. (See the list of suggested exemplary texts at the end of this chapter.) Read the introductions and appendices of these studies carefully in order to understand the authors' choices in regard to literary form, structure, theory, and conclusions. This kind of reading allows you to see models of how others have composed their work. You might find in this reading some language or style or structure that sparks your imagination for your own writing.

In addition to reading exemplary studies, read other forms of writing such as fiction and investigative reporting in order to "loosen up" your writing muscles. The goal is to get limber with your use of language. As Hammersley and Atkinson put it, "One may ask how different authors conjure up the spirit of a place, evoke its inhabitants, and construct cultural forms."[2] The way in

---

2. Ibid., 244.

which you write matters: it affects the cogency and readability of the ethnography. Well-chosen and vibrant language can help you bring a vivid and engaging narrative into being.

Also read scripture, commentary, and theology — found in both your research setting and in your own library. This kind of reading can help you become more agile in the work of theological reflection that is integral to the writing project. While theological reflection constitutes one of the steps in the rubric offered below (see Figure 6, p. 205), your use of religious stories or the vocabulary of faith should not be limited to one small section of the ethnography. Through reading and reflection upon the faith literature of your group, you will replenish the well of words, images, verses, stories, doctrines, and hymns from which you can draw throughout the writing process. By attending to your own religious or spiritual reading, you will enhance your ability to write theologically about your reflexive experience of the research.

Audience

Who is your audience? The answer to this question will shape your writing profoundly. Authors who write different accounts of the same research for different audiences illustrate this point well.[3] The work of sociologist Samuel Heilman offers a good example of this dynamic in the study of religious practices. In 1983, Heilman published *The People of the Book,* a scholarly account of his research on the Orthodox Jewish practice of *lernen,* the review and ritualized study of sacred Jewish texts.[4] In this engaging narrative, told mostly in the third person, Heilman utilizes the theoretical categories of Erving Goffman,[5] among others, to analyze the Orthodox Jews he studied. Heilman refers to his role

3. See Laurel Richardson, *Writing Strategies: Reaching Diverse Audiences* (Newbury Park, Calif.: SAGE Publications, 1990).

4. Samuel C. Heilman, *The People of the Book: Drama, Fellowship, and Religion* (Chicago: University of Chicago Press, 1983), 1.

5. See, for example, Erving Goffman, *The Presentation of Self in Everyday Life* (New York: Doubleday, 1959); and Goffman, *Strategic Interaction* (Philadelphia: University of Pennsylvania Press, 1972).

in the research with the practiced distance of a scholar, coolly describing his parts in the social drama he depicts. Only briefly, in the epilogue, does Heilman acknowledge that the research had any effect on him.[6] Clearly, in this book, Heilman's primary audience is an academic one.

A few years later, in 1986, Heilman wrote another book about the same research, this time focusing on his personal and religious experience in conducting the study. In this account, *The Gate behind the Wall: A Pilgrimage to Jerusalem*,[7] Heilman tells quite a different story: here he describes his research as his own religious pilgrimage. This book is written for an audience of coreligionists. The tone, style, and to some degree the substance of the two books differ dramatically. The first might be considered an example of "realist" writing, and the second might be called "confessional."[8] These are two well-written accounts, offered to distinctly different audiences.

Think about the audience that you have in mind for your ethnographic writing. Your primary audience may be your professor and your academic class, a group with whom you share particular assumptions, language, and interests. Your audience may be your peer group of researchers in congregational or hospital settings. You might also be considering publishing your work in any one of a variety of forms: an academic journal or monograph, a popular magazine or trade journal, or a more personal book for a general audience. Your decision about your audience will affect your writing style, your word choice, and the material you cover.

If this is your first attempt at pastoral ethnography, you may be writing primarily for yourself in order to gain clarity about your congregation or agency, your calling, and your relationship with the people you serve. Even if you do not plan to publish your work, once the ethnography is written and submitted, there is always the possibility that someone else may see it. As you write, bear in mind the effect that your account might have on any

---

6. Heilman, *The People of the Book*, 295–96.
7. Samuel Heilman, *The Gate behind the Wall: A Pilgrimage to Jerusalem* (New York: Penguin, 1986).
8. Hammersley and Atkinson, *Ethnography*, 260.

potential readers, including your research participants or other members of the group. Take care to honor your consent agreements and represent your findings in a way that is respectful to your research participants.

Your choice of audience will also influence the way that you frame the narrative. Nancy Ammerman and her colleagues explain some examples for possible frames or perspectives that can be used with congregational studies. These include: the *ecological frame,* which focuses on the congregation in relationship to its neighborhood, region, or denomination; the *cultural frame,* which concentrates on group rituals, practices, theology, and identity; the *resources frame,* which studies the financial and social capital of the group; and the *process frame,* which concentrates on the internal dynamics and flow of the organization.[9] Pastoral ethnography can involve any of these, or some combination of them. There are other possible frames as well, ranging from macro frames that take the larger socioeconomic picture into consideration, to micro studies that focus in on a very close-up analysis of one particular aspect of personal experience. Frame your writing in such a way that it will be comprehensible and useful to your chosen audience.

Forms and Conventions

Ethnographic writing involves particular forms and conventions. Ethnography is best understood as a narrative form of writing, which means that it is organized as a story and told in prose, describing events that involve characters and a plot. This narrative form is not to be confused with fiction. A work of fiction is an invented story that has its own distinct structural elements or modes of delivery. In writing pastoral ethnography, we strive to offer reliable, valid, and sensitive portrayals of real people and their religious practices. While reading fiction can help stir up the imagination for writing clear and vibrant prose, we do not want to get carried away with the idea of writing a good story to the point of embellishing the data.

---

9. Ammerman et al., *Studying Congregations,* 13–16 et passim.

Ethnographic writing aims to tell the truth. In truth, we know that our accounts are constructions, representations of social worlds that involve our perceptions and interactions in the setting. There are imagined elements in our limited understandings that we will never be able to completely avoid. There are also personal and political interests involved in ethnographic writing that influence the way we tell the story, the slant we give it, the parts we highlight, the parts we hide. We make disciplined efforts to tell a reliable and comprehensive story, though we are aware of our limitations. In ethnography, we tell *our* story about the group, but it ought it to be a true story, like a memoir, told as accurately and honestly as possible.[10]

Of course, there are exceptions. In one of the exemplary texts recommended as further reading in chapter 4, *Mama Lola,* author Karen McCarthy Brown intentionally uses fiction in every other chapter. In doing this, she is "true" to the form of the Vodou practice that she is describing, which involves prodigious story-telling. Brown's shorter fictive chapters tell stories that convey the gist of numerous stories Brown heard told and retold in various bits and pieces during her years of research. These stories are Brown's own imaginative constructions. She says that writing them that allowed her to "tap a reservoir of casual and imagistic knowledge, which all people who have done fieldwork have but do not ordinarily get to use."[11] The form and structure of Brown's pivotal book serves to push questions of epistemology, truth, politics, and poetics in the study of religion. Suffice it to say that these questions remain alive.[12]

---

10. While ethnography is like a memoir in the ways suggested above, these two forms are not identical. Ethnography involves more authorial distance than memoir does. Though the degree to which authorial distance is appropriate or possible in ethnography is much debated, the practices of research, data collection, and rigorous analysis foster a degree of critical distance in this form of writing. In a memoir, which is primarily based on the author's personal experience, there is less room for and expectation of authorial distance.

11. Brown, *Mama Lola,* 18.

12. See, for example, James V. Spickard, J. Shawn Landres, and Meredith B. McGuire, eds., *Personal Knowledge and Beyond: Reshaping the Ethnography of*

Pastoral ethnography also seeks to speak the truth in love (Eph. 4:15). Whatever the form and style you decide upon, strive to be clear about it — transparent — in your writing. If you are planning to alter identifying details for the protection of your research partners, state this clearly up front. Explain the use of pseudonyms. These efforts belong to the ethical dimensions of writing ethnography. Seek to tell the fullest story you know, with respect and care for your research partners.

Ask yourself questions such as these: What is the warp and woof of life in this setting? Who are the main characters and what is the action or plot unfolding? What are the underlying themes of group life here in this place and time? The goal of most pastoral ethnography is not so much to create a theory as it is to offer a "thick description" that increases the readers' understanding of these people and their practices.

Thick Description

"Thick description" is a classic term made popular through the work of the anthropologist Clifford Geertz. For Geertz, thick description named the particular intellectual effort involved in ethnography.[13] A thick description is a detailed and interpretive description that conveys your understanding of the deep meanings of your observations. Thick description goes beyond the literal and expresses the tacit import of a gesture, word, or action in this particular context.

Geertz borrowed this term and a great example from Gilbert Ryle.[14] According to Ryle, thick description is a thorough and detailed description of a sign that reveals all of its possible meanings.

Religion (New York: New York University Press, 2002); and Robert A. Orsi, *Between Heaven and Earth: The Religious Worlds People Make and the Scholars Who Study Them* (Princeton, N.J.: Princeton University Press, 2005).

13. Geertz, *The Interpretation of Cultures*, 1–30. Thick description is also used in theology, notably in George Lindbeck's cultural-linguistic approach. See George A. Lindbeck, *The Church in a Postliberal Age*, ed. James J. Buckley (Grand Rapids: Wm. B. Eerdmans, 2002).

14. Gilbert Ryle, "Collected Papers," cited in Geertz, *The Interpretation of Cultures*, 6.

Ryle used the example of a "wink of an eye" to explain his point. "When a man winks, is he merely 'rapidly contracting his right eyelid,' or is he 'practicing a burlesque of a friend faking a wink to deceive an innocent into thinking conspiracy is in motion'?" Is a wink "an involuntary twitch" or "a conspiratorial sign"?[15] Writing ethnography involves decoding signs, behaviors, and stories, in such a way as to "read" the culture that they represent. This is no easy task. As Geertz put it,

> Doing ethnography is like trying to read (in the sense of "construct a reading of") a manuscript — foreign, faded, full of ellipses, incoherencies, suspicious emendations, and tendentious commentaries, but written not in conventionalized graphs of sound but in transient examples of shaped behavior.[16]

Thick description is an attempt to tell the story of your group in its social setting that draws from all of your data — "transient examples of shaped behavior" — an interpretation of culture.

Swinton and Mowat add that good qualitative descriptions should be both *thick* and *rich*. Though this may sound like an advertisement for ice cream, the term rich here is used to denote creditability. A rich description is a faithful and recognizable description of a setting or an experience.[17] One mark of creditability would be that other people could recognize the setting or the experience described, if they encountered it, after only reading your study.[18] Your description should resonate with what another observer might experience. A thick and rich description will be a trustworthy account, one that conveys to the reader the fullness of the social setting and the range of meanings that words and practices connote in this context.

---

15. Ibid.

16. Ibid., 10.

17. Swinton and Mowat, *Practical Theology and Qualitative Research*, 122.

18. Ibid., citing M. Sandelowski, "The Problem of Rigour in Qualitative Research," *Advances in Nursing Science* 8, no. 3 (1986): 27–37.

Literary Conventions

As you write your ethnographic narrative, you will be trying to describe and summarize large amounts material in a relatively few pages.[19] You will naturally make use of writing conventions such as figures of speech or tropes. These might include analogy, metaphor, simile, and synecdoche. Such rhetorical devices help convey or evoke meaning in precise and compelling ways.

Metaphor is that figure of speech whereby "we speak of one thing in terms suggestive of another."[20] We find metaphors in everyday conversation and in every form of writing. They help us comprehend complicated information clearly and quickly. Metaphors sometimes arise in the author's mind during the process of reflection and writing, while she tries to find words to describe something. A metaphor does not describe a phenomenon directly, but illuminates meaning by suggesting a comparison to something else. As Janet Soskice puts it, "A strong metaphor compels new possibilities of vision."[21] It has an impact on our understanding. When the psalmist writes, "The Lord is my shepherd" (Ps. 23:1), for example, he is speaking metaphorically. The metaphor conjures up the protective care of a shepherd toward sheep, suggesting a vivid understanding of the care of the Lord.

Simile is a close relative of metaphor. Simile also suggests a comparison, but usually in a different grammatical form. Similes use the words "like" or "as" to illustrate or model comparisons. "The sanctuary was as dark as a cave," is an example of simile, though not a very inspiring one. "God, who brings them out of Egypt, is like the horns of a wild ox for them" (Num. 23:22). This is a more vibrant and surprising simile.

While the right figure of speech will convey meaning with stunning clarity, like a digital photograph, most writers' first drafts are considerably murkier. Anne Lamott, in her endearing writing manual *Bird by Bird*, uses the analogy of a Polaroid photograph

---

19. For the first-time pastoral ethnographer, I suggest a limit of twenty-five pages of text with additional materials attached in an appendix.

20. Janet Martin Soskice, *Metaphor and Religious Language* (Oxford: Clarendon Press, 1985), 1, 54.

21. Ibid., 58.

to describe most writers' first drafts.[22] For those readers who are too young to remember, Polaroid cameras have a special kind of film that begins to develop itself moments after the picture is taken. Polaroid films start out all green and gooey and murky-looking, but as you hold them in your hand, the colors brighten and the picture gradually becomes clear. When you begin to write descriptively, your early drafts may seem more like a gooey, developing Polaroid than a sharp digital image.

If your first drafts seem murky, don't despair. Writing is a recursive practice; you have to go back over your drafts many times before the picture fully develops. Tell your ethnographic story in the descriptive language that comes to you naturally. Do not try to make up metaphors or similes, but allow yourself to use the words and ideas that bubble up from your immersion in your data and from your analytic thinking. Then, after some time has passed, go back and scrutinize your use of language and writing conventions. Is your meaning made crisp and vivid by your comparisons, or is it still a bit gooey?

Hammersley and Atkinson suggest that you test your use of metaphors against your ethnographic data, using the following criteria to evaluate your choices: simplicity, cogency, and range. A simple comparison is economical; it doesn't waste words. It is easier to follow than a long and complicated comparison. A cogent metaphor is one that efficiently extends meaning, without ambiguity. Range has to do with the capacity of the metaphor to draw together different domains of data under a single theme.[23] To say that an organization is mired in controversy, for example, is a simple and cogent use of metaphor. It suggests a group that is characterized by anxious debates, frantically striving but getting nowhere. When reviewing your use of metaphor, think about the logical conclusions to which it might lead. If the implied comparison is crisp and apt, keep it. If, on the other hand, you realize that

22. Anne Lamott, *Bird by Bird: Some Instructions on Writing and Life* (New York: Anchor, 1994), 39–43.
23. Hammersley and Atkinson, *Ethnography,* 246–47, citing G. W. Noblit and R. D. Hare, *Meta-Ethnography: Synthesizing Qualitative Studies* (Newbury Park, Calif.: SAGE Publications, 1988), 34.

a metaphor or simile introduces connotations that are confusing or contradictory, drop it like a hot potato!

Another figure of speech used in ethnography is synecdoche. A synecdoche is a term denoting a part of something that comes to stand for the whole. While synecdoche is most commonly used in poetry, ethnographers also make use of this device in order to exemplify or illustrate their findings. As Hammersley and Atkinson put it, "The metaphor transforms and illuminates while the synecdoche describes and exemplifies."[24] As you do the work of analysis, you are often thinking about the relationship of various parts of your data to the whole of your study. When you cite one example from the data to give an illustration of a typical case, this is a form of synecdoche. You cannot possibly cite all the data or tell every story. So you choose one that you find particularly representative. The use of synecdoche can help make your ethnography more precise and more telling.

Sometimes a synecdoche seems to come to you as you try to describe your broad findings. One part of the data seems to suggest a deep insight about the whole story. When such a synecdoche occurs to you, test it against the data to make sure that it offers a valid glimpse of the whole. Use the synecdoche if it rings true in an overall way. If you find exceptions or challenges to this idea, note them as well.

Be careful not to get carried away with redundant or showy language, as in another famous Yogi Berra quotation: "It's like déjà-vu, all over again." Redundancies occur naturally in first drafts, when you are struggling to understand the material yourself even as you are trying to describe it to others. As you go back over your drafts, eliminate repetition as much as possible. This will conserve space and keep your reader's interest. Beware of fancy language. Remember Strunk and White's famous admonition against "putting a hat on a horse."[25] Just as a horse would look ridiculous in a hat, some words look silly when you add "ly"

---

24. Hammersley and Atkinson, *Ethnography,* 248.
25. William Strunk Jr. and E. B. White, *The Elements of Style,* 3rd ed. (New York: Macmillan, 1979), 76.

thusly. Do not dress up your language; instead work for clarity and flow.

Example: A Tower Clock

A doctor of ministry student submitted a particularly well-written pastoral ethnography entitled *The Tower Clock Has Stopped*.[26] In this paper, a newly appointed senior pastor narrates the "family history" of his congregation in order to try to understand how the church developed into what he terms, "a very low commitment congregation."[27] The author, whom we will call Art, relied on several forms of research, including unstructured interviews and the review of archival material in order to reconstruct the story of this nearly two-hundred-year-old small-town Protestant congregation, located in the Northeast.

In the very first paragraph, Art describes the bell tower vividly: "Looking out from all four sides, the white clock faces with black hands, encased with bright silver bezels and Plexiglas covers, look like giant pocket watches suspended from the tower parapets."[28] Note his use of the image of suspended pocket watches, in a simile that helps the reader imagine the look of the tower. More significantly, the image of the broken clock, introduced first in the title, "The Tower Clock has Stopped," metaphorically suggests the stopped or stuck life of the congregation itself. From his interviews and documentary research, Art pieced together a developmental story marked by several incidents of betrayal and unsavory "family secrets" in the life of the congregation. Art's interpretation is that these old wounds, unresolved and kept secret, function to block "the works" of congregational life. The title suggests a bold comparison between the very graphic and public display of stopped time on the tower clock and a profoundly low level of commitment of the members inside the building. The congregation is stuck, held back in time.

---

26. "Art," "The Tower Clock Has Stopped," unpublished paper, Wesley Theological Seminary, March 28, 2007.
27. Ibid., 3.
28. Ibid., 1.

This well-chosen metaphor is derived from the setting itself. It powerfully conveys a deep if painful understanding of the life of the group. At the same time, no one metaphor can say it all. In Art's research, he also heard some stories of faithfulness amid the betrayals and stuckness. He heard stories of individuals' integrity and courageous responses to God's call in their lives. Art includes these stories in his ethnography and suggests that they are evidence of the Holy Spirit at work in this congregation. Art brings forth this alternative or "counterstory,"[29] interpreting it theologically as a sign of hope in the midst of the serious difficulties he has discovered. The tension between the clock metaphor and the counterstory does not need to be fully resolved. The narrative form of ethnography can hold this complexity well.

As a pastor new to this setting, Art is sobered by what he has learned about the church's history. Yet he finds hope in the counterstory and in the candid way in which the members shared their memories with him. He uses another revealing metaphor to describe his growing relationship to the congregation. "I came to understand that I was experiencing a postnuptial ritual of sorts. I was being told about all the crazy in-laws by the in-laws who had already come to accept me and had begun to love me."[30] This new understanding helps Art to discern the particular kind of pastoral leadership that this congregation needs from him at this time in history.

A Rubric for Pastoral Ethnography

Writing ethnography as a pastoral practice involves bringing together several aspects of your ethnographic journey. Figure 6 presents a step-by-step rubric suitable as a class assignment in a pastoral ethnography course. The rubric lists the basic components of pastoral ethnography in a logical progression. Because writing is a creative and fluid process, the order of the steps is flexible. Your construction of the narrative may take a more creative

---

29. For an explanation of the therapeutic and theological importance of counterstories, see Neuger, *Counseling Women*, 134–37.

30. Ibid., 21.

or artistic shape. Moreover, the social setting you are studying might suggest a different, more compelling writing structure. As long as you include the components in the rubric and offer them in a coherent sequence, feel free to follow the muse.

Steps one through four of the rubric constitute part 1 of your ethnography. This introduction should orient the reader to the people in their social setting. Remember that this introduction to your setting is also the introduction to the story of your research journey. In the very first paragraph, give the reader at least some intimation or foreshadowing of your main conclusion. What is the theme of this story? Allude to findings if you do not state them outright.

Introduce yourself, explaining your role in relationship to the group, be it as a pastor, rabbi, member, student intern, staff member, chaplain, teacher, dean, board member, director, friend, or neighbor. How long have you been there? What is the nature of your current relationships there? Include any pertinent information about your social location that has a bearing on your relationships in this group. Briefly describe how you are like the people in this setting and how you are unlike them.

Step two involves laying out your basic research question and the theory, strategy, and methods you used to study a particular practice. You can look back to your original research plan when you are writing this section. Explain the type of intellectual puzzle you are working with and why you chose the research methods that you did. Delineate the scope of your study, explaining your sample selection — who and how many people you set out to interview or survey — and who you actually ended up interviewing, how many surveys came back, and so on. Give a broad description of the events that you observed, their properties and dimensions.

Step three asks you to recall your theological motivation at the start of this study. Even if your understanding of the theology-in-practice of the group has evolved in the course of your research, help the reader understand your starting point. Again, consulting your original research plan might be helpful. Try to push yourself a bit, to go beneath the surface. If you began with strong feelings

Figure 6. A Rubric for Writing Pastoral Ethnography

Part One

1. Write an introduction to your ethnographic study, beginning with a brief description of the congregation or group you studied (social, historical, cultural, and theological background) and your usual role there.

2. Explain your research question or questions and the strategy and methods you used to obtain knowledge in this setting. What is the religious practice that you set out to query? Give the rationale for your choice.

3. Explain your motivation for the study, your theology, and the expectations that you began with.

4. Describe how the research went for you, what you were able to accomplish, and what roadblocks you ran into along the way. Include a brief description of the ethical safeguards you used for the protection of your research participants, highlighting any new ethical issues that emerged in the research process and explaining how you addressed them.

Part Two

5. State your main research findings. Write a thick and rich description of how you came to this conclusion. Cite data and examples along the way, building an argument for your interpretation. Be sure to include some reflection on social capital and power dynamics.

6. Include a section on reflexivity: How do you think your presence influenced your results? Were there any surprises? What touched you or moved you? What did you learn about the people? Yourself?

7. How has your experience of conducting the research made an impact on your relationships with the persons in the study? What, if anything, has changed?

8. What are the pastoral-theological implications that your research suggests? What new understandings of God's presence in the community emerge for you? What new energy for transformation can you perceive or anticipate at this time?

Part Three

9. Summarize your paper, tying steps six through eight back to your stated conclusions.

10. Include in an appendix:

    ✓ Copies of signed consent forms (or an unsigned copy if confidentiality agreements require this)

    ✓ Lists of questions used in interviews or surveys

    ✓ Any graphs or tables of quantified data that you have c

    ✓ Any illustrations or diagrams that help present the data

    ✓ Copies of photographs or videos that are key to your a

about the subject matter, describe these convictions. Maybe the practice of infant baptism really bothered you; maybe your vision of justice was at stake. Share your convictions, acknowledging any biases that you are aware of bringing to this study. What did you expect to find?

With step four, tell the story of how the research went. Were there any obstacles or detours along the way? What did you make of them? Sometimes the detours are the most interesting part of the journey. If, in the course of your research, the questions or the methods were revised, explain how these decisions unfolded. The reader should be able to follow the path of your research journey and understand your rationale for the major decisions you took along the way. Also in this section, describe your research ethics and the approach you took to caring for the safety and privacy of your research participants. Describe any ethical questions that came up for you in the process of the research or the writing and explain how you handled them. Include your deliberations regarding the use of any visual media.

Steps five through eight of the rubric comprise part 2, the body of the paper. This is where you will be offering an answer to your main research question. For step five, try to formulate a simple and concise statement of your main conclusion. How did you arrive at this conclusion? Did you use deductive, inductive, or abductive reasoning? How did you decide to read your data (literally, interpretively, reflexively)? Lay out your analysis, showing rather than telling the reader how you arrived at your conclusions, citing examples from the data to illustrate the story. Include critical reflection on issues of power and social capital in this setting.

The best way to start this process is to go back to your original puzzle. The different types of intellectual puzzles lend themselves to different kinds of arguments. If yours is a developmental puzzle, you will be trying to find an explanation in the group's history for the development of the current religious practice or other phenomenon that you are studying. Your explanation might take the form of a story, as in the case of Art's ethnography, described above. The story must be substantiated by your findings. Explain to the reader how you arrived at the particular version of history that you are proffering. How did you piece it together? How did you evaluate the diverse stories people told? Did you use triangulation, bringing documentary evidence together with insiders' accounts? How did you analyze interviews? If there are key themes that numerous sources in your data pointed to, describe them vividly and refer to quotations and images (and perhaps photographs) from your data to help make your case. Use your imagination to help convey and evoke the tacit meanings that you have identified through your research experience.

If your puzzle is a mechanical one, describe what you take to be the best explanation for how this religious practice really works in your particular setting. Of course, there are usually multiple functions and meanings behind any one religious practice. Explain the possible and likely functions, letting the reader know what you learned from the data and how you came to your conclusions. What categories did you use to analyze your data, how did you compare various explanations, and what in your observations, reading, or reflection finally convinced you that your understanding is compelling? Again, use examples from your data that help give the flavor of your research experience. Include enough contextual detail to help the reader get a feel for the setting and an appreciation for the logic behind the practices you are attempting to explain.

If your puzzle is a comparative one, explain the main axis of comparison in your study and how your research sample did or did not help you arrive at any conclusions. Explain how you organized, analyzed, cross-referenced, and interpreted your data. Don't draw simple comparisons, but flesh them out with thick description. Add nuance to your argument by explaining what you make of the exceptions or contradictions in your data.

For example, if you are comparing the worship styles at two services, you might have come to the conclusion that one service is wildly successful and well attended, while the other is small and far less energetic. You could offer a detailed description of how you arrived at this conclusion, making a compelling case for the vibrancy of the first service and supporting it with illustrations from your data that demonstrate high levels of committed participation. By comparison, you could point out that the second service is repetitive and relatively dull. You could offer evidence of low attendance, cite occasions when you could see (and maybe even hear) people sleeping through the worship, and make a case that there are few, if any, signs of spiritual growth in this service. This analysis offers a simple and clear contrast. However, you have also been puzzling over some exceptions or contradictions to your main conclusion: a few of the most committed church leaders always choose the small service; they say it feeds their souls. Also, on certain occasions, the otherwise apparently dull, small service always draws a crowd. This doesn't support your main conclusion, but it is an interesting part of the story that merits mention and analysis. This might even be considered a counterstory that challenges the majority view. Including it and your reflections on it adds depth and nuance to your narrative.

A predictive puzzle involves more use of deductive reasoning. In this case, you started by asking a question, offering a theory or a hunch — a hypothesis — and then doing research to test the theory. Tell the reader which categories you used to sort the data and to cross-reference it. If this resulted in a number of graphs and tables, include them in an appendix. More important, though, explain how you read these tables and what conclusions you draw from them and why. Does your data really speak to your theory, or does it suggest something a little different from what you were expecting? What further study is needed to fill out our understanding of this phenomenon? As in the other kinds of puzzles, let readers see how you went about putting the pieces together in the way that you did to arrive at this particular conclusion.

Step six spirals back to reflexivity. How do you think your presence in the research field influenced your findings? Presumably, you have been "prewriting" for this section all along, in your research journal. Here you want to bring your presence more explicitly into the narrative. Do you think that people were on their best behavior in the interviews, saying what they thought you wanted to hear? Or did you feel hurt at their brutal honesty?

Were there any surprises? Surprises are important because they signal the places where your assumptions are up-ended. This is often where real learning occurs. When you are surprised, pay attention, reflect, and wonder. Ask yourself: what is really going on? Allow yourself to be moved by what you are learning.

Sometimes new insight dawns during the actual writing process, when you take the time to find words for your formerly inchoate hunches. If you feel that this is happening, say a prayer, light a candle, and stay with it. This is one of the goals of doing pastoral ethnography: that new understandings of the people, the faith, or even of God might break through into conscious awareness. What are you learning about the people? What are you learning about yourself? Write about this experience as openly and honestly as possible. When writing the first draft, pour out your insights freely. Later, use discernment to determine what parts of this introspective writing you want to include in the narrative.

Step seven asks you to bring a similar kind of energy to the work of reflecting on any changes that your research may be prompting in relationships at your research site. This might involve you and a sense of a shift in the dynamics of your relationship with the people you serve. You might notice some changes in the ways that people in the setting are getting along with each other or interacting with newcomers. Many of my students have reported that their research participants expressed gratitude for the chance to speak and be heard. A few students have reported some difficulty negotiating the shift in their pastoral role to that of a researcher. Describe whatever changes you perceive, for good or for ill, and explain how you think they came about.

Step eight invites you to move back along the spiral to more theological reflection. While your theology is at least implicitly present in the entire narrative, now articulate it explicitly again (as you did at the start of your writing), explaining any shifts or new understandings that have emerged along the way. As you reflect on the larger story of this group of people, yourself, and your research journey, where do you sense the presence of God? Where have you experienced "effects and traces" of the holy?[31] It may be helpful to follow a prescribed model for theological reflection. Among the many good models available, Pamela Cooper-White's proposal is particularly well suited for ethnography, especially in light of our emphasis on reflexivity.[32]

Cooper-White's model involves three steps. The first is free association. Adapting her phrase, we might ask, "What theological or spiritual themes pop into my mind as I sit with this research?"[33] A biblical story, image, or saying may come to mind. A theological theme from your particular tradition may pop up. Here is where all of your preparatory reading will be helpful. A sacramental theme, a piece of poetry, a hymn, an image, or a metaphor from a novel or even a piece of political commentary may come to mind. Maybe you will remember a phrase or a story from an interview or a movement in a ritual you observed. Write it all down. Take dictation from the deep. Do not censor anything in this phase of reflection.[34]

The second step in Cooper-White's model for theological reflection is critical thinking. If one of the images or theological ideas seems particularly fitting, work with it for a while. Ask yourself whether it really fits the social setting you have been studying. Does this image seem to illuminate your understanding of the people and their experience of God? Does it suggest any "deeper and more empathic ways" of engaging in authentic pastoral practice?[35]

Step three in Cooper-White's model entails planning for pastoral practice in this setting. How does the theological theme or image inform your care for the people in this time and place? This kind of reflection helps you reassess your own pastoral practice in light of your dawning theological understandings.[36] Given what

---

31. Graham, *Transforming Practice*, 207.
32. Cooper-White, *Shared Wisdom*, 74–79.
33. Ibid., 74.
34. Ibid., 74–76.
35. Ibid., 76–77.
36. Ibid., 77.

you have learned, is there a metaphor, image, or model that illuminates what your group needs from its leaders? In the example of Art's congregation, noted earlier in the chapel, he decided his role ought to be that of a "wounded healer,"[37] helping people come to terms with their hidden history that has kept them frozen in time, like their tower clock.

This last phase of theological reflection leads naturally to describing the broader pastoral-theological implications that your research suggests. What have you learned about religious leadership in this setting? Here is where you may wish to bring in some of the secondary reading you have been doing about your particular topic. Be careful not to overgeneralize. Instead, offer some of the "situated wisdom" of your setting. Hold your new wisdom lightly; offer it gently as a gift, not arrogantly as a rule. For example, if you think you have achieved a new level of trust in your group because you took the time to listen, explain how you might build more time and opportunities for dialogue into your organization's life. Maybe you will not decide to add new programs, but rather revise the approach taken to existing programs and procedures. For instance, you might come up with a way to make sure that each person attending a council meeting routinely gets a chance to speak without interruption. Share your practical ideas about how you might plan to offer patient listening and support the voices of those who are marginalized in your community's life together.

Now think about the level of energy and enthusiasm of your group at the present time. Has your research process sparked any new energy for transformation in the community? For example, is one person encouraged or enlivened in his spiritual life? Describe the changes that you witness or hear that person describe. Perhaps a group practice is receiving renewed attention. If your research has opened a vein of vitality, describe this, reflect on it, and spin out some possibilities for supporting and enhancing

---

37. This metaphor for ministry comes from the work of Henri Nouwen, *The Wounded Healer: Ministry in Contemporary Society* (New York: Image, Doubleday, 1979).

this potential growth in the community. If this has not happened, but instead you have gained a fuller understanding of a "low-commitment" group, explain any ideas you have for helping the group get "unstuck."

Step nine invites you to summarize your learning and your reflections, being sure to tie the work of steps six through eight back to your concise statement of research findings. Highlight its connection to your theological reflections. Leave the reader no doubt as to your interpretation of your study, summarizing your reasoning and conclusions in a brief and compelling way. Let your words convey your sense of the holy, made known to you in sacred story and in the stories you have heard, and beckoning forth new and faithful chapters of shared life.

Step ten reminds you to include supporting documents in one or more appendices to the paper: signed consent forms, lists of questions used, graphs or tables of data, illustrations or diagrams, photographs or videos.

In the next chapter, we will explore the work of intentionally sharing some or all of your findings with the people in your research setting. This careful process can be a catalyst for continuing growth in the community of faith. This sharing can open up the riches of your learning through new forms of conversation and faithful practice.

For Further Study

Hammersley, Martyn, and Paul Atkinson, *Ethnography: Principles in Practice.* 2nd ed. New York: Routledge, 1995, chapter 9.

Lamott, Anne. *Bird by Bird: Some Instructions on Writing and Life.* New York: Anchor Books, 1994, part 1.

Strunk, William, Jr., and E. B. White. *The Elements of Style.* 3rd ed. New York: Macmillan, 1979, especially chapter 5.

Exemplary Texts

Eiesland, Nancy L. *A Particular Place: Urban Restructuring and Religious Ecology in a Southern Exurb.* New Brunswick, N.J.: Rutgers University Press, 2000.

Fishburn, Janet F., ed. *People of a Compassionate God: Creating Welcoming Congregations*. Nashville: Abingdon Press, 2003.

Frederick, Marla F. *Between Sundays: Black Women and Everyday Struggles of Faith*. Berkeley and Los Angeles and Los Angeles: University of California Press, 2003.

Heilman, Samuel. *The Gate behind the Wall: A Pilgrimage to Jerusalem*. New York: Penguin, 1986.

Heilman, Samuel C. *The People of the Book: Drama, Fellowship, and Religion*. Chicago: University of Chicago Press, 1983.

Tribble, Jeffery. *Transformative Leadership in the Black Church*. New York: Palgrave Macmillan, 2005.

- N I N E -

Sharing Results

Weaving a Theological Narrative

It's not the heat; it's the humility.

— YOGI BERRA

After the huge accomplishment of writing your ethnography, take a deep breath. Pause and ponder the journey you have undertaken with your research partners thus far. You have entered into a practice of giving thoughtful attention to the words and ways through which the people proclaim their faith. You have constructed a narrative about the group's shared culture and religious practices. You have engaged in pastoral theological reflection. It is fitting to take some time to absorb these shifts in your approach to pastoral leadership as you contemplate the next phase of the pastoral practice of ethnography: sharing your research results with the group you have been studying.

The goal of this phase is to offer your ethnographic research to the group in such a way as to prompt honest and searching conversation about your findings. You will be sharing what you can see from where you stand, in order to invite dialogue about the group's faith in action and instigate reciprocal learning, growth, and transformation. Once again you must relinquish the role of religious expert and be among the people as an honest, engaged human being. You will need to listen to the members' feedback calmly, with an open heart. As Yogi Berra's malapropism suggests, "it's the humility" that is needed for this phase of pastoral ethnography.

Students have often expressed trepidation about this part of the work, because it involves revealing thoughts about the group

214

to the group. Eventually, the process also leads to hearing group members tell you more candidly their thoughts and feelings about you, your theology, and your leadership. While some of this speaking and listening may be difficult, the very sharing process itself can become a catalyst for greater mutual love and theological commitment within the community.

Think of this work as analogous to the reflective listening that is part of a pastoral conversation, but reflective listening with an entire group, rather than just one person. "This is what I heard," you will be saying to your community. "Have I got that right?" You will need to listen carefully to the responses that come back to you, responses that may challenge or move you in some way. According to Don Browning, transformation involves a dialogical process, a mutual process.[1] You model and foster this process as you share your results, setting a tone of mutual respect, care, and connection between you and the group and among members of the group. You might even be able to frame the disciplined listening and speaking process in terms of your group's theological identity. For example, a Protestant leader might speak of "the priesthood of all believers," reminding the group of the importance of each member. As the community becomes adept at this shared reflective conversation, the conditions are created in which deeper faith, integrity, and agency can grow.

Sharing Results — Weaving Connections

Sharing your research results with your community can also be thought of as a way of weaving theological and interpersonal connections in the life of the group. The threads of the weaving are the stories — the yarns — that the community offers. Many colorful yarns have already been heard, analyzed, and thoughtfully woven into your written ethnography. Through theological reflection — both the people's and your own — you have brought threads of biblical stories, images, and theological insights together into the fabric of your ethnography. Now you will be sharing this

---

1. Browning, *A Fundamental Practical Theology,* 279.

fabric that you have woven and inviting the group to add on to it, perhaps to unravel and redo parts of it, and to join in a community-wide practice of weaving the group's future together.

The connections you have woven together among personal stories, group stories, and divine stories can help guide the life and purposeful work of the congregation or organization. Anderson and Foley call attention to the critical task of integrating narratives human and divine. They point out that in many faith communities, human stories are heard and people nurtured through pastoral care, while divine stories are proclaimed through worship and preaching, and "never the twain shall meet." These authors suggest that this unnatural separation be remedied by bringing "mighty stories" and "dangerous rituals" back together in the context of worship, "a particularly privileged space in which the divine-human relationship is rehearsed and realized."[2] By sharing your ethnography in the context of worship or in other contexts of group life, you can participate in this integrative work.

How can we go about weaving together our human stories with divine stories? This is a theological question as well as a practical one. Theology can influence the stories you choose and the ways in which you weave them together. What is theology like in your setting? Is there a set pattern to the theology you weave together, like the precise patterns of industrial weaving, which can create beautiful, clear, and coherent tapestries of faith? Or is this theological weaving a more open-ended process, such as the Saori way of weaving, an example of which is pictured on this book's cover? Saori "means weaving without rules, without tears, without 'errors.' In Saori we weave from a place deep within our hearts. We create because the act of creating calls us. The colors sing. The textures warm us."[3] Or does your group weave theology in a more mixed way, using some rules and patterns while also allowing for some improvisation?

---

2. Anderson and Foley, *Mighty Stories, Dangerous Rituals*, 42.
3. Taken from the website *weavingaway.com*. See the link for the Saori Way (accessed December 19, 2007).

Your approach to the work of weaving stories together will depend, in part, on your particular faith and your particular theology. Some Christians, for example, regard the canon of the Bible as God's self-narrated story, containing the preset patterns into which personal and group stories of the church should be woven, and to which they should conform. This kind of weaving, known as canonical narrative theology, calls on people to change their lives, to bring them into accord with the patterns understood as consistent with the weave of God's own story. Proponents of this approach, such as Stanley Hauerwas, emphasize stark differences between human ways and divine ways. These authors envision an ethical community patterned after a straightforward reading of scripture.[4] This approach clarifies (and some believe, strengthens) Christian identity as a distinct culture of its own, over and against the ways of the world.[5]

Others believe that theology is a more fundamentally contextual endeavor, and so expect more variation in the weave — in the way stories of the divine are told and interpreted within and among diverse communities of faith. These theologians consider the straightforward interpretation of biblical stories and the classical doctrinal formulations of the church to be only one version of God's story, shaped and limited by Western culture. Contextualists understand the community of faith less as a cohesive culture of its own, set apart from the world, and more as a culturally embedded response to a God who is found among all people.[6] For leaders using a more contextual theological approach, the patterns in the weave of divine and human stories will be more complex and

---

4. Elaine Graham et al., *Theological Reflection: Methods*, 78. See chapter 3, "Telling God's Story," for a thoughtful exposition and evaluation of authors who use this approach, 78–108. See for example, Stanley Hauerwas and William Willimon, *Resident Aliens: Life in the Christian Colony* (Nashville: Abingdon Press, 1989).

5. See Tanner, *Theories of Culture*, especially chapter 5, "Christian Culture and Society," 93–119.

6. Graham et al., *Theological Reflection: Methods*. See chapter 8, "Theology in the Vernacular," 200–229. For a good example of a constructive, intercultural pastoral theology, see Emmanuel Lartey, *Pastoral Theology in an Intercultural World* (Cleveland: Pilgrim Press, 2006).

fluid. The resulting theology will not be as neat and clear; it will be messy, maybe even torn or unraveled in places.[7] The patterns that emerge will be unique, reflecting diverse local identities and theologies. Robert Schreiter, whose work reflects extensively on cross-cultural data from Catholic mission and ministry in Africa, is a perceptive advocate of contextual theology.[8]

Your particular faith and your theology will inflect the way in which you do this sharing and weaving work in your community. In any case, the process of bringing human and divine stories together is crucial: it enlivens the interplay between faith and religious practice and makes this interrelationship more visible in the community. In weaving these threads together, leaders create the conditions for more intentional and salutary faith-actions. Or, as Anderson and Foley put it, "we live our stories best when we understand them in relation to the larger human story, the stories of our faith traditions, and the story of God."[9]

Whatever your theological approach to the sharing of your research results and the weaving of stories human and divine, remember that the basic ethical rules of ethnography must apply whenever you share human stories (see chapter 4). The weaving process that you are now about to teach your group must include regard for privacy, confidentiality, and the right to refuse to speak or to participate. It is wise to explain these ethical guidelines to the community explicitly, lest inadvertent harm is done. For example, you might stress the duty to show respect for the views that have been described in the ethnography, even if people disagree, so that no participant will suffer insulting or dismissive comments. Additionally, you might need to describe the consent agreements that you made, in order to specify the limitations of confidentiality or anonymity that you are working with and the

---

7. "As Roemer has suggested, many of the best and most powerful stories that draw us closest to the mystery of the sacred in the midst of life are ambivalent, painful or strange." Graham et al., *Theological Reflection: Methods*, 73.

8. Robert J. Schreiter, *Constructing Local Theologies* (Maryknoll, N.Y.: Orbis Books, 1985).

9. Anderson and Foley, *Mighty Stories, Dangerous Rituals*, 48.

rationale for these.[10] In sharing stories with a faith community, ethical concerns are heightened because of the high degree of trust and the reasonable expectation of spiritual sensitivity that people bring to this setting.

While the interplay of personal, communal, and social change remains mysterious on some levels, it is clear that the theological transformation of a community involves all of these elements. Growth at the level of community requires the honest and brave speech of individual members, as described in chapter 6. The telling of group narratives in different voices and versions (not an amalgamated or smooth narrative that glosses over conflict or evil) initiates the practice of more honest speech in the community. This, in turn, provides the conditions for more rigorous engagement with stories of God found in the group's history and its religious traditions. As members of the group engage in this conversation with you and with each other, their energy and spiritual growth will likely increase.

The communal experience of growth both supports and relies upon the continuing spiritual growth and development of individual members of the group. These are reciprocal processes: strong and agile groups foster creative and honest individuals; likewise persons who offer authentic speech and original ideas contribute to the health and energy of their communities. While we cannot expect that every member of the group is open to spiritual growth, we can try to add some nutrients to the soil of group life.[11] In a healthy and open community, members know that they are free to speak the truth of their experience, that their speech will be heard and engaged theologically, and that they can have a role in co-creating the group's actions in the present and in the future.

The Sharing Process: Practical Approaches

After some time has passed, reread your ethnography. Try to imagine how reading this document or hearing parts of it spoken

10. For a helpful presentation of some of these ethical issues in ministry, see Bush, "Permission for Mission," in *Gentle Shepherding*, 44–69.

11. See Kornfeld, *Cultivating Wholeness*.

aloud might feel to members of your group, both those who participated actively in the research and those who did not. This written document represents your word of truth to this community. How can you begin to make it known?

Plan for a sharing event as carefully as you planned for the earlier stages of research. Consider this event another opportunity to "observe a lot by watching,"[12] as you offer the group the corporate story that you have composed. Be prepared to record people's responses carefully, because you may be so caught up in the dialogue that follows your sharing that you miss some of the details. Keep your notebook at hand. Later you will be able to recall and analyze the sharing event as you go over the various responses of members of the group.

There are numerous venues for the work of ethnographic sharing. Among the contexts and media my students have tried are sermons, videos, PowerPoint presentations, workshops, exhibits, written reports, and public forums. We will look at some of these examples, but this will not be an exhaustive guide. Knowing your group as you do now, you probably have the best insight as to how you might begin the work of results sharing. Take your time in deciding how best to proceed.

Offering a Sermon

Offering a sermon is one way to begin to share your ethnographic narrative. This is a powerful vehicle for sharing because it brings together "mighty stories" with the "dangerous ritual" of proclamation.[13] The weight of tradition imbues the ritual of preaching with sacred value and religious authority in many faith communities. When preaching is combined with the emotional and spiritual power of narrative sharing, the conditions are ripe for theological engagement. Though preaching has traditionally been performed in a one-sided way — that is, the leader preaches to the people rather than engaging in a shared conversation —

12. Yogi Berra.
13. Anderson and Foley, *Mighty Stories Dangerous Rituals*, 163–66.

this form can be altered or embroidered over with new practices that make it more participatory. We can also observe that using an ethnographic narrative in preaching already makes the ritual more participatory because the voices of members of the group will be heard in or through the sermon.

Sharing ethnographic narratives through preaching can spark transformation in a group in at least two ways: through conceptual stirrings and through the formation or strengthening of interpersonal (intersubjective) connections. By conceptual stirrings, I am referring to the way that hearing stories can spark the listener's imagination, giving rise to new understandings and commitments. When the narratives offered bring the members' story together with your theological reflection, the new conceptual stirrings will be tinged with the awareness of God. This is the power of giving testimony: it brings together "what one has seen" with "what one believes."[14] Sharing ethnographic narratives can reveal and evoke understandings of the divine-human relationship in the experience of both the teller and the hearers.

Sharing ethnographic narratives through preaching can weave bonds of social connection in the community. When those hearing a narrative experience a sense of recognition — involving not only the sense of understanding the narrative but also an awareness of being understood by it — a connection to the group will become woven into the experience. To the extent that ethnographic narratives ring true and people recognize themselves as part of the larger group, named in some aspect of the story and in tune with at least some of the group's values or shared theology, this sense of recognition develops. The fabric of this community of faith becomes more apparent; its colors and patterns and textures can be recognized and felt. People can see it now and feel that they are part of it.

This can be viewed, in Elaine Graham's terms, as the work of groups forming "narrative identities that enable them to move

---

14. See Anna Carter Florence, *Preaching as Testimony* (Louisville: Westminster John Knox Press, 2007), xx.

forward through time in healthy and creative ways without for-getting the past."[15] This is why we share ethnographic narratives: in order to support the corporate body in moving forward in healthy and creative ways without forgetting the past. The past, when it is remembered and retold with honesty and hopefulness, becomes a springboard for change in the present and the future. Fuller accounts of the past must be articulated and woven anew into the current community's identity, so that the weight of its remembered history becomes less restrictive. The past, and its residue in the present — the *habitus* — can then function nei-ther as an invincible mythology that stymies innovation, nor as an invisible enemy that the group must rebel against.

By sharing your narrative interpretation of the group's his-tory through preaching you can help the group move forward in healthy and creative ways. This is the essence of narrative leader-ship, and the pulpit is a highly privileged space from which you can offer it. When you explicitly link your well-honed under-standing of the group's history to its current processes of identity formation, connecting all of this to your prayerful reflection upon the scriptures of the day, you are exercising an empowering kind of leadership. This leadership supports and calls forth the people's own theological wisdom, in conversation with sacred texts.[16]

Ethical and Practical Matters

In preaching, as in any kind of results sharing, your presentation of your research findings must be consistent with the informed

15. Graham et al., *Theological Reflection: Methods,* 66. Here Graham is building on the work of Paul Ricoeur, as found in M. J. Valdes, ed. *A Ricoeur Reader: Reflection and Imagination* (Hemel Hempstead: Harvester Wheatsheaf, 1991). Ricoeur speaks of becoming "the narrator of our own story, without completely becoming the author of our life," 437. See also the three-volume work of Paul Ricoeur, *Time and Narrative,* vols. 1–2, trans. Kathleen McLaugh-lin and David Pellauer, vol. 3, trans. Kathleen Blamey and David Pellauer (Chicago: University of Chicago Press, 1984, 1985, and 1988).

16. For a helpful resource on narrative preaching, see Mike Graves and David J. Schlafer, eds., *What's the Shape of Narrative Preaching? Essays in Honor of Eugene L. Lowry* (St. Louis: Chalice Press, 2008).

consent agreements that you made with your research participants. Reread these agreements, and select carefully the material
that you are free to offer publicly. If you did not anticipate that
your sharing event might take the form of preaching when you
made the agreements, you will either need to restrict your remarks
accordingly, or seek explicit permission from your participants
for the use of their stories. This permission is critical, especially
in the event that you wish to quote from or refer explicitly to one
particular story.

One way to avoid some of the ethical problems that could arise
is by preaching reflexively about what you have learned from the
ethnographic study and writing process. When you share your
own experience, you allow others to see you, thus turning the
research relationship around for the moment and bearing the vulnerability of the one who is being studied. This is where "the
humility" comes in. You must model the kind of honest reflection on your own religious practice that you are trying to teach
your community. When you talk about your own experience of
learning from the group and how this has changed you, there is
far less risk of making your research participants uncomfortable.

The use of reflexivity is consistent with the tradition of giving
testimony. As you reflect on the day's scripture and the word
of God for this community, relate it to what you have learned
about *yourself* through this ethnographic study process. Choose
a theme or image from your ethnography that is related to your
reflexive learning and one that also connects to the meaning you
have identified in the scriptures. In light of the group's story and
your own story and the divine story as you understand them,
what change in action or practice is called for now? As you recall
your ethnographic learning experience, let it inform and guide
your insights and your proclamation.

If you think this form of preaching will be too difficult, either
for you or for the people, stop and ponder the reasons for your
hesitation: Is it too difficult because this is a new and unfamiliar
approach to preaching for you? Is it too difficult because you
fear that what you have to say is too harsh or challenging for
the group to hear? Or is the word you have to offer troublesome

because it touches on a part of the group's history that is sensitive and usually not discussed? These are three different scenarios.

In the first case, where custom or habit has inculcated different expectations of preaching in this setting, you need to do the work of discernment. Pamela Cooper-White's theological reflection process (described in chapter 8) or Edward Wimberly's wonderful book on remembering one's own call may be helpful to you at this juncture.[17] Sort out the sources of your reluctance to speak out honestly in the community. What is at risk for you in this sharing? Try to stay grounded in your understanding of your calling. What does this community, entrusted to your care, need to hear from the scriptures and from their leader? What are the threads in the fabric of the faith tradition and the scriptures that are woven through the cultural life of the group and through your own life as well? Be patient as you sort through your resistance and search for spiritual wisdom. Perhaps you will decide to consult with one or two trusted members of the community as part of your discernment process.

In the second scenario, where you fear that the word you have to offer will be too challenging to be helpful, think over some options. Rather than offering one dramatic and potentially overwhelming sermon, consider taking a more gradual approach to this shift in your leadership and preaching style. Perhaps you can break down your message and offer a little piece of your ethnographic learning this week through this sermon. Consider turning this sharing event into a sermon series, where you patiently, over time, build a case for the new direction or new practices that your ethnographic research and theological reflection suggest.

As regards the worry that your word may be too harsh, this is a legitimate concern. The tone that you take in telling this story matters a great deal. Tone comes through in both word choice and speaking voice. One can preach boldly and confidently without using "shoulds" and "oughts." If you preach in the tradition

---

17. Cooper-White, *Shared Wisdom*, 74–79; Wimberly, *Recalling Our Own Stories*.

of testimony, you might mention the ways in which this new insight has been a struggle for you to see and accept. Don't expect that everyone will agree with what you say, but proclaim your testimony to the spiritual stirring in your life. Your tone of voice can help convey both clarity and humility.

When offering a sermon that you think might be challenging or controversial, it is wise to plan time for a "talkback" session afterward (or even during the sermon, if the group's worship style will allow it). When people know that they will have a chance to speak, they may be more receptive listeners.[18] Humility doesn't mean that you water down your vision of the truth, but that you offer it in such a way that it invites and makes room for others' narratives and wisdom to be shared as well. By doing this, you will be living into the dialogue and the change in the community that is the hope of pastoral ethnography.

In the third scenario, where you hesitate to share your research results through preaching because your ethnography touches on a sensitive part of the group's history, your hesitation is warranted. Think of the congregation as analogous to a family: if you discover a long-buried family secret, what do you do with it? Most of us don't want to blurt it out at a holiday dinner or on the Jerry Springer television show. On the other hand, we don't do well to keep a shameful secret hidden and festering forever, either. Ideally, we proceed cautiously, and find caring ways to begin to open the hidden story. We take time to discern what needs to be shared and how to begin the process.[19]

In a case like this, where the congregation has one or more big hidden secrets, it is probably wise to exercise caution and refrain from using the pulpit as a venue for disclosure. Nevertheless, you can preach in such a way as to acknowledge that you are aware that painful historical events are still affecting the community.

---

18. Inviting e-mail responses is another way to elicit feedback, and an electronic message board allows for a limited form of ongoing conversation among members of the group.

19. For an excellent book on dealing with family secrets, written for a general audience, see Evan Imber-Black, *The Secret Life of Families* (New York: Bantam Books, 1997).

Deception and shame are not unfamiliar themes in the biblical stories. The stories of Joseph and his brothers, for example (Gen. 37–50), offer ample instances of family strife, replete with secrets hidden and revealed. Working with these themes and doing your reflexive sharing in a sensitive and gentle way could help prepare the group to reexamine its history in more detail later in more contained and supportive forums.

Whether in preaching or in other contexts of ministry, we need to tend a balance between discretion and honesty. Ethnography as a pastoral practice brings us right into the heart of this challenge. Ethical considerations are always of primary concern: if we violate the confidentiality of personal sharing, we break trust and do harm; if we are insensitive in the way we characterize individual or group stories, even when we do have permission, we could do unwitting harm. At the same time, pastoral ethnography is meant to promote openness and honesty in the group. Strive to create a climate in the community where people are free to tell their stories, listen to others' stories, and encounter divine stories with candor and mutual trust. Through story-sharing, we signal to the members of the community that it is okay, and in fact good, to be real.

My hunch is that the best way to share study results through preaching is to leave some loose threads, some unraveled edges, in the fabric you weave. In your research, you have likely uncovered multiple views of the group's story. Allowing some of the contested interpretations to be heard, without harming or shaming anyone, is part of the challenge in this form of preaching. Don't try to smooth over problems in a text or in a community for the sake of narrative resolution. Anderson and Foley talk about the importance of a community learning to "practice reconciliation without resolution."[20] They note the importance of developing the capacity of holding multiple interpretations of reality in view.[21] In terms of the weaving metaphor, preaching should communicate that the fabric is not finished, that

20. Anderson and Foley, *Mighty Stories Dangerous Rituals*, 168.
21. Ibid.

the people are capable co-weavers with you, and that dramatically different threads can coexist and become interwoven in this community.

At the same time, do not be shy about sharing your view or adding your thread of wisdom to the communal fabric. Here is an opportunity to proclaim the presence of God in relationship to this particular community. Here is a chance to describe the truth of this community as you understand it and to articulate your vision for its future. Where do your research and reflection and prayer suggest that the divine energy is leading you and this mortal band of believers? What is going to be the theme of the next chapter of this group's shared life? In the words of Habakkuk, "Write the vision. Make it plain" (Hab. 2:2). Then speak it out loud, with clarity and conviction.

Because you are in an honest relationship to the people, it doesn't matter so much that you get or say everything right. What matters is that you make a faithful and honest effort and that you stay open to the responses that people offer. We have already mentioned the value of providing "talk-back" sessions. Alternatively, students such as Eleanor (in chapter 7) have taken the tack of distributing written feedback forms in advance of the sermon, and asking listeners to write down their responses to what they hear. This can be done through electronic mail as well; and it may or may not be anonymous.

By offering a format through which people can give feedback, you invite them back into the conversation. Even if things go poorly and people hate what you say, they will have a chance to communicate that to you, and you will be getting to know them better through the process. If you are worried, bear in mind that it is more than likely that at least one person will have something positive to say or write on the response forms. This can comfort you in the event that you begin to feel anxious after the sermon. Whatever folks may have to say, listen attentively and stay in the conversation with them. In terms of the journey metaphor, we can say that once this kind of conversation gets going, you have arrived at a new place with the people you serve.

In-House Forums

Another good setting for sharing your ethnography is in an in-house forum. If your research protocol and consent forms allow it, you may present your research findings in the context of a workshop for members of the group, a retreat, a staff meeting, or an ongoing adult study group. Your sharing event can take the form of a large, highly structured presentation or a small, more intimate gathering. In-house forums give you the freedom to design contained and safe "holding environments"[22] for your results sharing, in which you can promote interactive conversations.

For large-scale events, consider the use of visual aids such as graphs, maps, photos, illustrations, or video clips to highlight the key findings of your study.[23] These materials can help you convey your findings in a clear, appealing, and engaging way. Do not overwhelm the group by sharing every detail, image, or statistic you have gathered. Rather than giving the event the feel of a lecture or a monologue, try to create an experience that invites dialogue and conversation.

Allow time for questions and conversation after your presentation. Depending on the size of the group, you might suggest breaking up into smaller groups for discussion. You might also recommend that the groups adopt some guidelines aimed at increasing participation, such as going around the group and allowing each person to speak once before anyone speaks twice. Ask each group to appoint a scribe so that you can get a record of what was said.

Whatever the size of the group(s), you can help focus the conversation by preparing some of the questions for reflection ahead of time. Begin by asking people to raise any questions that have to do with the clarity of the presentation. Then ask questions that elicit people's responses to your findings, both positive and negative. If one or more persons express disagreement, try to avoid becoming defensive or insisting that you know your data. Instead,

---

22. This term comes from the work of D. W. Winnicott, *The Maturational Processes and the Facilitating Environment* (New York: Karnac Books, 1990).
23. For helpful guidelines on the presentation of research findings, see Ammerman et al., *Studying Congregations*, 234–35.

ask the person(s) to elaborate and take notes on what they say. Include at least some questions that invite pastoral theological analysis. For instance, "In light of this presentation, where do you perceive that God is leading us now?"

Make sure that you have a way to record responses, perhaps by writing them down on newsprint pads and taping them to the walls of the room or making an audio recording of the session (with prior permission). Think of this event as an opportunity for imagining new ideas and possibilities. Do not move the group into the work of voting on issues or program plans during this session. Allow this to be a time for people to express their thoughts and wonder out loud, without fear of being shot down. Teach the group how to hear its own collective wisdom as it emerges. If you do happen to hear a clear consensus on the group's identity, theology, or mission emerging, try to name this. Then ask the group to correct or refine its evolving vision.

On the other hand, if disagreement or rancor follows your presentation, try to stay calm. Use this as an opportunity to teach the group how to listen and acknowledge differences respectfully. If two clearly opposing views seem to be emerging, try suggesting that people divide up into two camps, so that they get to stay with their like-minded colleagues for a while. Ask each group of like-minded folks to work together to articulate (and record) its case more clearly. Then have each group report back to the larger gathering. Carefully list all the points each group makes, side by side, in plain view. Ask the larger group to reflect on the two neighboring lists. What is the gist of the disagreement? What areas of common concern, if any, can be found in these lists? Alternatively, ask the two groups with opposing views to meet separately, but this time with the task of trying to articulate the other side's case as well as they can. Have them record their debating points, and then share these back with the larger group. Activities such as these can paradoxically help clarify differences of opinion while simultaneously bringing people together.[24]

---

24. Some of these ideas are taken from a Wabash Workshop given on June 14, 2006, in Crawfordsville, Indiana.

When it is time to end the event, close with a shared ritual. Do not expect all differences to be resolved, nor attempt to create a compromise. Look carefully at what has been written on the lists around the room. Ask if anyone can point to some areas of common ground. In Kathryn Tanner's words, "Agreement should be looked for with utmost patience."[25] Even where there is basic theological or practical disagreement, usually there will be some area of overlapping belief or values. Lift up the points of commonality in your ritual of closing. The point is not to smooth over differences, but to help the members come together with their distinctions intact, able to care for each other anyway.

Small Forums

Smaller gatherings may allow for more intimate sharing in a contained and safe space. Recall the story of In Sun in chapter 6, who created a warm and pleasant evening for her research associates. In Sun opened her home for this occasion, served special foods, and invited the women who wished to take part in this event to come together. She began by sharing her own personal, reflexive learning with the small group of Korean students' wives in a gentle and sensitive way. This then encouraged the other women to speak to each other, to compare notes, and to think further about their stories, the main characters in their lives, and their experiences of God's presence and call. Though this was not a formal group or organization, the women created richer relationships as they reflected together on their shared stories and hopes for the future.

Sharing Painful Stories

In more formal organizations and congregations, similar small group forums might be especially helpful for the sharing of sensitive stories, such as naming painful events in the group's history.

---

25. Tanner, *Theories of Culture*, 172.

This work is difficult, and depending on the nature and severity of the traumatic events, the use of an outside consultant who has experience with the particular issue can be helpful.[26] Work to create a safe and contained environment for recollecting difficult aspects of the group's history or experience. Continue to think of yourself as a witness, one who sees and hears and accompanies the group through this experience with calm strength.

Elaine Graham writes:

> There will be many times when helping people to tell their stories will lead to healing and peace. However, there will be other moments in which a pastoral response will mean entering alongside into the death of meaning and loss of coherence.... We may use rituals, symbols, or music to allow pain to be communicated rather than constructing stories that promise an illusory reconciliation of tragic circumstance.[27]

When a group recalls and tells its painful history, allow for the expression of that pain through some poetic or expressive means. For example, when a congregation comes to terms with the sexual misconduct of a previous leader, the people may speak of trauma, loss, betrayal, or shame. Try to respond in a way that allows the group to process the emotional burden of this event in their history. This might involve singing a hymn of mourning or reading a Psalm or a poem that captures the anguish and expresses it. When a group has endured such a breach of faith, the outcry must be uttered, maybe in a way that is too deep for words. Rather than "healing the wound lightly," try to support the deep cleansing that the community needs and acknowledge, too, that some wounds leave us changed. Music, art, and creative expression can be means of grace that begin a process of deeper healing.

---

26. For example, The Faith Trust Institute in Seattle, Washington, trains consultants to work with congregations and groups affected by clergy sexual misconduct. See the website at *www.faithtrustinstitute.org*.

27. Graham et al., *Theological Reflection: Methods*, 73.

Eventually, the open sharing of stories of a traumatic event in the group's history can prove a huge relief. Recall Ken's experience of bringing the subject of race out into the open in an all-white congregation in which several men had once belonged to the Ku Klux Klan. Speaking this secret out loud helped defuse its power to isolate and shame individuals. Instead of pretending that the pastor's race didn't matter, members of the congregation could admit that it did and confess that race had been an enormous stumbling block in their relationship to him. Once freed to acknowledge this honestly, the men also found words to express their nascent admiration for their pastor, whom they believed had loved them into faithfulness. This sharing of history and cultural identity cleared the way for a more honest relationship and a greater commitment to ministry.

Public Forums

A public forum is another possible way to share your research results, not only with your participants, but also with a wider community. This approach holds out the potential of sparking transformative change on a larger scale. Of course, the necessary ethical procedures must be followed to ensure that you have informed consent for any public form of sharing. When these conditions are met, you are free to share the learning you glean from your study and the hope of transformation with a wider audience.

One of my students, whom I shall call Belinda, accomplished this feat. Belinda is a single African American woman, the owner and director of a child development center in Southeast Washington, D.C. Southeast is the most economically depressed quadrant of the District, and many of the families that the center serves are single-parent families with limited incomes. Belinda's research began out of her concern for the well-being of African American boys, whom she sees in her day care center, being raised primarily by the women in their lives — mothers, aunts, grandmothers, or great aunts — frequently without the direct involvement of the boys' fathers. Belinda worried about this, as she believed that two-parent families were the ideal and that these boys could not grow up well without their fathers taking an active role in their lives. Through her research, Belinda wanted to probe this dynamic, to understand where the men were and how the women were coping. She also intended that the research would support the women in the study, helping each "give voice to her joys and struggles in rearing her sons and/or grandsons in Southeast Washington."[28]

Through her ethnographic research, Belinda learned a great deal about these women, who were all connected to her childcare center in some way. She did a careful study, using reflexivity, which enabled her to understand how her own economic privilege may have blinded her to the strength and resilience of the women who were working so hard to raise the boys. As Belinda puts it, her ethnography narrates how "an educated 'sistah' gets a real-life education."[29] Rather than judging her research participants, or reproaching them because of her belief in the importance of two-parent families, Belinda came to understand the women she interviewed with renewed respect. She came to appreciate them as creative and thoughtful caregivers to their sons, nephews, and grandsons: women who were not perfect, but who managed well as the sole financial, spiritual, and emotional supports of their families.

Belinda also did her theological reflection and introspective work, immersing herself in the stories of the "Exodus women," the women who helped birth Moses and keep him alive. She started to see some similarly "brave, intelligent, and spirit-filled" qualities in the African American women she interviewed. Belinda also reflected on the critical role of her own father, now deceased, in her life. She saw that her love for him and her grief over his loss influenced her desire that the black boys in her center could have a strong and caring father in their lives. Belinda further reflected on her own longing to be a mother, realizing that she did

28. "Belinda," "When Five 'Sistahs' Keep the Promise Alive," unpublished paper, Wesley Theological Seminary, May 7, 2007, 2.
29. Ibid., 6.

not want to take on the burden of single parenthood herself. Her soul-searching reflections helped her understand her biases and gain greater appreciation for the single parents at her center.

Belinda decided to share her findings in three different ways. First, she decided to hold a special Mother's Day luncheon for the research participants to give them a chance to hear and discuss the results of the study and to talk further about their lives as caregivers. Belinda also wanted to provide a pleasant and soothing interval for these women, who were constantly giving and supporting their families but rarely had opportunities to receive supportive care themselves. Belinda's center provided the meal and childcare for this event. The center also supplied a bouquet of flowers and the offer of a seated massage for each of the five participants in the study as forms of literal and symbolic care.

Second, Belinda decided to use her research results to help her make her childcare center into a more supportive environment for single mothers rearing their sons and grandsons. She modeled this shift on the concept of *homeplace* as a place "where people support each other's development and where everyone is expected to participate in developing the homeplace."[30] She asked the women in her study to help her brainstorm about how to do this best.

Third, with the permission of her participants, Belinda shared her research findings in a more public forum. She applied for and received a chance to present her findings at an area-wide meeting of an association of local childcare providers, of which she is a member. Belinda shared her results through a PowerPoint presentation that highlighted her main findings, using pseudonyms for the particular women in her study. She also shared her reflexive work, bravely admitting how some of her preconceived notions about the necessity for two parents in a family had been up-ended. She publicly described how she had moved to a place of greater appreciation for the women in her center, many of whom were raising their African American sons, nephews, or grandsons, with great devotion and limited resources.

---

30. Belenky et al., *A Tradition That Has No Name*, 3.

Belinda also invited two childcare providers from her staff to tell their stories of their programmatic efforts to reach out to the fathers of the boys in the center. One story involved a Father's Day program, which the staff created for the boys in the center, in order to bring them together with their fathers or other African American men who could serve as surrogates — such as a friend, uncle, grandfather, or even the brother of a staff member. The program involved a simple meal and an activity — a small building project that each boy and his father or mentor could work on together. The results of this event were striking, as both the boys and the men enjoyed themselves tremendously and formed or renewed bonds to each other. They often asked when there was going to be another project time.

After two such moving stories were shared with the large group of childcare providers, Belinda invited the audience to enter into discussion in small groups around the lunch tables. She suggested that people share their own experiences with creative programs and ideas that supported good parenting for both the women and the men in their centers. Sitting at one of these tables, I heard the energized conversation of the professional childcare providers, as they came up with creative ideas about how to improve their services for the families they serve. The conversation also turned to local politics and the advocacy work that must go on constantly in Ward 8 in the District of Columbia to maintain funding for childcare and for the extremely modest level of other public services for the residents of area.

This story exemplifies an approach to sharing ethnographic findings with a wider public in the hope of sparking transformation in the lives of children growing up in poverty. Belinda's work combines deep personal and spiritual reflection, careful listening to her research participants, and public sharing followed by opportunities for feedback, more story-sharing, and small-group conversation. The potential for life-giving change that includes, but is not limited to, participation in the political process is evident in this pastoral ethnography.

Sharing your ethnographic learning can set the stage for bold and committed work for change. In agencies or in congregations, genuine dialogue can lead to more thoughtful and intentional faith practices, not only internally, among the membership, but beyond the group as well, through public forums for proclamation and conversation about the common good.

For Further Study

Anderson, Herbert, and Edward Foley. *Mighty Stories, Dangerous Rituals: Weaving Together the Human and the Divine.* San Francisco: Jossey-Bass, 1998, chapter 3.

Belenky, Mary Field, Lynn Bond, and Jacqueline S. Winestock. *A Tradition That Has No Name: Nurturing the Development of People, Families, and Communities.* New York: Basic Books, 1997, chapters 6–9.

Graham, Elaine L. *Transforming Practice: Pastoral Theology in an Age of Uncertainty.* Eugene, Ore.: Wipf and Stock, 1996, chapters 2–4.

– T E N –

Ethnography for Change

Co-authoring the Future

The future ain't what it used to be.

— YOGI BERRA

The telling of lives changes lives.[1] The humble journey of listening to the religious and spiritual lives of people through pastoral ethnography can lead to a place of life-giving change within a faith community and beyond it. In this chapter, we return to this premise and examine the links between pastoral ethnography and prophetic change in, with, and through faith communities. In particular, we will explore the connection between creativity and change. By honoring creativity throughout the research process and beyond it, religious leaders help spur their organizations forward into a future that, in Yogi Berra's words, "ain't what it used to be."

Ethnography as a pastoral practice forms and informs religious leaders in the art of co-authoring the future in and with a community of faith. This co-authoring process is similar to what narrative therapists call "re-authoring."[2] Two dynamic activities are involved in this kind of "writing": first, constructing one's life story in a new way, using new themes, metaphors, and story lines; and second, actually living into these new themes and plot lines that were not previously imagined or tried. The goal of narrative therapy with individuals is that persons become free to think and

---

1. Davidman, "Truth, Subjectivity, and Ethnographic Research," 19.
2. See White and Epston, *Narrative Means to Therapeutic Ends,* 13; and Wimberly, *Recalling Our Own Stories,* 73–88.

237

act in new ways, departing from old constraining scripts. Pastoral ethnography with congregations or groups similarly has the goal of freeing groups of people to revise their narratives — their ways of thinking about and living out their faith — collectively and corporately.

I use a more modest term, "co-authoring," to describe this process in order to acknowledge that the future is always uncertain and that we are finite and contingent beings.[3] The language of co-authoring names the reality that no one composes a life story alone, or from scratch, or with full *author*-ity. In religious life, we recognize our dependence upon God, our reliance upon and responsibility toward the earth, and our interrelatedness with our human counterparts, near and far. We are born into worlds of meaning, and we are formed by and embedded in particular cultural stories. We cannot fully extricate ourselves from these stories that shape us and to some degree limit the scope of our imaginations and our actions.

While we human beings do not have the complete freedom to write our own stories and direct our own lives, individually or collectively, we do have some degree of agency. Theologian H. Richard Niebuhr wrote that we have a way of freeing ourselves from the past, which he calls the way of *reinterpreting* it.[4] The way of reinterpreting, according to Niebuhr, "recalls, accepts, understands, and reorganizes the past instead of abandoning it."[5] When we reinterpret our stories and traditions, we open up paths to prophetic change. We become free to change our patterns by coming to terms with our stories and traditions, by consciously examining such faith as we have been given, and by improvising new riffs of theological insight and faithful action. Understanding our historical, religious, and cultural particularity through ethnography strengthens our clarity and resolve as we

---

3. For theological reflections on human contingency from a Christian perspective, see Daniel L. Migliore, *Faith Seeking Understanding: An Introduction to Christian Theology*, 2nd ed. (Grand Rapids: Wm. B. Eerdmans, 2004), 101–3.

4. H. Richard Niebuhr, *The Responsible Self: An Essay in Christian Moral Philosophy* (San Francisco: Harper and Row, 1978), 102; italics in the original.

5. Ibid.

strive to co-author a more faithful, just, and life-giving future. Whether in the context of families or congregations, in denominations or in neighborhoods, or in broader social and political arenas of life, we have at least some freedom to alter the scripts we speak and the actions we perform.

Through the research process, individuals and groups begin to experience greater author-ity through telling their own stories about themselves, their faith traditions, and their experiences of the Holy. Leaders and groups expand their imaginations and insight when they join in "sacred conversations" about race, for example.[6] Likewise persons and groups come to understand, through honest discourse, that they have the power to "change the subject," to open up the worth of women.[7]

Religious leaders, by virtue of their experience of divine call and the authority that their faith communities vest in them, have additional social influence that they may not fully recognize. Clergy, for example, have "the power to speak" and to be heard when they address their congregations and communities.[8] With this power comes the responsibility to speak wisely and fairly, to exercise power *with* the people, helping people find voice, rather than speaking *for them,* or exercising power *over* them. Religious leaders must listen to the wisdom of the people, who have the experience of living with certain questions and challenges, who have the capacity to recognize solutions and paths of action that are "genuine, authentic, and commensurate with their experience."[9]

Using pastoral ethnography, leaders can compose narrative chapters that are theologically grounded in prophetic witness to God's mercy, justice, and love for the world, as well as culturally grounded in the stories and the lives of the faith community. Pastoral ethnographers thus support movement and growth from

---

6. The term "sacred conversations" alludes to the United Church of Christ's call for a denomination-wide "sacred conversation on race," begun in May 2008. See *www.ucc.org* for more information.

7. See Mary McClintock Fulkerson, *Changing the Subject: Women's Discourses and Feminist Theology* (Minneapolis: Fortress Press, 1994), 12.

8. Chopp, *The Power to Speak.*

9. Schreiter, *Constructing Local Theologies,* 17.

within the community. They do this by entering into deeper and more honest conversations with the people, by employing new religious metaphors that name God's presence afresh, and by moving forward into revised or improvised faith practices with the people they serve.

Honoring Creativity

Pastoral ethnography is a challenging and creative form of religious leadership. In order to navigate with charts of change, leaders must move deftly through the currents of organizational life. Pastoral researchers navigate not in such a way as to avoid conflict or upheaval, but rather by working with these forces and harnessing their energy for change. This kind of leadership requires not just knowledge and practice, but also imagination, flexibility, and deep, abiding faith. The creative insight that yields wise decisions in this work is always a little bit mysterious. In this, creativity is like the Spirit: no one can possess or control it. Yet leaders can learn to recognize, nurture, and affirm creative ideas and actions as they emerge through the process of pastoral ethnography. Leaders can practice welcoming and honoring creativity.

The interrelatedness of creativity and change is most obvious when we think about the work of artists. Artists have the power to represent (re-present) religious symbols and ideas in ways that inspire and evoke transformation on many levels — personal, communal, and societal. Religious leaders who recognize and honor their own creativity, as well as that of the people they serve, will be able to "catch the wave" of transformation. Pastoral ethnographers can honor their own creativity by beginning to think of themselves as artists as they watch, weave, write, and rehearse the group's evolving story. While the work of conducting research is rigorous and analytic, it also involves "thinking on one's feet," listening, responding, and understanding in deep ways that draw upon creative intelligence and empathic imagination. In the work of writing ethnographic narratives and sharing them and entering into honest conversations with members, leaders search for language that is both precise and poetic. In moving forward with the community into a wave of change, a leader's creativity lends both lift and ballast.

As a pastoral leader, you can practice honoring your own creativity by listening for the Holy in the midst of pastoral research, as well as in moments of respite from the work. Make it a practice to go back to the well of spiritual wisdom, for reflection, prayer, or meditation to help replenish your creative and spiritual energy. Some might call this practice keeping the Sabbath.[10] Pausing, taking a break, and engaging in restorative play or recreation (re-creation) can help inspire the courage to move forward into the untried idea, the previously unimagined or unexpected future.[11]

The art of leading change is a mysterious and unpredictable endeavor. We sow the seeds of change as we move along the spiral ethnographic journey. We do not always see immediate results. What makes this journey difficult is that we are moving along a path that leads into unknown territory. This kind of leadership is hard, creative work. It is like putting on a play, in that it requires a great deal of practice and imagination.[12] With pastoral ethnography and the conversations it spurs, we rehearse our way into change, by speaking new words and practicing new actions. We work at what Karen Thorkilsen calls "the edge of knowing" as we attempt to give form to the emerging shared wisdom.[13] It takes time to find a new way of doing things that incorporates the evolving convictions of the community. Even when a group

---

10. See Dorothy C. Bass, "Keeping Sabbath," in *Practicing Our Faith: A Way of Life for a Searching People,* ed. Dorothy C. Bass (San Francisco: Jossey-Bass, 1997), 75–89.

11. See Michael S. Koppel, *Open-Hearted Ministry: Play as Key to Pastoral Leadership* (Minneapolis: Fortress Press, 2008).

12. See Karen Thorkilsen, "The Edge of Knowing," 4–5, cited in Sharon Daloz Parks, *Leadership Can Be Taught: A Bold Approach for a Complex World* (Boston: Harvard Business School Press, 2005), 247–48.

13. Karen Thorkilsen, "The Edge of Knowing," *In Context* no. 5 (Spring 1984): 4–5.

achieves consensus or near consensus on a new course of faithful action, it will take time and perhaps a few false starts before the shift takes hold emotionally and spiritually.

Leaders and groups need time to practice change, to rehearse it until it begins to feel natural and authentic. Trying out new actions is usually risky and tentative at first. For instance, offering a vegetarian church supper (hypothetical case, chapter 1) would probably be difficult for the church that was accustomed to serving red meat. Adding a new practice of member participation in the worship service (Eleanor's case study in a retirement home, chapter 7) could disturb some residents even as it comforted others. Leaders need to name the grief that change brings and allow for the time that it takes to let go of what is lost in order to move forward into accepting the new.[14] Through listening and interpersonal connection, leaders and groups together find the new words to say and new ways to live with clarity, faithfulness, and purpose.

The art of leadership through pastoral ethnography is akin to what Ronald Heifetz of the Harvard Business School terms "adaptive leadership." Adaptive leadership involves, among many other things, the art of paying attention to conflicts, learning when to take action, when to pause, and how to marshal and support the "collective creativity" of the group.[15] The art of pastoral ethnography is adaptive in that it involves recognizing and getting on board with the wisdom that emerges in the faith community. This wisdom cannot be known in advance, nor can it be finally settled once and for all. This wisdom emerges over time in the context of the particularity of the people and the relationships being formed. Since the conditions of group life are always changing, leaders must remain flexible and open to the new wisdom that emerges in the group's faith in action.

---

14. Ronald Heifetz and Marty Linsky write: "People do not resist change, per se. They resist loss." *Leadership on the Line* (Boston: Harvard Business School Press 2002), 11 and 92–95, cited in Sharon Parks, *Leadership Can Be Taught,* 66–67.

15. Parks, *Leadership Can Be Taught,* 227, 230.

The work of co-authoring new theological narratives requires this kind of adaptive and artistic skill. Robert Schreiter points out that while he sees the community itself as the prime author of theology in a local context, there are individuals — such as prophets, poets, and teachers — in each local community of faith who shape into words the wisdom and spirit of the community.[16] It is here that the religious leader's trove of theological knowledge becomes a resource: in order to shape the local wisdom into words, leaders need to understand and articulate the theologies and practices of the larger religious tradition. Steeped in such knowledge, leaders can skillfully call upon the power and wisdom of broader faith stories and bring them into critical conversation with the local community's practical theological wisdom.

Leading a community in this co-authoring process also involves recognizing and calling upon the group's artists and poets, who can evoke and proclaim the emerging local theology. Creative expression through visual art, music, or theater can convey a depth of emotion that awakens people to the wonder and beauty of creation, to the compelling human needs of the day, and to God's indwelling love. Hymns, for example, or musical performances can touch us at an embodied level, calling forth memory, faith, and commitment.[17] Artistic productions also offer a venue for a group to communicate its story with a wider public, drawing more people together into movements for justice and social change.

The arts are also a resource for supporting the development of mind and voice, a key goal of pastoral ethnography.[18] Consider the words of Jane Sapp, the founding director of the Center for Cultural and Community Development, a center devoted to "cultural work" in what she calls the Black Belt of the southern United States. Describing the power of singing, Sapp writes:

---

16. Schreiter, *Constructing Local Theologies*, 17.
17. For a discussion of the impact of bodily practices on memory, see Paul Connerton, *How Societies Remember* (Cambridge: Cambridge University Press, 1989), 72–104.
18. Belenky et al., *A Tradition That Has No Name*, 235.

There is something about singing. It is not that singing washes away thoughts but it opens up the mind to let something new come in. Like sleep and dreams, music relaxes the barriers of the mind. Music is a way to unlock what is waiting to come out. Music shakes up all of your preconceived notions. We have those tapes of set ideas that we play in our heads. Music shuts out those tapes and allows you to hear new ideas.[19]

For Sapp, and for others she has observed, music opens the mind to truly new ideas, new ways of thinking. People working for social and political change need to be spiritually nurtured with the deep inspiration and creative freedom that Sapp identifies. Indeed, music played a significant role in the cultural workers movement that Sapp founded. The role of music in the American civil rights movement and in other freedom movements around the world is also well documented.[20]

Music and the arts have the potential to empower leaders and communities to improvise new variations on traditional faith practices. We have seen how the *habitus,* the accumulation of past understandings that is operative in the shared social culture of a group, can weigh down a group's present faith-in-action. Through ethnography, we lean into these past understandings and traditions so that they may become a springboard into a better and more faithful future.[21] Music, in particular, is a vehicle that can carry us through this process of leaning back into memory of the past and then springing forward with originality and inspiration for change. The deep emotional resonance of singing and hearing religious music involves us at a visceral level in the proclamation of faith that is both rooted in history and open to the new needs of the world. In the words of the psalmist, "O sing to the LORD a new song; sing to the LORD, all the earth" (Ps. 96:1).

---

19. Jane Sapp, cited in ibid., 235.

20. Belenky et al., *A Tradition That Has No Name,* 36–37. For a specific instance, see Taylor Branch, *Parting the Waters: America in the King Years 1954–63* (New York: Simon and Schuster, 1988), 531–32.

21. D. W. Winnicott writes, "In any cultural field, it is not possible to be original except on a basis of tradition." Winnicott, *Playing and Reality,* 99.

Visual art as well offers opportunities for communities to transcend old barriers and experience a taste of transformation. Both in the making and the viewing of artistic products, there are opportunities to imagine and realize theological longings for a better world. In participatory artwork, communities can be drawn together to co-create beautiful and rich representations of their faith and longings for transformation. The tangible and visual products that result take on a life and power of their own, moving the community forward and potentially influencing larger publics.

The "Diversity Quilt" project at Wesley Theological Seminary offers an example of the power of artwork as a vehicle of transformative theological expression. Wesley is a school that publicly proclaims the goodness, the grace, of human diversity. The community of scholars and staff at Wesley reflects many kinds of human difference, such as diversities of theology, denomination, gender, age, culture, race, language, sexual identity, economic status, and dis/ability.[22] Wesley celebrates its diversity even while in everyday life, some members of the school community experience struggle or stress related to this diversity, such as a struggle to communicate across a language barrier, or an experience of feeling marginalized by the larger group. Wesley's Diversity Committee addresses the legal and practical work of justice in policies such as enrollment and hiring. In recent years, the committee has also taken on the proactive work of helping to promote mutual understanding among diverse persons and groups within the community.

In the spring semester of 2008, the Diversity Committee, with the help of artist-in-residence Robert Peppers, embarked upon the creation of a "Diversity Quilt." The committee set up a table near the entrance to the refectory in order to invite a good number of students, staff, and faculty to participate in the quilt's creation. Individuals walking by the table were invited to design a square

---

22. The term "dis/ability" indicates that persons with physical and mental dis/abilities are also persons with abilities and gifts. See Janet Schaller, "Confronting 'the Stare': Women with Dis/abilities, Negative Cultural Representations, and Resistance" (Ph.D. dissertation, Claremont School of Theology, 2004), 22–28.

featuring their first names and first initial of their last names. Participants used decorative paper, which they stenciled, cut out, and glued onto ninety card-stock patches. With the artistic guidance of Robert Peppers, students from his Art Practicum class assembled the quilt, mounting the patches onto high quality blue banner paper and marking it with stylized "stitches" that appear to hold the patches together. The finished product is ninety inches long and fifty-six inches wide. It will soon be displayed at Wesley so that the entire community as well as visitors will be able to view it.

Kelly Wilkins, a recent graduate and former member of the Diversity Committee, describes what the quilt means to her:

> This Diversity Quilt reminds me of the discussions we had on the Trinity this year in class. We learned that God's own being is in community and the different diverse persons in the Trinity are dependent on one another. So when I look at each unique patch on the quilt I am reminded that God is diverse and that we are created in the image of God, in the same kind of diversity and relationship that is in God's own heart. We are profoundly different and that is what God intended.
>
> Also, the stitching in this quilt reminds me of how connected and dependent we are on each other. We are not able to live in this world alone or solve our problems by ourselves; we are gathered together by a common thread of unity and love. The quilt represents our community's expression of diversity, but more importantly, it reminds me of the image of God in us, which is diversity, relationship, and connection.[23]

Kelly's words demonstrate the way that an artistic project can communicate and enlarge upon theological insight in a community. Kelly Wilkins found in the quilt an expression and a representation of the theology that she had been honing carefully in her theology class.

---

23. Kelly Wilkins, speech at the presentation of the Diversity Quilt, Wesley Theological Seminary, Washington, D.C., May 9, 2008.

The project of creating the quilt was a participatory one. It drew together members of the community, in Kelly's words, "to try something new that they don't normally do. It was an unpretentious way of people coming together to have conversation." The act of trying something new, supported in this case by the Diversity Committee's leadership and Robert Peppers's artistic guidance, resulted in the creation of a lasting visual work that will continue to influence the persons who view it. The project drew upon the creativity and the theological wisdom of members of the community. The visual power of the quilt goes beyond words, but it also inspires more of them, as members of the community continue to converse about the theological value of diversity proclaimed in this work of art.

This project exemplifies the way in which artistic creativity and theological insight flow together when leaders intentionally work to help the group embody and enact its shared theological values. Pastoral ethnographers can support similarly creative projects in their communities as they seek to guide groups forward into change. While the beauty and compelling power of artistic productions are important, equally significant are the opportunities for members of the group to come together, in Kelly's words, "to try something new that they don't normally do." The understanding of community formation that Kelly describes is much like the kind of community that pastoral ethnography seeks to create.

Worship and religious rituals provide natural venues for creative and artistic expression in congregations. Herbert Anderson and Edward Foley offer helpful guidelines for both creating new rituals and enlivening existing rituals through the use of stories human and divine.[24] Artist and theologian Catherine Kapikian describes some of the many ways in which art can be brought into "service of the sacred."[25] In particular, Kapikian describes a

---

24. Anderson and Foley, *Mighty Stories, Dangerous Rituals,* 125–66.
25. Catherine Kapikian, *Art in Service of the Sacred,* ed. Kathy Black (Nashville: Abingdon Press, 2006).

process she calls "participatory aesthetics," which is a way of engaging a congregation or group in a shared artistic project in the context of sacred space, such as a sanctuary.[26] These texts offer rich resources for harnessing the creative energy and artistic gifts of the community for its shared ritual spaces and practices. The experience of enlivened ritual can help the group come to terms with the change it is trying to bring into being.

Creativity surrounds and undergirds the ethnographic journey. Wise pastoral ethnographers will honor their own creativity in listening, writing, speaking, and moving forward into new faith practices. They will also recognize the creativity of other leaders in their group and in their communities and adapt to the ever changing conditions of shared life. Artistic endeavors arising in the midst of the journey provide a natural avenue for expressing and enacting the group's faith-in-action as the process of transformation unfolds.

Ethnography for Transformation

Religious leaders can begin to think of ethnography as a series of key practices that form and inform their capacity to foster transformation. These ethnographic practices include: listening for God and identifying important questions; listening to persons and tending to the ethics of research relationships; listening to groups — reading local theology through research and rigorous analysis; composing shared stories that begin the work of pastoral-theological interpretation; sharing these narratives with the group and entering into dialogue and conversation; weaving and reweaving new theological insights and practices into the life of the group; and finally, honoring creativity throughout the process.

As we have seen, these practices are not consecutive steps along a sure path. Rather, they are key elements of a spiral journey: we return to each one over and over again, as each element informs

26. Ibid., 107–18.

all of the others and calls for deeper understanding and new actions. Even after moving through all the chapters of this book and completing all of the steps involved in pastoral ethnography, the work of prophetic leadership is not done. Leaders and people must actually try out the faithful practices they are imagining and co-authoring and then reflect upon the new experiences and insights that emerge as the community moves forward. As each of these components of pastoral ethnography becomes learned in the bones, through practice, leaders develop the capacity to help create transformative, prophetic change.

According to pastoral theologian Edward Wimberly, one of the assumptions of narrative therapy is that "transformation is possible, but not easy."[27] Student ethnographers and other researchers cited in this book demonstrate that, even in the midst of difficulty, change is possible. Often, the changes that take place at first are small and the growth is incremental. At other times, a group experiences more fundamental transformation, and a spring of enthusiasm begins to flow. When we make even small changes in the stories that we tell (to ourselves and to each other), a space opens up for a trickle of new insight or a slightly different way of acting, or both. It is with these tiny and sometimes fragile attempts to change that larger and more fundamental transformation can begin to flow in and through a community.

For example, recall Ken's congregants (in chapter 1) who had been driving away new members. When Ken gently asked them what size church they like, several people said they liked a small church. They then shared with him stories of loss and fears of losing their power in the church. Ken, consciously attempting to listen with compassion rather than judgment, was able to appreciate the people who were speaking to him so openly. Ken noticed the tender places in the conversation, the places where the potential flow of energy for change in the church began with the trickle of tears.

Through more research, Ken learned that these longstanding members, many of whom were farmers and former farmers, had

---

27. Wimberly, *Recalling Our Own Stories*, 74.

indeed suffered significant losses of land to a government buy-out in their recent local history. Seeing this story in its fullness helped Ken understand the people's desire to hold on to their power in the church. As his understanding and compassion grew, there was a shift in the way he addressed the people and shared scripture with them. He no longer blamed them for failing to obey the "great commission" (Matt. 28:18–20). Together, the pastor and the people wove a new story about faithfulness in this local church story, a story that enabled them to grow and change together. The people altered their practices of alienating newcomers, consciously choosing to become a more hospitable and welcoming congregation, with dramatic results. Some years later, Ken reported that church was transformed, not just numerically, but in its faithfulness and love. Because Ken taught the people how to engage in faithful listening and new story-weaving as they went along, the transformation that took hold during his tenure at the church has lasted years beyond his departure.[28]

Though change is possible, it is often difficult. Not every attempt at pastoral ethnography leads to the dramatic transformation that Ken witnessed. In chapter 9, we saw how Belinda, the leader of a child development center, through her interviews with mothers and grandmothers raising African American boys without fathers present in their homes, came to feel less judgment and more respect for the single mothers in her center. In this case, change began with Belinda, as she shifted her leadership style toward deeper listening. Staying grounded in her faith, Belinda could see links to the biblical story of Hebrew midwives in the lives of these mothers. Belinda also added creative programs that reached out to the boys' fathers and father figures, who did become more present in the boys' lives.

These shifts seem small. It is not as though justice has started rolling down like the waters (Amos 5:24) in Southeast D.C. This is still the most economically depressed quadrant of the District, which is also plagued by unacceptably high rates of violence in the streets. Many African American children growing up here still

---

28. "Ken," e-mail communication, May 23, 2006.

suffer undue and unjust stresses, as do their parents. Yet to the local group of parents involved in the child development center, these small shifts in understanding and practice matter. The experience of being heard by Belinda gives the mothers more voice in the way the center is run. The mothers' stories were magnified — enlarged — when shared with a larger community of childcare providers. Belinda's creative PowerPoint presentation, along with her generous and artful provision of a luncheon for the providers, helped inspire the group. Creative strategies for organizational and political change were voiced at this meeting, which took place in a local church basement. New speech and new actions can lead incrementally to renewed lives.

We can also imagine ways to expand upon Belinda's good work in Southeast D.C. In her book on child poverty, practical theologian Pamela Couture uses the term "rhizomatic ministry" to describe the ways in which congregations, denominational groups, and persons of faith are joining with secular organizations and individuals in order to advocate for the rights and welfare of children living in poverty. Rhizomes are the root systems of plants — such as grass — that spread horizontally to form connections to each other underground. Couture uses rhizomes as a metaphor for horizontal linkages between religious ministries and social and political agencies that also work on behalf of poor children.[29] We can imagine how connections between congregations and childcare centers and other social agencies might strengthen and spread creative efforts to promote the welfare of children in Southeast D.C.

Rhizomatic ministries to promote the welfare of children could then become the focus for further theological and spiritual reflection. For example, Couture, a United Methodist, suggests that the work of ameliorating child poverty is nothing less than a Christian discipleship practice and that "the awareness of God's concern for children and the poor takes permanent

---

29. Pamela Couture, *Child Poverty: Love, Justice, and Social Responsibility* (St. Louis: Chalice Press, 2007), 148–60.

residence in the disciple's heart."[30] By continuing to practice observation, theological reflection, narration, conversation, creative new practices such as rhizomatic ministries, and ongoing spiritual reflection, Belinda and other religious leaders could advance the larger faith goal of supporting local parents and children holistically in their sacred work of raising the next generation.

Challenges

Teaching, learning, and practicing pastoral ethnography present many challenges for scholars, students, and religious leaders. One challenge is in drawing together insights from disparate schools of thought, such as ethnography and theology. These disciplines have different starting points, epistemologies, and methods.[31] There is a risk of misunderstanding these distinctions and engaging in sloppy or disrespectful borrowing. This is a challenge that we all come up against whenever we attempt interdisciplinary or multi-perspectival research and teaching. Because pastoral theology has always been a hybrid field, scholars and students must read widely across the theological disciplines anyway. Adding the literature of congregational studies, sociology of religion, ethnography, and examples of religious studies from diverse fields, and then the task of weaving all of these diverse kinds of insight back into a pastoral theological framework, makes the workload challenging for scholar-teachers as well as for students and pastoral researchers. At the same time, the choice of risking interdisciplinary complexity for the sake of opening up congregational stories may also be viewed as strength.[32]

A second challenge inherent in conducting ethnographic research in the context of ministry is that of role confusion, as the pastoral role and researching role sometimes collide. Negotiating ethical boundaries around these roles is difficult work. Matters of

---

30. Ibid., 175.
31. Swinton and Mowat, *Practical Theology and Qualitative Research*, 73–98.
32. See Lisa M. Hess, "Theological Interdisciplinarity and Religious Leadership," *Journal of Religious Leadership* 5, no. 1 (Spring 2007): 1–37.

permission, informed consent, and confidentiality are not simple to teach or to practice. And in any ethnography, even if research is conducted well, the narratives composed have the potential to inflict harm upon the participants. Ethnographic portraits, like mirrors, may startle or confuse as well as empower or liberate. The challenge is to practice pastoral research in humility and with care for participants and members of the group.

A third challenge in the practice of pastoral ethnography involves the ongoing modeling role of the religious leader, who must strive to teach the group the habits of narrative listening and theological conversation. This is the work of community formation, in which the process — the way we go about communicating and caring for one another — is just as important as the content of the community's shared vision and plan for action. Pastoral ethnographers must try to teach the work of story-weaving to lay leaders and members of the community who will be there in the future, after the pastoral researcher departs. As life goes on and new challenges and needs arise, calling for new understandings of God and new patterns of faithful practice, the members of the local community of faith need to know how to flexibly move forward together.

Much of this teaching takes place through the pastoral ethnographer's modeling of the many practices of research and leadership we have discussed. The challenge is to embody the new theology and practice in the daily interchanges and life in leadership of the group. This is not unlike the modeling that parents offer children all the time, willy-nilly. The work of modeling involves listening, recognizing and celebrating creative gifts, sharing leadership as people grow, and adapting to changing understandings and conditions. As any parent knows, this continuous work of modeling is harder than it looks.

Conclusion: Listening as an Act of Love

Ethnography as a pastoral practice can be understood in many ways. It can be viewed as a form of leadership bent toward prophetic change. It can be understood as a kind of pastoral ministry that seeks to empower faithful persons, groups, and communities. It can be considered a vehicle for contextual theological reflection. Fundamentally, though, the theological value of pastoral ethnography can be summed up in the words of Dave Isay, radio producer and founder of the Storycorps Project: listening is an act of love.[33] Listening is that crucial act of love for which human beings long. With careful listening can come the gifts of being heard, known, understood. Ethnography as a pastoral practice offers a path toward deep, loving, and empowering listening to persons, congregations, and other religious agencies.

Ethnographic listening begins with relationships to individual persons. When we ask individual research participants to reflect deeply on their faith practices, we give them an opportunity to name their experience, to find new words to describe it, and to become more conscious and intentional about their theology-in-action. Honoring the person, and the presence of God in each person, can lead to change that comes from the heart, change that inspires commitment and collaboration rather than compliance or rebellion. Listening also becomes an act of love through the researcher's careful attention to the ethics of research and the well-being of the persons who are partners and participants in the study.

Listening to the congregation or group as a whole is also an act of love. We try to "catch" the sense of a culture holistically, with all of its complexity, in order to be in the position to develop truly responsive theological narratives.[34] Weaving individual stories together, and identifying intersections between stories human and divine, helps reorient the community back to God, and back to its faith and calling. When we share our findings and perceptions with the group, we open dialogues and conversations that

33. Dave Isay, ed., *Listening Is an Act of Love: A Celebration of American Life from the Storycorps Project* (New York: Penguin Press, 2007). The Storycorps Project, begun in 2003, has conducted over ten thousand recorded interviews of ordinary Americans' personal and family stories. Many of these interviews have been aired on National Public Radio programs such as *This American Life.*

34. Schreiter, *Constructing Local Theologies,* 28.

can lead to more creative understandings of the holy and more expressive, new, and just ways of living. Pastoral ethnographers strive to co-author the future *with* the community and with God.

Along with many challenges, there is great promise in the practice of pastoral ethnography. The promise lies in the honest connections that we forge with each other through research, and the honest sharing that brings us face to face with persons in the fullness of their hopes and fears and struggles. The promise lies in the shifts to which pastoral leaders submit: the shift from masquerading as religious experts to becoming students of the embodied and enacted wisdom of the people; the shift from asserting one's authority and power over others to respecting and listening as an act of love; and the shift from demanding uniformity of opinion or practice toward supporting creative energy and genuinely new approaches to theology-in-action.

Through ethnography as a pastoral practice, we encounter persons and communities of faith in greater fullness. We hear stories and songs that move us, and move us forward toward greater justice and wholeness in the world. We discover images and words with which to co-author the future, and we develop the shared communal capacity to engage in ministries of transformation. These are the gifts of God, given for people of the world.

For Further Study

Belenky, Mary Field, Lynn Bond, and Jacqueline S. Winestock. *A Tradition That Has No Name: Nurturing the Development of People, Families, and Communities.* New York: Basic Books, 1997, chapters 10–11.

Kapikian, Catherine. *Art in Service of the Sacred.* Ed. Kathy Black. Nashville: Abingdon Press, 2006, especially chapter 7.

Select Bibliography

Ammerman, Nancy Tatom, Arthur E. Farnsley, et al. *Congregation and Community*. New Brunswick, N.J.: Rutgers University Press, 1997.

Ammerman, Nancy T., Jackson Carroll, Carl S. Dudley, and William McKinney. *Studying Congregations: A New Handbook*. Nashville: Abingdon Press, 1998.

Anderson, Herbert, and Edward Foley. *Mighty Stories, Dangerous Rituals: Weaving Together the Human and the Divine*. San Francisco: Jossey-Bass, 1998.

Augsburger, David W. *Pastoral Counseling across Cultures*. Philadelphia: Westminster Press, 1986.

Bass, Dorothy C. "Keeping Sabbath." *Practicing Our Faith: A Way of Life for a Searching People*. Ed. Dorothy C. Bass. San Francisco: Jossey-Bass, 1997.

Becker, Penny Edgell, and Nancy L. Eiesland, eds. *Contemporary American Religion: An Ethnographic Reader*. Walnut Creek, Calif.: Altamira Press, 1997.

Belenky, Mary Field, Lynne A. Bond, and Jacqueline S. Weinstock. *A Tradition That Has No Name: Nurturing the Development of People, Families, and Communities*. New York: Basic Books, 1997.

Billman, Kathleen D. and Daniel L. Migliore. *Rachel's Cry: Prayer of Lament and Rebirth of Hope*. Cleveland: United Church Press, 1999.

Bourdieu, Pierre. *The Logic of Practice*. Cambridge: Polity Press, 1992.

Branson, Mark Lau. *Memories, Hopes, and Conversations: Appreciative Inquiry and Congregational Change*. Herndon, Va.: Alban Institute, 2004.

Brizee, Robert. *The Gift of Listening*. St. Louis: Chalice Press, 1993.

Brown, Karen McCarthy. *Mama Lola: A Vodou Priestess in Brooklyn*. Berkeley and Los Angeles: University of California Press, 1991.

Browning, Don S. *A Fundamental Practical Theology: Descriptive and Strategic Proposals*. Minneapolis: Augsburg Fortress, 1991.

Bush, Joseph E. *Gentle Shepherding: Pastoral Ethics and Leadership*. St. Louis: Chalice Press, 2006.

Cameron, Helen, Philip Richter, Douglas Davies, and Frances Ward, eds. *Studying Local Churches: A Handbook*. London: SCM Press, 2005.

Carroll, Jackson, Barbara Wheeler, Daniel Aleshire, and Penny Long Marler. *Being There: Culture and Formation in Two Theological Schools*. New York: Oxford University Press, 1997.

Chopp, Rebecca. *The Power to Speak: Feminism, Language, God*. New York: Crossroad, 1989.

Clinebell, Howard. *Basic Types of Pastoral Care and Counseling: Resources for the Ministry of Healing and Growth*. Rev. ed. Nashville: Abingdon Press, 1984.

Connerton, Paul. *How Societies Remember*. Cambridge: Cambridge University Press, 1989.

Cooper-White, Pamela. *Shared Wisdom: The Use of the Self in Pastoral Care and Counseling*. Minneapolis: Fortress Press, 2004.

Couture, Pamela. *Child Poverty: Love, Justice, and Social Responsibility*. St. Louis: Chalice Press, 2007.

Davidman, Lynn. "Truth, Subjectivity, and Ethnographic Research." In *Personal Knowledge and Beyond: Reshaping the Ethnography of Religion*. Ed. James Spickard, J. Shawn Landres, and Meredith B. McGuire. New York: New York University Press, 2002.

Denzin, Norman K. *Interpretive Ethnography: Ethnograpic Practices for the 21st Century*. Thousand Oaks, Calif.: SAGE Publications, 1997.

Dittes, James E. *Pastoral Counseling: The Basics*. Louisville: Westminster John Knox Press, 1999.

Doehring, Carrie. *Taking Care: Monitoring Power Dynamics and Relational Boundaries in Pastoral Care and Counseling*. Nashville: Abingdon Press, 1995.

———. *The Practice of Pastoral Care: A Postmodern Approach*. Louisville: Westminster John Knox Press, 2006.

Dorff, Elliot N. *The Way into Tikkun Olam (Repairing the World)*. Woodstock, Vt.: Jewish Lights Publishing, 2005.

Dudley, Carl, and Nancy Ammerman. *Congregations in Transition: A Guide for Analyzing, Assessing, and Adapting in Changing Communities*. San Francisco: Jossey-Bass, 2002.

Dunaway, David K., and Willa K. Baum, eds. *Oral History: An Interdisciplinary Anthology*. 2nd ed. Walnut Creek, Calif.: Altamira Press, 1996.

Dykstra, Craig, and Dorothy C. Bass. "A Theological Understanding of Christian Practices." In *Practicing Theology: Beliefs and Practices in Christian Life*. Grand Rapids: Wm. B. Eerdmans, 2002.

Eiesland, Nancy L. *A Particular Place: Urban Restructuring and Religious Ecology in a Southern Exurb*. New Brunswick, N.J.: Rutgers University Press, 2000.

Erlandson, David A., Edward L. Harris, Barbara L. Skipper, and Steve D. Allen. *Doing Naturalistic Inquiry: A Guide to Methods*. Newbury Park, Calif.: SAGE Publications, 1993.

Fishburn, Janet, ed. *People of a Compassionate God: Creating Welcoming Congregations*. Nashville: Abingdon Press, 2003.

Florence, Anna Carter. *Preaching as Testimony*. Louisville: Westminster John Knox Press, 2007.

Frank, Thomas Edward. *The Soul of the Congregation*. Nashville: Abingdon Press, 2000.

Frederick, Marla F. *Between Sundays: Black Women and Everyday Struggles of Faith*. Berkeley and Los Angeles: University of California Press, 2003.

Freire, Paulo. *Pedagogy of the Oppressed*. 30th anniversary ed., trans. Myra Bergman Ramos. New York: Continuum International, 2000.

Friedman, Edwin H. *Generation to Generation: Family Process in Church and Synagogue*. New York: Guilford Press, 1985.

Fulkerson, Mary McClintock. *Changing the Subject: Women's Discourses and Feminist Theology*. Minneapolis: Fortress Press, 1994.

Gaede, Beth Ann, ed. *When a Congregation Is Betrayed: Responding to Clergy Misconduct*. Herndon, Va.: Alban Institute, 2005.

Geertz, Clifford. *The Interpretation of Cultures: Selected Essays*. New York: Basic Books, 1973.

Gorringe, T. J. *A Theology of the Built Environment: Justice, Empowerment, Redemption*. Cambridge: Cambridge University Press, 2002.

Graham, Elaine L. *Transforming Practice: Pastoral Theology in an Age of Uncertainty*. Eugene, Ore.: Wipf and Stock, 1996.

———, Heather Walton, and Frances Ward. *Theological Reflection: Methods*. London: SCM–Canterbury Press, 2005.

Graham, Larry Kent. *Care of Persons, Care of Worlds: A Psychosystems Approach to Pastoral Care and Counseling*. Nashville: Abingdon Press, 1992.

Graves, Mike, and David J. Schlafer, eds. *What's the Shape of Narrative Preaching?: Essays in Honor of Eugene L. Lowry*. St. Louis: Chalice Press, 2008.

Hall, David D., ed. *Lived Religion in America*. Princeton, N.J.: Princeton University Press, 1997.

Hammersley, Martyn, and Paul Atkinson. *Ethnography: Principles in Practice*. 2nd ed. New York: Routledge, 1995.

Hareven, Tamara. "The Search for Generational Memory." In *Oral History: An Interdisciplinary Anthology,* ed. David K. Dunaway and Willa K. Baum. Walnut Creek, Calif.: Altamira Press, 1978.

Hauerwas, Stanley, and William Willimon. *Resident Aliens: Life in the Christian Colony.* Nashville: Abingdon Press, 1989.

Heilman, Samuel C. *The People of the Book: Drama, Fellowship, and Religion.* Chicago: University of Chicago Press, 1983.

——. *The Gate Behind the Wall: A Pilgrimage to Jerusalem.* New York: Penguin, 1986.

Hiltner, Seward. *Preface to Pastoral Theology.* New York: Abingdon Press, 1958.

Hopewell, James F. *Congregation: Stories and Structures.* Minneapolis: Fortress Press, 1987.

Hummel, Leonard M. *Clothed in Nothingness: Consolation for Suffering.* Minneapolis: Augsburg Fortress, 2003.

Imber-Black, Evan. *The Secret Life of Families.* New York: Bantam Books, 1999.

Isay, Dave, ed. *Listening Is an Act of Love: A Celebration of American Life from the Storycorps Project.* New York: Penguin Press, 2007.

Kapikian, Catherine. *Art in Service of the Sacred.* Ed. Kathy Black. Nashville: Abingdon Press, 2006.

Koppel, Michael S. *Open-Hearted Ministry: Play as Key to Pastoral Leadership.* Minneapolis: Fortress Press, 2008.

Kornfeld, Margaret Zipse. *Cultivating Wholeness: A Guide to Care and Counseling in Faith Communities.* New York: Continuum International, 2000.

Lamott, Anne. *Bird by Bird: Some Instructions on Writing and Life.* New York: Anchor, 1994.

Lartey, Emmanuel. *Pastoral Theology in an Intercultural World.* Cleveland: Pilgrim Press, 2006.

Lawless, Elaine J. *Holy Women, Wholly Women: Sharing Ministries through Life Stories and Reciprocal Ethnography.* Philadelphia: University of Pennsylvania Press, 1993.

Loder, James. *The Transforming Moment.* 2nd ed. Colorado Springs, Colo.: Helmers & Howard, 1989.

MacIntyre, Alasdair. *After Virtue: A Study in Moral Theory.* Notre Dame, Ind.: University of Notre Dame Press, 1981.

Madison, D. Soyini. *Critical Ethnography: Method, Ethics and Performance.* Thousand Oaks, Calif.: SAGE Publications, 2005.

Mason, Jennifer. *Qualitative Researching.* 2nd ed. Thousand Oaks, Calif.: SAGE Publications, 2002.

McDannell, Colleen. "Interpreting Things: Material Culture Studies and American Religion." *Religion* 21 (1991): 371–87.

———. *Material Christianity: Religion and Popular Culture in America*. New Haven: Yale University Press, 1995.

McKinney, Lora-Ellen. *View from the Pew: What Preachers Can Learn from Church Members*. Valley Forge, Pa.: Judson Press, 2004.

Mellott, David. "Ethnography as Theology: Encountering the Penitentes of Arroyo Seco, New Mexico." Ph.D. dissertation, Graduate Division of Religion, Emory University, 2005.

Miller-McLemore, Bonnie J. "The Living Human Web: Pastoral Theology at the Turn of the Century." In *Through the Eyes of Women*, ed. Jeanne Stevenson-Moessner, 9–26. Minneapolis: Fortress Press, 1996.

———, and Brita Gill-Austern, eds. *Feminist and Womanist Pastoral Theology*. Nashville: Abingdon Press, 1999.

Migliore, Daniel L. *Faith Seeking Understanding: An Introduction to Christian Theology*. 2nd ed. Grand Rapids: Wm. B. Eerdmans, 2004.

Morton, Nelle. *The Journey Is Home*. Boston: Beacon Press, 1985.

Moschella, Mary Clark. "Food, Faith, and Formation: A Case Study on the Use of Ethnography in Pastoral Theology and Care." *Journal of Pastoral Theology* 12, no. 1 (January 2002): 75–87.

———. *Living Devotions: Reflections on Immigration, Identity, and Religious Imagination*. Eugene, Ore.: Pickwick Publications, 2008.

Naples, Nancy A. *Feminism and Method: Ethnography, Discourse Analysis, and Activist Research*. New York: Routledge, 2003.

Neuger, Christie Cozad. *Counseling Women: A Narrative, Feminist Approach*. Minneapolis: Fortress Press, 2001.

Niebuhr, H. Richard. *The Responsible Self: An Essay in Christian Moral Philosophy*. San Francisco: Harper and Row, 1978.

Nouwen, Henri. *The Wounded Healer: Ministry in Contemporary Society*. New York: Image, Doubleday, 1979.

Orsi, Robert A. *Between Heaven and Earth: The Religious Worlds People Make and the Scholars Who Study Them*. Princeton, N.J.: Princeton University Press, 2005.

Parks, Sharon Daloz. *Leadership Can Be Taught: A Bold Approach for a Complex World*. Boston: Harvard Business School Press, 2005.

Patton, John. *Pastoral Care in Context: An Introduction to Pastoral Care*. Louisville: Westminster John Knox Press, 1993.

Pauw, Amy Plantinga. "Attending to the Gaps between Beliefs and Practices." In *Practicing Theology: Beliefs and Practices in Christian Life*, ed. Miroslav Volf and Dorothy C. Bass, 33–48. Grand Rapids: Wm. B. Eerdmans, 2002.

Pink, Sarah. *Doing Visual Ethnography: Images, Media, and Representation in Research.* 2nd ed. Thousand Oaks, Calif.: SAGE Publications, 2007.

Ramsay, Nancy, ed. *Pastoral Care and Counseling: Redefining the Paradigms.* Nashville: Abingdon Press, 2004.

Rendle, Gil, and Alice Mann. *Holy Conversations: Strategic Planning as a Spiritual Practice for Congregations.* Herndon, Va.: Alban Institute, 2003.

Richardson, Laurel. *Writing Strategies: Reaching Diverse Audiences.* Newbury Park, Calif.: SAGE Publications, 1990.

Ricoeur, Paul. *Time and Narrative.* Vols. 1–2: trans. Kathleen McLaughlin and David Pellauer. Vol. 3: trans. Kathleen Blamey and David Pellauer. Chicago: University of Chicago Press, 1984, 1985, and 1988.

Savage, John. *Listening and Caring Skills: A Guide for Groups and Leaders.* Nashville: Abingdon Press, 1996.

Scalise, Charles J. *Bridging the Gap: Connecting What You Learned in Seminary with What You Find in the Congregation.* Nashville: Abingdon Press, 2003.

Scheib, Karen D. *Challenging Invisibility: Practices of Care With Older Women.* St. Louis: Chalice Press, 2004.

Schreiter, Robert J. *Constructing Local Theologies.* Maryknoll, N.Y.: Orbis Books, 1985.

Seasoltz, R. Kevin. *A Sense of the Sacred: Theological Foundations of Christian Architecture and Art.* New York: Continuum International, 2005.

Soskice, Janet Martin. *Metaphor and Religious Language.* Oxford: Clarendon Press, 1985.

Strauss, Anselm, and Juliet Corbin. *Basics of Qualitative Research: Techniques and Procedures for Developing Grounded Theory.* 2nd ed. Thousand Oaks, Calif.: SAGE Publications, 1998.

Stringer, Ernest T., et al. *Community-Based Ethnography: Breaking Traditional Boundaries of Research, Teaching, and Learning.* Mahwah, N.J.: Lawrence Erlbaum Associates, 1997.

Strunk, William, Jr., and E. B. White. *The Elements of Style.* 3rd ed. New York: Macmillan, 1979.

Swidler, Ann. "Culture in Action: Symbols and Strategies." *American Sociological Review* 51 (April 1986): 273–86.

Swinton, John, and Harriet Mowat. *Practical Theology and Qualitative Research.* London: SCM Press, 2006.

Tanner, Kathryn. *Theories of Culture: A New Agenda for Theology.* Minneapolis: Fortress Press, 1997.

Taylor, Charles W. *The Skilled Pastor: Counseling as the Practice of Theology*. Minneapolis: Augsburg Fortress, 1991.

Thorkilsen, Karen. "The Edge of Knowing." *In Context* no. 5 (Spring 1984): 4–5.

Tooley, Michelle. *Voices of the Voiceless: Women, Justice, and Human Rights in Guatemala*. Scottdale, Pa.: Herald Press, 1989.

Tribble, Jeffery. *Transformative Leadership in the Black Church*. New York: Palgrave Macmillan, 2005.

Turner, Victor W. *The Ritual Process: Structure and Anti-Structure*. Chicago: University of Chicago Press, 1969.

Tweed, Thomas A. "Introduction: Narrating U.S. Religious History." In *Retelling U.S. Religious History*, ed. Thomas A. Tweed, 1–23. Berkeley and Los Angeles: University of California Press, 1997.

———. *Our Lady of the Exile: Diasporic Religion at a Cuban Catholic Shrine in Miami*. New York: Oxford University Press, 1997.

van Beek, Aart M. *Cross-Cultural Counseling*. Minneapolis: Augsburg Fortress, 1996.

Van Manen, Max. *Researching Lived Experience: Human Science for an Action Sensitive Pedagogy*. Albany: State University of New York Press, 1990.

VandeCreek, Larry, Hillary Bender, and Merle R. Jordan. *Research in Pastoral Care and Counseling: Quantitative and Qualitative Approaches*. Decatur, Ga.: Journal of Pastoral Care Publications, 1994.

Volf, Miroslav, and Dorothy C. Bass, eds. *Practicing Theology: Beliefs and Practices in Christian Life*. Grand Rapids: Wm. B. Eerdmans, 2002.

Watkins Ali, Carroll. *Survival and Liberation: Pastoral Theology in African American Context*. St. Louis: Chalice Press, 1999.

White, Michael, and David Epston. *Narrative Means to Therapeutic Ends*. New York: W. W. Norton, 1990.

Wimberly, Edward P. *Recalling Our Own Stories: Spiritual Renewal for Religious Caregivers*. San Francisco: Jossey-Bass, 1997.

Winnicott, Donald Woods. *The Maturational Processes and the Facilitating Environment*. New York: Karnac Books, 1990.

———. *Playing and Reality*. New York: Routledge, 1971.

Index

265